编委会

高等职业教育"十四五"规划旅游大类精品教材
福建省职业教育旅游大类示范专业精品教材

总主编

郑耀星　全国旅游职业教育教学指导委员会委员，福建师范大学旅游学院原院长

顾问

刘松林　福建省旅游行业职业教育指导委员会秘书长，福州职业技术学院原副院长

编委（排名不分先后）

林　东　福州职业技术学院文化创意学院院长，教授，省级精品在线开放课程主持人
曾　咪　漳州职业技术学院文化旅游学院院长，教授，省级精品在线开放课程主持人
崔筱力　厦门南洋职业学院外国语与旅游学院执行院长，教授，省级精品在线开放课程主持人
李晓雯　黎明职业大学外语与旅游学院副院长，副教授
黄宇方　闽西职业技术学院文旅创意学院旅游管理专业主任，省级精品在线开放课程主持人
李　心　福建信息职业技术学院文化创意与旅游学院副院长，副教授
周富广　漳州职业技术学院文化旅游学院副院长，副教授，省级精品在线开放课程主持人
叶城锋　泉州职业技术大学文化旅游与体育学院副院长，省级精品在线开放课程主持人
黄朝铭　厦门东海职业技术学院航空旅游学院院长，省级精品在线开放课程主持人
刘少艾　闽江师范高等专科学校人文社科系副主任，省级精品在线开放课程主持人
陈月珍　泉州幼儿师范高等专科学校外语旅游学院导游专业副主任，省级精品在线开放课程主持人
张清影　漳州职业技术学院文化旅游学院副院长，副教授
黄冬群　漳州职业技术学院文化旅游学院副教授
薛秀云　漳州职业技术学院文化旅游学院副教授
李　青　福建信息职业技术学院文化创意与旅游学院副教授，中国职业教育新媒体专业联盟常务理事
严亦雄　福州职业技术学院旅游管理专业副教授，福州市先进教育工作者
佘艺玲　黎明职业大学外语与旅游学院副教授，旅游管理专业带头人
毛爱云　漳州科技学院教育与航空旅游学院副教授
黄丽卿　漳州职业技术学院食品工程学院副教授，省级精品在线开放课程主持人
包晓莉　闽西职业技术学院文旅创意学院副教授
许爱云　厦门南洋职业学院外国语与旅游学院教授
黄斐霞　黎明职业大学外语与旅游学院副教授，省级精品在线开放课程主持人
朱赛洁　厦门南洋职业学院外国语与旅游学院副教授
邢宁宁　漳州职业技术学院文化旅游学院副教授
吴艺梅　漳州职业技术学院文化旅游学院办公室主任
廉晓利　漳州职业技术学院文化旅游学院空中乘务专业主任

福建省"十四五"职业教育规划教材

高等职业教育"十四五"规划旅游大类精品教材(总主编 郑耀星)

导游英语

DAOYOU YINGYU

黄冬群 佘艺玲 薛秀云 主编

华中科技大学出版社
http://press.hust.edu.cn
中国·武汉

内 容 提 要

《导游英语》分为上篇和下篇。上篇遵循情境功能原则和任务为本原则,以涉外导游工作流程的典型工作任务为依据,对教材内容进行模块划分。上篇共设计9个项目,分别为接站服务、酒店入住、餐饮服务、都市服务、前往景点途中、景点讲解、旅游购物与娱乐、离站服务、问题与紧急情况处理。通过案例导入、情境创设、情景模拟、小组活动等活动载体来落实教学内容,让学生动起来,倡导学生在"做"中"学",实现做学一体化。下篇根据旅游资源特点,分为名山之旅、胜水之旅、古建筑之旅、古代园林之旅、古城古镇之旅、中国特色文化之旅、红色文化之旅、都市风光之旅8个项目。进行分门别类的介绍,既有助于学生了解祖国的各类旅游资源,也有助于他们积累同类别旅游资源讲解的素材。

《导游英语》适用于高等旅游院校旅游英语、导游英语、旅游英语口语等课程的教学,也可供对英语导游工作感兴趣、希望加入英语导游队伍的社会人员作为自学和培训教材。

图书在版编目(CIP)数据

导游英语/黄冬群,佘艺玲,薛秀云主编.—武汉:华中科技大学出版社,2022.8(2024.8重印)
ISBN 978-7-5680-8542-7

Ⅰ.①导… Ⅱ.①黄… ②佘… ③薛… Ⅲ.①导游-英语-教材 Ⅳ.①F590.633

中国版本图书馆 CIP 数据核字(2022)第 126823 号

导游英语
Daoyou Yingyu

黄冬群　佘艺玲　薛秀云　主编

策划编辑:	汪　杭
责任编辑:	陈　然
封面设计:	原色设计
责任校对:	李　弋
责任监印:	周治超
出版发行:	华中科技大学出版社(中国·武汉)　电话:(027)81321913
	武汉市东湖新技术开发区华工科技园　邮编:430223
录　排:	华中科技大学惠友文印中心
印　刷:	武汉科源印刷设计有限公司
开　本:	787mm×1092mm　1/16
印　张:	18
字　数:	576千字
版　次:	2024年8月第1版第2次印刷
定　价:	59.80元

本书若有印装质量问题,请向出版社营销中心调换
全国免费服务热线:400-6679-118　竭诚为您服务
版权所有　侵权必究

出版说明

伴随着我国的社会和经济在"十四五"期间步入新的发展阶段,中国的旅游业迎来了转型升级与高质量发展的新局面,并将在推动并形成以国内经济大循环为主体、国际国内双循环相互促进的新发展格局中发挥独特的作用。

《中国教育现代化 2035》及《加快推进教育现代化实施方案(2018—2022 年)》明确提出"推动高等教育内涵式发展、形成高水平人才培养体系"。"职教二十条"和"双高计划"的相继发布,也对中国旅游高等职业教育的发展提出了新要求。

中国旅游业面临的这些崭新局面,客观上对我国旅游高等职业教育和专业人才培养提出了更高的要求。基于此,出版一套把握新形势、反映新趋势、面向未来的高质量旅游高等职业教育教材成为迫切需要。

基于此,教育部直属的全国"双一流"大学出版社华中科技大学出版社汇聚了国内一大批高水平旅游院校的资深教授、学科带头人、双师型教师、旅游行业专家以及 1+X 职业技能等级证书评价机构联合编撰了高等职业教育旅游大类"十四五"规划精品教材。本套教材从选题策划到成稿出版,从编写团队到出版团队,从内容组建到内容创新,均做出了积极的突破,具有以下特点。

一、名师团队担任编委

本套教材编写者主要来自高水平旅游职业院校的教授、教学名师、学科带头人、双师型教师、旅游行业专家以及 1+X 职业技能等级证书评价机构。他们有着丰富的执教或从业经验,紧跟教育部、文旅部的权威指导意见,充分整合旅游领域的最新知识点,确保本套系教材的权威性、准确性、先进性。

二、课程思政贯穿全书

本套教材引进"课程思政"元素,落实立德树人的根本任务,在每个学习单元除了设置"知识目标""能力目标"外,还注重"素质目标"和"思政目标",通过案例分析、课后训练等形式,将社会主义先进文化与中华优秀传统文化,以及忠诚担当的政治品格、严谨科学的专业精神等内容贯穿于教材内容,旨在培养学生掌握相关岗位技能操作中必备的思政元素,践行社会主义核心价值观。

三、依托省级精品在线开放课程建设

本系列教材大多数有全国各省份的省级精品在线开放课程以及国家精品在线开放

课程的支撑，能够支持适合新学情的O2O混合式教学模式。依托各省级精品在线开放课程的在线教学平台，结合导学、在线讨论、在线答疑、在线测试等环节，可实现线上线下教学相融合，可实现以学习者为主体的"教、学、做一体化"。教材与在线开放课程结合，能够让教师的教学更便捷，让学生的学习更主动和可控。

四、校企融合编写贴近岗位实际

本系列教材建设伊始即实施了产教融合、校企共同设计与开发的路径，课程和教材建设均注重与企业实际工作过程相对接，与旅游行业代表性企业合作，邀请行业知名经理人以及1+X职业技能等级证书评价机构联合编写，从教材顶层设计到分步实施，每一个学习单元都与企业实际典型工作任务对接，既关注旅游基础理论，也重点突出了企业应用的实际。此外，教材还融通了1+X职业技能等级证书的知识、案例、真题等。

五、配套丰富教学资源形成立体化教材

华中科技大学出版社为本套系教材建设了线上资源服务平台，在横向资源配套上，提供教学计划书、教学课件、习题库、案例库、参考答案、教学视频等系列配套教学资源；在纵向资源开发上，构建了覆盖课程开发、习题管理、学生评论、班级管理等集开发、使用、管理、评价于一体的教学生态链，打造了线上线下、课堂课外的新形态立体化互动教材。

中国旅游业发展前景广阔，中国旅游高等职业教育任重道远，为中国旅游业的发展培养高质量的人才是社会各界的共识与责任，相信这套凝聚来自全国骨干教师和行业一线专家们的智慧与心血的教材，能够为我国旅游人才队伍建设、旅游职业教育体系优化起到一定的推动作用。

本套教材在编写过程中难免存在疏漏、不足之处，恳请各位专家、学者以及广大师生在使用过程中批评指正，以利于教材水平进一步提高。也希望并诚挚邀请全国旅游院校及行业的专家学者加入我们这套教材的编写队伍，共同促进我国旅游高等职业教育事业向前发展。

华中科技大学出版社
2022年5月

前言
Preface

随着旅游业发展方式的转变,旅游服务更加注重质量的全面提高和个性化服务,这对导游人员的工作能力、职业素养提出了更高的要求。为了帮助学校、社会培养更多高素质、实践能力强的英语导游,结合当今旅游市场对导游人才在知识和能力方面的需求,特编写此书,以飨读者。

《导游英语》各单元均严格按照图文导入、情景对话、实践操练、模拟讲解、延伸阅读的体例安排,力求方便教学的顺利推进及学生学习的循序渐进;力求图文并茂,书中重要景点、重要文化元素均配有实景图片,增强了直观性,提高了可读性;注重语言和文化的融合,对每一景区提及的重难点附有中文阐述,拓展了学生的知识面。本书每单元都编写了练习题,有助于学生巩固知识,提升语言应用能力,在内容上做到专业学习与导游资格证考试内容结合,各地景点解说与全国代表性景点结合。充分开发文本、图像、音频等多模态一体化的学习资源,给学生提供丰富的实践机会,强化实际应用能力训练。文字、图像、音频为一体,视听说有效结合,努力创造一个真实的导游工作环境。

本书体例新颖,内容翔实,"宽""专"结合。"宽"是指重视导游基础知识学习,包括中国历史文化、民族风情、自然科学等普及性知识的学习;"专"是指突出英语导游服务知识,强化导游人员专业技能和操作能力的训练,如导游服务规范、导游应变能力、旅游景点英文讲解、导游情景英文对话等。

课程思政贯穿始终,特别突出文化自信,介绍中国特色文化(中国节日之旅、地方戏剧之旅、中国陶瓷文化之旅、中国文房四宝、中国水墨画、地方特产),并添加了红色文化之旅。教材内容与时俱进,加入了共享单车、移动支付、网络购物等内容。

黄冬群老师负责教材的大纲和样章撰写、分工安排、上篇1—3章节编写、下篇10—12章节编写,并最终统稿审核。薛秀云老师负责案例收集,上篇4—6章节、下篇15—17章节编写,音频录制。佘艺玲老师负责上篇7—9章节、下篇13—14章节编写。

目录
Contents

PART I　Service Procedures of English Tour Guide　/001

Module 1　Meeting the Tourists　/003

Task 1　Meeting the Tourists at the Airport　/004
Task 2　On the Way to the Hotel　/008

Module 2　Hotel Check-in　/015

Task 1　Room Reservation　/015
Task 2　Check In　/020
Task 3　Itinerary and Morning Call　/025

Module 3　Food and Beverage Service　/030

Task 1　Meal Arrangement　/031
Task 2　Special Meal Requirements　/037

Module 4　City Service　/043

Task 1　Public Transportation　/043
Task 2　Shared Bike　/049
Task 3　Currency Exchange　/054
Task 4　Booking Tickets　/059

| Module 5 | **On the Way to the Scenic Spot** | /066 |

Task 1　Narration on Tour　/066
Task 2　Organizing Activities on the Bus　/073
Task 3　Reminding Before Getting off the Coach　/078

| Module 6 | **Visiting Scenic Spot** | /082 |

Task 1　Brief Introduction of a Scenic Spot　/082
Task 2　A Visit to Fujian Tulou　/088

| Module 7 | **Shopping and Entertainment** | /094 |

Task 1　The Four Treasures of the Study　/094
Task 2　Chinese Painting　/097
Task 3　 Introducing Local Specialties　/100
Task 4　Recreation Activities　/105

| Module 8 | **Seeing the Tour Group off** | /110 |

Task 1　Preparation for Seeing Off Tourists　/111
Task 2　Check out of the Hotel　/115
Task 3　Making a Farewell Speech　/119
Task 4　At the Airport　/123

| Module 9 | **Handling Emergencies** | /127 |

Task 1　Certificate Loss　/128
Task 2　Personal Property Loss　/132
Task 3　Dealing with Sudden Illnesses　/136
Task 4　Tourists Missing　/141
Task 5　Dealing with Emergencies En Route　/146

PART II Scenic Spots Interpretations /151

Module 10 Tour of Famous Mountains /153

Task 1 A Trip to Mount Taishan /153
Task 2 A Trip to Mount Huangshan /158
Task 3 A Trip to Mount Wuyi /163

Module 11 Tour of Water Landscape /168

Task 1 A Trip to the Three Gorges of the Yangtze River /168
Task 2 A Trip to Jiuzhaigou /173
Task 3 A Trip to Qinghai Lake /177

Module 12 Tour of Historic Buildings /182

Task 1 A Trip to the Forbidden City /182
Task 2 A Trip to the Confucian Temple, Qufu /187
Task 3 A Trip to the Museum of Terracotta Warriors and Horses /192
Task 4 A Trip to the Potala Palace /197

Module 13 Tour of Ancient Gardens /202

Task 1 A Trip to the Summer Palace /202
Task 2 A Trip to the Humble Administrator's Garden /207
Task 3 A Trip to Qinghui Garden /210

Module 14 Tour of Ancient Cities and Ancient Towns /215

Task 1 A Trip to Wuzhen /215
Task 2 A Trip to Zhouzhuang /219
Task 3 A Trip to the Old Town of Lijiang /223
Task 4 A Trip to the Ancient City of Pingyao /226
Task 5 A Trip to the Three Lanes and Seven Alleys /231

Module 15　Tour of Chinese Culture　/235

Task 1　Traditional Chinese Festivals　/235
Task 2　Traditional Chinese Operas　/240
Task 3　Chinese Ceramics　/245

Module 16　Red Tour　/250

Task 1　A Trip to Mount Jinggang　/250
Task 2　A Trip to the Memorial Hall of the First National Congress of the CPC　/254
Task 3　A Trip to the Site of the Gutian Congress　/257

Module 17　City Tour　/261

Task 1　A Trip to the Oriental Pearl TV Tower　/261
Task 2　A Trip to Kulangsu　/264
Task 3　A Trip to Chimelong Tourist Resort　/268

参考文献　/272

PART I Service Procedures of English Tour Guide

Module 1
Meeting the Tourists

Learning Objectives

1. Learn the basic procedures and specifications of pick-up service.
2. Communicate with the guests effectively, confirm the identity of the guests and ask about the travel matters.
3. Present a welcome speech.
4. Deal with unexpected situations, such as wrong connection, late arrival, empty connection etc.

Case Introduction

Case 1:

A tour group arrived in Xiamen at 16:20 on October 25 by flight MH456 as planned. The local guide, Xiao Wang, arrived at the airport 20 minutes in advance. The flight arrived on time, but Xiao Wang didn't receive the guests.

What should Xiao Wang do to deal with the accident?

Case 2:

The local tour guide went to Xiamen airport at 10:00 am to pick up the group. After arriving at the airport, he learned that the flight was four hours late.

What should the local tour guide do?

Task 1 Meeting the Tourists at the Airport

Warming Up

1. Read and Match

a. airport   b. enquiry   c. luggage claim area   d. coach

(1)

(2)

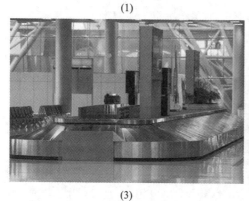

(3)

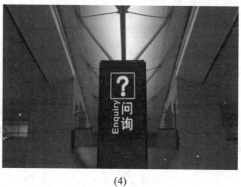

(4)

2. Question

What should a tour guide do to meet the tourists on arrival?

Tips for reference:

(1) Arrive at the meeting sites ahead of time.
(2) Identify the tourists or the tour group.
(3) Greet the group leader and give self-introduction.
(4) Remind the tourists to check the baggage.
(5) Lead the tourists to the coach.

Situational Dialogues

➤ Dialogue 1

Meeting the Tour Group at the Airport

(As a local guide, Xiao Li is picking up a group from the UK led by Mrs. Grant at Xiamen Gaoqi International Airport. He is holding a welcome sign with "Mrs. Grant" and the company's name on it.)

L: **Xiao Li, the local guide**   G: **Mrs. Grant, the tour leader**

L: Excuse me, but are you Mrs. Grant, the tour leader of Happy Tour from the UK?

G: Yes. You are?

L: My name is Xiao Li, the local guide from China International Travel Service. Nice to meet you.

G: Nice to meet you, Xiao Li. Thank you for coming to meet us.

L: It is my pleasure. We've been looking forward to your visit. How was your flight? It's such a long journey.

G: Not too bad, but a bit tired. The food on the plane is terrible.

L: I am sorry to hear that. But don't worry, Xiamen is a city famous for delicacies and delicious snacks. You will have a good chance to feast your stomach. Well, is everybody here now?

G: Let me see. Yes, we have 12 members in total. Now everyone's here.

L: Shall we go to the hotel now? It takes only twenty minutes to get there. And then you can have a good rest.

G: That is good. Thank you.

(Xiao Li turns to the tour group)

L: Hello, everyone. Welcome you all to China. I hope you will have a pleasant stay here. My name is Xiao Li. I am a tour guide from China International Travel Service, one of the biggest travel services in China. It is nice to see all of you. Our bus is waiting outside the airport. Now please check your luggage. If there is no problem, please follow me. Everybody, shall we go now?

G: Yes, we have been ready.

L: Please follow me. This way, please.

➤ Dialogue 2

Being Late for Meeting the Tour Group

(As a local guide, Zhang Yuan gets a last-minute notice of change of plan which

扫码
听听力

扫码
听听力

requires her to rush to the airport to meet a tour group. The tourists have been waiting for a long time when she gets there and they are full of grumbles.)

Z: Zhang Yuan, the local guide   B: Mr. Black, the tour leader

Z: Hello, you must be Mr. Black, the tour leader from China Smith Tour in New York?

B: Yes, I am. And you?

Z: Oh, Mr. Black, I am Zhang Yuan, your local guide from CITS, Xiamen Branch. You can call me Xiao Zhang.

B: Oh, here you are. Do you know how long we have been waiting here? We have been waiting here for one hour. That is really too much.

Z: I am very sorry for that. The traveling plan has changed and your group left for Shanghai ahead of time. The operator of the Hangzhou travel agency forgot to inform us on time. Our travel agency did not receive the notice until one hour ago.

B: Whatever the reason, we have been waiting here for a long time. It is lunch time. We are so hungry and thirsty.

Z: We do apologize for the trouble. We will go to the hotel directly and have lunch at the hotel. We have arranged some soft drinks for you as compensation. Our manager has been waiting for you in the hotel to express our sincere apology. And after lunch, you can have a short rest.

B: Oh, it sounds not bad. I hope there will be no other trouble for our next traveling.

Z: I will do my best to make your trip pleasant and comfortable. If you have any problem, please don't hesitate to let me know. I will be always at your service.

Useful Expressions

1. Are you Mrs. Grant, the tour leader of Happy Tour from the UK?
您是英国来的"快乐之旅"的领队格兰特女士吗?

2. We've been looking forward to your visit.
我们一直在盼望着你们的到来。

3. How was your flight?
你们的旅途顺利吗?

4. Is everybody here now?
大家都到齐了吗?

5. Our bus is waiting outside the airport. Now please check your luggage.
我们的大巴在机场外面等着。现在请确认一下你们的行李。

6. Please follow me.
请跟我来。

7. The traveling plan has changed and your group left for Shanghai ahead of time.
旅行计划有变,贵团提前出发去了上海。

8. We do apologize for the trouble.

对给你们带来的麻烦,我们深表歉意。

9. We have arranged some soft drinks for you as compensation.

我们已经为你们安排了一些软饮料作为补偿。

10. Our manager has waited for you in the hotel to express our sincere apology.

我们的经理已经在酒店等你们,以表达我们诚挚的歉意。

III Exercises

1. Match the following Chinese with the correct English versions

(1) 国际机场   a. tour guide
(2) 导游   b. international airport
(3) 领队   c. exit
(4) 中国国际旅行社   d. coach
(5) 中国青年旅行社   e. tour leader
(6) 接机   f. China Youth Travel Service
(7) 行李   g. luggage
(8) 行李认领处   h. luggage claim area
(9) 出口   i. China International Travel Service
(10) 大巴车   j. pick sb. up

2. Translate the following Chinese into English

(1) 您是从美国来的莉斯小姐吗?
(2) 我是中青旅的导游。
(3) 车子在外面等候。
(4) 我的名字叫珍妮。很高兴认识你。
(5) 一路上怎么样啊?
(6) 所有的行李都在这里了吗?
(7) 你们总共有多少件行李?
(8) 经过漫长的旅途,你们一定很疲倦了。

3. Fill in the blanks with appropriate words and expressions

A: Excuse me, but are you Joy Tour Group from New York?

B: Yes, we are. I'm Mary Smith, the tour ____(1)____. And you?

A: Hello, Ms. Smith. I'm Fang Lin, your local guide from CITS, Xiamen Branch. ____(2)____ to Xiamen.

B: How do you do, Mr. Fang?

A: How do you do? How was your ____(3)____?

B: Very pleasant. Thanks.

A: There are 16 persons in your group. ____(4)____?

B: Oh, some are still claiming their luggage. We've got altogether 20 ____(5)____ of check-in luggage.

A: We have a coach and a luggage truck waiting for us outside at the parking lot.

B: That is great. Let me see … yes, everyone is here now. ____(6)____, please, everyone. This is Mr. Fang, our local guide in Xiamen. Please follow his blue flag to the bus.

A: Ladies and gentlemen, please ____(7)____ me.

4. Role play

Situation 1: Suppose you are the local guide and are now picking up a tour group of 15 members from USA. You are now talking with the tour leader. Make a dialogue with your partner and your dialogue should include the following points: exchange of greetings, inquiring about the journey, guiding the way.

Situation 2: Suppose you are the local guide and you are now picking up Mr. Alma in the airport. Due to the bad weather and heavy traffic jam, you are late for ten minutes. Make a dialogue with your partner and your dialogue should include the following points: exchange of greetings, make apologies, calm down the guests, and promise that the similar thing will never happen again.

5. Questions & Answers

Question 1: How to make preparations in terms of the language and knowledge before guiding the group?

Question 2: How to identify a tour group when the local guide is picking up the tour group?

IV Extended Reading

Passport and Visa

Passport and Visa

Task 2   On the Way to the Hotel

I Warming Up

1. Read and Match

a. Xi'an Wild Goose Pagoda   b. Oriental Pearl TV Tower
c. CCTV Headquarter Building   d. Twin Towers in Xiamen

Module 1　Meeting the Tourists

(1)　　　　　　　　　　(2)

(3)　　　　　　　　　　(4)

2. Questions

Question 1: What content should a welcome speech usually include?

Tips for reference:

(1) Self-introduction.

(2) Introduction of the driver.

(3) Introduction of the hotel that the tourists are going to stay at.

(4) Simple itinerary presentation and notes.

Question 2: What should be introduced to the guests by the local guide en route to the hotel?

Tips for reference:

There is no fixed mode. The main buildings, shopping malls, landmark attractions and unique scenery along the way are usually introduced.

Ⅱ Situational Dialogues

➢ Dialogue 1

Making a Welcome Speech

(Xiao Li, the local guide, has picked up the guests from Xiamen Gaoqi International Airport. On the way back to the hotel, Xiao Li makes a welcome speech to the tour group and answers relevant questions.)

L: Xiao Li, the local guide   G: the guest

L: Ladies and gentlemen, attention, please. Welcome to Xiamen. First, let me introduce myself. My name is Xiao Li, the local guide from China Comfort Travel. I am happy to be your guide here. This is Mr. Yang, our driver. Mr. Yang is a responsible and experienced driver, so you are in safe hands. We'll always use the same bus in the following days. So please remember the number of our bus, E20206. We'll do everything possible to make your visit pleasant. If you have any problems or requests, please don't hesitate to let us know. We will be always at your service. Now we are heading for the hotel, Hilton Hotel. It will take us about 40 minutes to get there.

G: Is the hotel in the center of the city?

L: Yes, it is located in the center of the city. It is one of the best hotels in the city. It has a restaurant bar, a barbershop, a beauty parlor and laundry service. The facilities inside are very modern and comfortable. I am sure you'll have a nice stay there.

G: It sounds great. Thank you. By the way, what is the time now? You know the time difference.

L: Thank you for your question. Now the flight has taken you from the western hemisphere to the eastern hemisphere. The time difference between the two cities is 16 hours. Please reset your watches to Beijing standard time, which is 4:15 pm. The entire country follows Beijing standard time.

(The tourists reset the watches)

L: Now let me introduce something of our city. Xiamen is a beautiful city along the southeast coast of China, with a total area of 1700.61 square kilometers and an urban population of less than 600000. The airport you just came out of is Xiamen Gaoqi International Airport, the seventh largest airport in China, which has opened 53 domestic routes and 8 international routes. 33 domestic and foreign airlines have set up offices in Xiamen to carry out various business operations. Xiamen has beautiful environment and interesting folk customs. It is also one of the top ten tourist cities in China. The biggest feature of Xiamen is "the city is on the sea, and the sea is in the city".

G: That is excellent. What is the best time to travel in Xiamen?

L: Xiamen is located in the subtropical zone. The annual temperature difference is not big. There is no bitter cold in winter and no severe heat in summer. The climate is pleasant and it is very suitable for tourism all the year round.

G: Wow, that is great. Thank you.

L: You are welcome.

Dialogue 2

Services en Route to the Hotel

(On the way to the hotel, Xiao Li introduces the scenery along the way and answers relevant questions of the guests.)

L: Xiao Li, the local guide   G: the guests

L: Ladies and gentlemen, please look out of the window. Our car is now passing Xiamen Bridge, which is the first sea-crossing bridge in China. It has a total length of 6599 meters and a total investment of 1.5 billion yuan. It was completed and opened to traffic in December, 1991. On one side of the bridge are many tall buildings; on the other side is the vast sea where ships are sailing. This is Xiamen. "The city is on the sea, and the sea is in the city." Now look at the birds flying above the sea. Do you know the name of the birds? Anyone knows it?

G: Are they egrets? I heard that egret is the city bird of Xiamen.

L: Yes, you are right. Egrets have a high requirement for their habitat, that is, ventilated and sunny woods, quiet and clean water. They are especially sensitive to the quality of air and water. So, egrets are regarded as the detection birds of air and water quality by the International Environmental Protection Organization Association. There are small fish, shrimps and shellfish around the beach and shallow sea in Xiamen, which provide enough food for egrets. The large and small reefs, dense pines and mangrove forest provide a very comfortable habitat for egrets. Therefore, Xiamen has become a favorite home for egrets, and Xiamen people also have deep feelings for egrets. OK, just now, we mentioned the city bird. Do you know the city tree and the city flower of Xiamen?

G: Is it possible that the beautiful trees along the way happen to be the city tree?

L: Bingo. The city trees of Xiamen are phoenix trees. When they bloom in summer, the trees are full of bright red flowers, just like the crown of phoenix. And the city flower of Xiamen is triangle plum, which symbolizes enthusiasm, perseverance and indomitable spirit of the Xiamen people. Now our car is on Zhongshan Road. Zhongshan Road is the most prosperous commercial street in Xiamen at present. It was built in 1920s and 1930s. The buildings along the street are of arcade style. The lower part of the building is made into a colonnade sidewalk to avoid the rain and shade the sun. As you see, Xiamen is located in the subtropical zone and it is very hot and often rains in summer. Pedestrians can protect themselves from the sun and rain under the arcade, they can walk freely and shopping at will.

G: I like shopping. Can we have a chance to go shopping on Zhongshan Road?

L: Of course. We have set a whole afternoon for shopping on Zhongshan Road in our itinerary.

G: That is exactly what I want.

扫码
听听力

L: OK, ladies and gentlemen, we have now arrived at the parking lot of the hotel. Please take your belongings and follow me to the lobby.

Useful Expressions

1. The city is on the sea, and the sea is in the city.

城在海上,海在城中。

2. This is Mr. Yang, our driver. Mr. Yang is a responsible and experienced driver, so you are in safe hands.

这是杨先生,我们的司机。杨先生是一位有责任心、经验丰富的司机,所以你们可以放心乘坐。

3. Please reset your watches to Beijing standard time, which is 4:15 pm.

请将您的手表调到北京标准时间下午4:15。

4. Xiamen is a beautiful city along the southeast coast of China, with a total area of 1700.61 square kilometers and an urban population of less than 600000.

厦门是中国东南沿海美丽的海滨城市,总面积为1700.61平方千米,城市人口不到60万。

5. There is no bitter cold in winter and no severe heat in summer.

冬无严寒,夏无酷暑。

6. If you have any problems or requests, please don't hesitate to let us know.

如果您有任何问题或要求,请随时告诉我们。

7. We'll do everything possible to make your visit pleasant.

我们将竭尽所能让您的旅行愉快。

8. We will be always at your service.

我们将随时为您服务。

9. Our car is now passing Xiamen bridge, which is the first sea-crossing bridge in China.

我们的车正在经过厦门大桥,这是中国第一座跨海大桥。

10. Zhongshan road is the most prosperous commercial street in Xiamen at present.

中山路是厦门目前最繁华的商业街。

Exercises

1. Match the following Chinese with the correct English versions

(1) 时差   a. city center
(2) 亚热带地区   b. provincial capital
(3) 海滨城市   c. time difference
(4) 市中心   d. international metropolis

Module 1 Meeting the Tourists

(5) 省会 e. subtropical zone
(6) 国际大都市 f. city tree
(7) 市花 g. coastal city
(8) 市树 h. pedestrian street
(9) 地标 i. city flower
(10) 步行街 j. landmark

2. Translate the following Chinese into English

(1) 我来介绍一下厦门的基本概况。
(2) 这是我们的司机陈师傅,他已经有20年的驾驶经验。
(3) 如果大家有任何问题,都可以与我联系。我很乐意为大家服务。
(4) 我们的车牌号是D5066H,请一定记得。
(5) 朋友们,请大家抬头往上看,现在在空中飞翔的正是厦门市鸟——白鹭。
(6) 这是一座冬无严寒、夏无酷暑的城市。
(7) 请大家往右边看,这是我市中心的地标。
(8) 这是最热闹的步行街。在这里,商品琳琅满目。

3. Fill in the blanks with appropriate words and expressions

A: Now, we are driving you to the Lakeview Hotel, the hotel you will live in during your stay in Hangzhou. This is our driver Mr. Zhang. He has over 10 years of ___(1)___, and is quite ___(2)___.

B: That is great. Is our hotel far from the airport?

A: It usually ___(3)___ 40 minutes to the Lakeview Hotel. This hotel is a very nice five-star hotel, located on the east bank of the West Lake. In your room, you can have a view of the beautiful lake.

B: This is our first ___(4)___ to your city. I was told it was a very popular scenic city among the Chinese cities. Right?

A: Yes. In China, there is an old saying which goes, "Up in heaven there is ___(5)___, down on earth there're Suzhou and Hangzhou." So, Chinese people consider Hangzhou as a paradise city.

B: Wow. That is gorgeous.

A: The history of the city can be ___(6)___ back to over 2200 years ago. You know, in classic Chinese, the word "Hangzhou" means a piece of land in water which is accessible by boat. Hangzhou saw its heyday during the Southern Song Dynasty about 800 years ago when it served as the capital of the country. Thus, Hangzhou is one of the six ancient capitals in China.

B: What is the population of the city?

A: The ___(7)___ is about 6 million including the suburbs. However, here in China, it is only a medium-sized city. Now we have entered the downtown area.

B: That huge building on the right looks very unique. What is it?

A: That is Hangzhou East Station. The total construction ___(8)___ of the station is more than 50000 square meters. It adopts a huge space wooden truss supporting the whole structure, reflecting the image of "white wall and dark tile" of folk houses in Southern China. It is notable for the ____(9)____ of the traditional architectural elements and the flavor of modern times.

B: When we leave Hangzhou for Shanghai, can we have a chance to take a train there?

A: Yes, we will go to Shanghai by express train from Hangzhou East Station.

B: That is excellent.

A: Now we are approaching the West Lake. It's called the West Lake because the lake is located on the west part of the city, surrounded by mountains on three sides, except the east side. The east side is the city proper. Ladies and gentlemen, here we are, at the Lakeview Hotel. I'll ask the ____(10)____ to take care of your luggage and I will help you to check in.

B: Thank you.

4. Role play

Situation 1: Make a welcome speech to the guests on the coach. The following parts should be included: say welcome, introduce yourself and the driver, willingness to serve the guests, expectation of a happy visit.

Situation 2: On the way to the hotel, the local guide introduces the main feature of the city and answers relevant questions raised by the guests.

5. Questions & Answers

Question 1: What should be included when the local guide makes a general introduction of the city en route?

Question 2: What should be the content of the welcome speech?

Ⅳ Extended Reading

Welcome to Fuzhou

Welcome to Fuzhou

Module 2
Hotel Check-in

Learning Objectives

1. Check-in for the guests.
2. Confirm or modify the room reservation.
3. Discuss or confirm itinerary.
4. Arrange morning call service.
5. Handle the guests' complaint about the room or the room arrangement.

Case Introduction

In the peak tourist season, Xiao Zhou, the local guide, took a group of 26 people to Huangshan. When the guests entered the hotel, some guests complained that the hotel didn't look like a five-star hotel and wanted to change to a better hotel.

What should Xiao Zhou do to deal with the situation?

Task 1 Room Reservation

 | **Warming Up**

1. Read and Match

a. front office   b. single room   c. twin room   d. suite

(1)　　(2)　　(3)　　(4)

2. Question

What information should be clarified in the room reservation?

Tips for reference:

(1) Room types.

(2) Number of rooms.

(3) Price or discount.

(4) Date of arrival and departure.

(5) Special requirements.

Ⅱ Situational Dialogues

> **Dialogue 1**

Confirmation of Room Reservation

(As a local guide, Xiao Li calls Hilton Hotel to confirm the room reservation before receiving the tour group.)

L: **Xiao Li, the local guide**　　R: **Receptionist at the front office**

R: Good morning. Hilton Hotel front office. May I help you?

L: Good morning. This is Xiao Li, a local guide from China International Travel Service. I would like to confirm my room reservation in your hotel.

R: Wait a moment, please, Mr. Li. Let me check the computer record.

L: Well, I reserved ten double rooms and five single rooms last Monday morning.

R: Let me see… Yes, you are right. You have reserved ten double rooms and five single rooms from October 1 to October 10.

L: And all my rooms face the park. Am I correct?

R: Exactly.

L: Thank you very much. And are all the rooms on the same floor?

R: Yes. Your double rooms are from Room 701 to Room 710, single rooms from Room 721 to Room 725, all on the seventh floor.

L: Great. My tour group is due to arrive at 10:30 tomorrow morning. You see, it is a one-hour drive from the station to the hotel. So we are probably going to get to the hotel at about 12:00 am tomorrow. Can you get all the rooms ready for us at that time?

R: Yes, of course. We are expecting your coming.

L: Thanks a lot. What's more, my guests have many pieces of big luggage. So can you arrange some porters to help us?

R: No problem. I will ask two bellmen to help you with your luggage.

L: That is very kind of you. Thank you.

R: Anything else I can do for you?

L: No, that is all. Thank you for your help. Bye.

R: Bye.

> **Dialogue 2**

Mistakes in Room Reservation

(As a local guide, Wang Lin calls Wyndham Hotel to confirm the room reservation and finds there is something wrong with the reservation.)

W: Wang Lin, the local guide   R: Receptionist

R: Good morning. Wyndham Hotel front office. What can I do for you?

L: Good morning. This is Wang Lin, a local guide from China Comfort Travel. I have a reservation for tonight. It is under Tina Williams. I would like to confirm the reservation.

R: Wait a moment, please. I will check it for you. Oh, yes, a Chinese suite for Jim Williams, right?

L: No, not Chinese suite. I remember I reserved five single rooms.

R: Let me check it again. Can you spell the guest's full name?

L: T-I-N-A, Tina, W-I-L-L-I-A-M-S, Williams.

扫码
听听力

R: Let me see. Yes, five single rooms for tomorrow.

L: Oh, no. They are for tonight, not tomorrow night.

R: There must be some mistake. I am awfully sorry for the mistake. Let me change the information for you. Five single rooms for tonight.

L: Can you arrange all the five rooms on the same floor?

R: I am sorry. You see, now it is the peak season and we have high occupancies in the hotel. I am afraid it is not possible to do that.

L: I see. That is OK.

R: Thank you for your understanding.

Useful Expressions

1. I would like to confirm my room reservation in your hotel.
我想确认一下预订信息。

2. My tour group is due to arrive at 10:30 tomorrow morning.
我的团队预计在明天早上10点30分抵达。

3. Can you get all the rooms ready for us at that time?
那时房间能全部准备好吗?

4. Can you arrange some porters to help us?
你能否安排一些行李员来帮助我们?

Exercises

1. Match the following Chinese with the correct English versions

(1) 房间预订　　　　　　　　　　a. porter, bellman
(2) 确定　　　　　　　　　　　　b. discount
(3) 单人间　　　　　　　　　　　c. agreement
(4) 双人间　　　　　　　　　　　d. room reservation
(5) 中式套间　　　　　　　　　　e. single room
(6) 日式套间　　　　　　　　　　f. presidential suite
(7) 总统套间　　　　　　　　　　g. double room
(8) 行李员　　　　　　　　　　　h. Japanese suite
(9) 折扣　　　　　　　　　　　　i. confirm
(10) 协议　　　　　　　　　　　　j. Chinese suite

2. Translate the following Chinese into English

(1) 喜来登酒店前台。有什么需要帮助的吗?
(2) 请稍等。我查一下。
(3) 一间双人房要多少钱?
(4) 我想确认一下预订信息。

(5) 我想加一间双人房、一间单人房。

(6) 我想把一间双人房改为套间。

(7) 双人房和套间的价格差多少？

(8) 我们是有协议价的。

(9) 可以打折吗？

(10) 很抱歉，这是我们的最低价。

3. Fill in the blanks with appropriate words and expressions

A：Good morning. Front office. What can I do for you?

B：Good morning. I made a ____(1)____ five days ago. I would like to confirm my reservation.

A：May I have your ____(2)____, please?

B：Tina，Fang.

A：Wait a moment. Let me ____(3)____. Yes, you reserved 5 French suites for October 11, right?

B：Yes. Can you arrange the suites with a view of the sea?

A：I am sorry. I can only ____(4)____ two suites with a view of the sea. You know, now it is the peak season.

B：I understand. That is OK. My guests will arrive at about 8：00 pm. Is the hotel restaurant still open then?

A：Don't worry. It is still ____(5)____.

B：That is great. Thanks a lot.

A：It is my pleasure.

4. Role play

Situation 1：Suppose you are the local guide and are now making a call to the front office of the hotel to confirm the room reservation. The day of the arrival happens to be the birthday of one guest. You ask the receptionist to prepare a bunch of flowers and a birthday cake to be sent to the room.

Situation 2：Suppose you are the local guide, two guests decided not to join the tour group. You call the front desk of the hotel to change the room reservation.

5. Questions & Answers

Question：What should a local guide do when his or her group is checking in at a hotel?

Ⅳ Extended Reading

Presidential Suites

Presidential Suites

Task 2 Check In

| Warming Up

1. Read and Match

a. passport   b. deposit receipt   c. QR code   d. room card

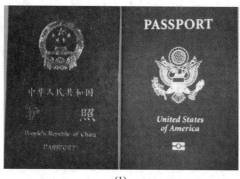

(1)

(2)

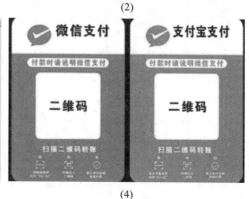

(3)   (4)

2. Question

What should a local guide do when checking in the tour group at the hotel?

Tips for reference:

(1) Help with the check-in procedure.

(2) Introduce the main facilities at the hotel.

(3) Tell the tourists the schedule for the day or the next day.

(4) Clarify the time and place for the first meal of the group.

(5) Clarify the time of the morning call for the next day.

Module 2   Hotel Check-in

📖 Ⅱ Situational Dialogues

➤ Dialogue 1

Check in for the Tour Group

(Xiao Li, the local guide, approaches the front office of Hilton Hotel to check in for her tour group.)

　　L: Xiao Li, the local guide　　R: Receptionist

　　R: Good morning. What can I do for you?

　　L: Good morning. I am Xiao Li from China International Travel Service. I would like to check in for my tour group.

　　R: OK, Miss Li. Have you got a reservation?

　　L: Yes. I made a reservation of ten double rooms, five single rooms and one Japanese suite from October 1 to October 10. All my rooms are all on the seventh floor.

　　R: Let me have a check. Yes, you are right. May I have the passports and landing cards of your tour members?

　　L: Of course. Here you are.

　　R: Thank you. A moment, please.

　　L: OK. Can you assign the rooms to my tourists according to the name list I faxed to you last Sunday?

　　R: No problem. Wait a moment, please. Let me check the fax.

　　L: Thank you very much. One more thing, we have about 10 pieces of luggage in the coach. They are big and heavy. I have called the front office yesterday to ask two bellmen to help us with the luggage.

　　R: Yes. Don't worry. We have arranged two bellmen for you.

　　L: Thanks a lot. All our rooms are on the seventh floor. So please ask the bellman to deliver the luggage to the corridor of the seventh floor.

　　R: That is OK. May I have 1500 yuan as deposit?

　　L: Can I pay with Alipay or WeChat?

　　R: Of course. You can scan the QR code here.

　　L: OK. One more thing, one of my tour members has sprained his ankle seriously just now. I am afraid he can not walk. I wonder if you can offer him a wheelchair.

　　R: I am sorry to hear that. But don't worry. The two bellmen will go to the parking lot with luggage carts and a wheelchair with you. Here is telephone number of the hotel clinic. Your guest can go there to see the doctor.

　　L: That is very considerate of you. Oh, you've finished all the check-in. What

扫码
听听力

efficiency! Thank you very much.

R: It's my pleasure. Here are your room cards and breakfast coupons. Please keep them. If you have any problems, please do not hesitate to let us know. We are always at your service.

➢ Dialogue 2

Guests Are not Satisfied with the Room Arrangement

(Xiao Li, the local guide, is leading Mr. Bellow to his room. But the guest is not satisfied with the room because it is facing the west and the window cannot be opened.)

L: Xiao Li, the local guide   B: Mr. Bellow, the guest

L: Mr. Bellow, this is your room. How do you like it?

B: I am afraid it is not very satisfying. You see, the room is facing the west. I hate sunset. It always makes me upset. What is worse, the window cannot be opened. How could I live in a room without natural air?

L: I am terribly sorry for the inconvenience. But this is the peak season for traveling here. There is high occupancy in the hotel. I cannot guarantee that there is still room left.

B: What should I do then?

L: Well, I will call the hotel manager to see if there is any vacant single room. Wait a moment, please.

(After the call)

L: Mr. Bellow, I am sorry to say that all the single rooms are booked up in the hotel. There is still a suite room left. It doesn't face the west and the windows in it could be opened. Would you like to change the room?

B: That is OK. A suite will do.

L: One more thing, a single room is 268 yuan, a suite is 368 yuan. So you have to pay extra 100 yuan. Is that acceptable to you?

B: That is OK.

L: I will go to the front office and change the room for you. So would you like to stay in this room or go to the hall with me?

B: I'd like to go to the hall with you.

L: OK. Let's go.

Useful Expressions

1. I would like to check in for my tour group.

我想办理我的旅游团的入住登记手续。

2. I made a reservation of ten double rooms, five single rooms and one Japanese suite from October 1 to October 10.

我预订了 10 月 1 日至 10 月 10 日的 10 间双人房、5 间单人房、1 间日式套房。

3. May I have your passports and landing cards of your tour members?

请出示护照和旅行团成员的入境证好吗？

4. Can you assign the rooms to my tourists according to the name list I faxed to you last Sunday?

你能根据我上周日传真给你的名单把房间分配给我的游客吗？

5. Here are your room cards and breakfast coupons. Please keep them.

这是你的房卡和早餐券。请保管好。

III Exercises

1. Match the following Chinese with the correct English versions

(1) 商务套房   a. room card
(2) 蜜月套房   b. deposit
(3) 海滨城市   c. occupancy
(4) 海景房   d. seaside city
(5) 房卡   e. business suite
(6) 押金   f. honeymoon suite
(7) 收据   g. peak season
(8) 早餐卡   h. sea-view room
(9) 旺季   i. breakfast coupons
(10) 入住率   j. receipt

2. Translate the following Chinese into English

(1) 请把护照给我。我去给你们办理入住。
(2) 我预订了 5 间单人房、5 间双人房。
(3) 这个房间是一个海景房。
(4) 很抱歉，酒店已经没有空房了。
(5) 我问一下前台还有没有空房。
(6) 如果您要换房间的话，需要支付 200 元的差价。
(7) 大家对房间有什么不满意的地方，请及时告知我。
(8) 这是你们的房卡和早餐券。

3. Fill in the blanks with appropriate words and expressions

A：Good morning. What can I do for you?

B. I am the tour guide from CITS. I want to check in for my tour group.

A：_____(1)_____?

B：My name is Li Ming.

A：Wait a moment, let me _____(2)_____. Oh, yes, you booked 8 deluxe suites from May 1 to May 4, right?

B: That's right.

A: Please give me ____(3)____.

B: Here you are. By the way, can you ____(4)____ all the suite on the same floor?

A: I am sorry to say that ____(5)____. You see, it is the ____(6)____ season. I can arrange 4 suites on the 10th floor and the other 4 suites on the 11th floor. Is that acceptable?

B: That is good.

A: Please pay 1600 yuan as ____(7)____. How would you like to pay? Alipay or credit card?

B: Credit card, please.

A: Here is the deposit receipt. Please ____(8)____ it.

B: Thank you.

A: These are the room cards and breakfast ____(9)____.

B: Thank you. What time will the breakfast be served?

A: From 6:30 am to 10:00 am. The dining hall is on the second ____(10)____.

B: Thank you for your information.

A: Is there anything else I can do for you?

B: That's all. Thanks a lot. Bye.

A: Bye.

4. Role play

Situation 1: Suppose you are the local guide and now are checking in for your group at the front desk of the hotel. Make a dialogue with the receptionist.

Situation 2: Suppose you are a local guide and one of your guests tells you that she has a sleeping problem and cannot share the room with other guests. Make a dialogue with the guest and try to solve the problem.

5. Questions & Answers

Question: How can a local guide keep in touch with the tourists after the group has checked in at the hotel?

Ⅳ Extended Reading

Check in Procedures

Check in Procedures

Task 3 Itinerary and Morning Call

| Warming Up

1. Read and Match

a. Bird's Nest
c. the Summer Palace
b. Water Cube
d. the Temple of Heaven

(1)　　(2)　　(3)　　(4)

2. Question

What should a local guide do when the itinerary on hand is different from the itinerary the tour leader has received?

Tips for reference:

(1) Apologize first.

(2) Clarify the reasons for the difference.

(3) Apologize again and promise not to make the same mistake again.

Situational Dialogues

Dialogue 1

Discussion of Itinerary and Time of Morning Call

(Xiao Lu, the local guide, is now discussing the itinerary and the time of morning call with Mr. Green, the tour leader.)

L: Xiao Lu, the local guide   G: Mr. Green, the tour leader

L: Mr. Green, I have come to discuss our itinerary. Could you spare me some time right now?

G: Sure. Go ahead.

L: On the morning of the first day, we will go and visit the Great Wall. We are going to have lunch in a local restaurant where we can have a taste of typical Beijing food. And after lunch, we will go and visit the Bird's Nest and Water Cube. The visit will last for 3 hours, and then we will go back to the hotel and have buffet in the Venice Restaurant on the second floor.

G: That is OK.

L: Good. What about the morning call? The coach will leave at 7:00.

G: 6:00 am will be reasonable. What do you think of it?

L: Well, I agree with you. So the hotel will wake us up at 6:00 am. Our coach will be waiting for us in the parking lot of the hotel. We are going to set out at 7:00 sharp. Everyone is required to get to the parking lot at 6:50. OK?

G: No problem. What about the arrangement on the second day?

L: We have a busy schedule on the second day. We will go to the Tian'anmen Square, the Palace Museum and Beihai Park.

G: What can we see in the park?

L: Beihai Park is located in the central area of Beijing and is an ancient Chinese royal garden with an area of 682000 square meters. The White Pagoda and Yong'an Temple, which symbolize the divine power, are set up in an important position on Qiongdao Island. They have the momentum of dominating the whole garden to reflect the feudal thought of "divine conferment of monarchical power", which is a major feature of the imperial palace.

G: That sounds interesting. On the third day, we will go to the Summer Palace and the Temple of Heaven. Am I right?

L: Yes. The Summer Palace is an ancient imperial garden in Beijing. It is located in the western suburb of Beijing, 15 kilometers away from the urban area, covering an area of 290 hectares. It is a large-scale landscape garden and draws the inspiration from the West Lake of Hangzhou. It is known as the "Royal Garden Museum". The Temple of Heaven was a place for the emperors of the Ming and Qing Dynasties to offer sacrifices and pray for abundant grain.

G: Those are spots really worth a visit. By the way, do we have a chance to go shopping?

L: This is a non-shopping tour. But if you like, you can go to Wangfujing Street at night, the liveliest street in Beijing. There are a variety of shops there.

G: Thank you. Is Wangfujing Street far from here?

L: No. It just takes 30 minutes to get there. You may take the subway or hail a taxi.

G: I see. Thanks a lot.

L: You are welcome. Any more questions about the itinerary?

G: No, the arrangements are satisfying.

L: If you have any problems, please feel free to let me know. I am always at your service. Have a pleasant evening.

G: Thank you. Goodbye.

➤ Dialogue 2

Morning Call Service

(Xiao Li, the local guide, is asking morning call service at the front desk.)

L: Xiao Li, the local guide   R: Receptionist

R: Good morning. What can I do for you?

L: I would like to ask for morning call service for my guests.

R: No problem. At what time?

L: At 6:00 am. The room numbers are 601, 602, 603, 801, 802 and 805.

R: 601, 602, 603, 801, 802 and 805. Six rooms in all. Right?

L: Yes, that is right.

R: OK. We will wake them up by phone at 6:00 am.

L: Thank you. Please make sure that the guests will all receive the call and answer the call. You know our schedule is tight. There is no time to be missed. If one guest is late, the whole schedule may have to be changed.

R: OK. We will take care of that.

L: At what time will the breakfast be served?

R: Our restaurant is open at 6:00 am.

L: I wonder if it is breakfast buffet.

R: Yes. It is breakfast buffet. We offer Chinese breakfast and Western breakfast. For Chinese breakfast, we have porridge, stuffed buns, steamed bread, deep-fried dough stick etc. For Western breakfast, we have milk, bread, sausages

扫码
听听力

and fried eggs. You can choose as you like.

L: That is excellent. Thank you for your introduction.

R: It is my pleasure.

Useful Expressions

1. We are going to set out at 7:00 sharp.

我们明天早上七点整准时出发。

2. The White Pagoda and Yong'an temple, which symbolize the divine power, are set up in an important position on Qiongdao Island. They have the momentum of dominating the whole garden to reflect the feudal thought of "divine conferment of monarchical power", which is a major feature of the imperial palace.

白塔和永安寺是神权的象征,在琼岛上占有重要地位。它们具有统领整个园林的气势,体现了封建"君权神授"的思想,这是皇家宫殿的一大特色。

3. The Temple of Heaven was a place for the emperors of the Ming and Qing Dynasties to offer sacrifices and pray for abundant grain.

天坛是明清两代皇帝祭祀、祈求粮食丰收的地方。

4. Please make sure that the guests will all receive the call and answer the call. You know our schedule is tight. There is no time to be missed.

请确保客人会接到电话并接听电话。你知道我们的日程很紧。不能错过任何时间。

5. For Chinese breakfast, we have porridge, stuffed buns, steamed bread, deep-fried dough stick etc. For Western breakfast, we have milk, bread, sausages and fried eggs.

中式早餐有粥、包子、馒头、油条等。西式早餐有牛奶、面包、香肠、煎蛋。

Exercises

1. Match the following Chinese with the correct English versions

(1) 行程　　　　　　　　　　a. schedule adjustment

(2) 叫早服务　　　　　　　　b. final version

(3) 最后版本　　　　　　　　c. itinerary

(4) 无购物行程　　　　　　　d. morning call service

(5) 行程调整　　　　　　　　e. no-shopping tour

(6) 行程差异　　　　　　　　f. itinerary difference

(7) 自助早餐　　　　　　　　g. Chinese breakfast

(8) 中式早餐　　　　　　　　h. breakfast buffet

2. Translate the following Chinese into English

(1) 我们来核对一下我们的行程安排。

（2）我们的行程不一致。

（3）这不是最后版本的行程表。

（4）我们的行程在10月6日做了调整。

（5）请安排早上六点半的叫早服务。

（6）很抱歉，一定是哪里出错了。我会尽快确认原因。

（7）我们第一天要去的是西湖和灵隐寺。

（8）第二天的行程很紧张，有三个景点。

（9）我们是无购物行程。如果客人要购买伴手礼的话，酒店的商店里就有售。

（10）我们明天早上七点在酒店大堂集合，请务必准时。

3. Fill in the blanks with appropriate words and expressions

A：Good morning. What can I do for you?

B．I am the tour guide from CITS. I want a morning call service for my guests.

A：At what ＿＿（1）＿＿ ?

B：At 6：30.

A：May I have the ＿＿（2）＿＿ ?

B：Room 101-110. Ten rooms in ＿＿（3）＿＿ .

A：Let me ＿＿（4）＿＿ the information with you. 6：30 tomorrow morning, room 101-110. Am I correct?

B：Yes. That is right.

A：Anything else I can do for you?

B：That's all. Thank you.

4. Role play

Situation 1：Suppose you are the local guide and now you are checking the itinerary with the tour leader. Make a dialogue with the tour leader.

Situation 2：Suppose you are the local guide and now you are arranging morning call service. Make a dialogue with the receptionist at the front desk.

5. Questions & Answers

Question：What should the local guide do when the guests want to change the itinerary?

IV Extended Reading

3-Day Private Zhangjiajie Tour

3-Day Private Zhangjiajie Tour

Module 3
Food and Beverage Service

Learning Objectives

1. Arrange the first meal and solve the relevant problems.
2. Introduce the main features of Chinese cuisine and Western cuisine.
3. Make special meal arrangement.
4. Deal with complaints about food and beverage service.

Case Introduction

Case 1:

In the meal time, an eight-month-old baby girl in the tour group grabbed the stew pot on the table and was scalded by the hot soup. At this time, she was lying in her mother's arms crying with her red hot fingers. Her mother was angry and kept complaining.

What should the local guide do to deal with the accident?

Case 2:

In the meal time, the local guide noticed that one of the guests ate very little. He quickly went forward to ask the reason and knew that the guest had something wrong with the stomach and dared not eat seafood. But most dishes on the table were seafood.

What should the local guide do?

Module 3　Food and Beverage Service

Task 1　Meal Arrangement

Warming Up

1. Read and Match

a. fork and knife　　b. soup spoon　　c. chopsticks　　d. wine glass

(1)

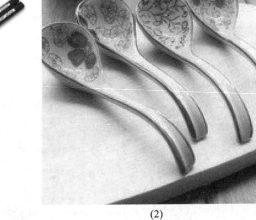
(2)

(3)

(4)

2. Question

What should a tour guide do in terms of meal arrangement?

Tips for reference:

(1) confirm the meal information in advance with the restaurant;

(2) tell the tourists in advance the time and place for the meal, the way the meal is served;

(3) clarify the regulations of the restaurant;

(4) introduce the tour leader to the restaurant manager or the head waiter.

Ⅱ Situational Dialogues

➢ Dialogue 1

The First Meal

(It is the first meal time. When eight dishes with a soup as stipulated in the contract are served, two tourists tell Mr. Wang, the local guide, that they are Buddhist vegetarians and ask Mr. Wang to arrange another meal for them. They say they mentioned this when they signed up for the tour.)

W: Mr. Wang, the local guide   S: Mr. and Mrs. Smith, the tourists

W: Attention please. The two tables at the corner are for our group. You can take your seat and wait for a minute. The dishes are coming.

(The dishes are served)

S: Mr. Wang, I have something to tell you. I am afraid you have to arrange another meal for us two.

W: Why? Anything happened?

S: You see, all the dishes here are not vegetarian dishes. But my husband and I are Buddhist vegetarians. We mentioned this when we signed up for the tour. Haven't you written it in the contract?

W: I am sorry, let me check with the travel agency first. Please wait a moment.

(Five minutes later)

W: Mrs. Smith, it is indeed the carelessness of our staff that caused the mistake. I am awfully sorry for the inconvenience we have caused.

S: What's to be done then?

W: Thank you for your understanding. To make up for it, we will talk with the restaurant to arrange vegetarian dishes for you as soon as possible. And of course our travel agency will bear all the cost. But first allow me to arrange the details with the restaurant. Would you please wait in the bar for a moment and have some drinks while waiting?

S: That is OK.

(After the vegetarian dishes are ready)

W: I am sorry to have kept you waiting. Your dishes are ready now. Please follow me to the table by the window.

S: OK.

(Mr. and Mrs. Smith taste the dishes)

W: I hope the dishes suit your taste. We have asked the restaurant to prepare some famous local vegetarian dishes for you. What do you think of them?

S: Thank you for the careful arrangement. They are perfect in color, aroma and taste.

W: I am glad to hear that. And I will arrange your diet more carefully in the following days. Take your time and enjoy your dinner.

➤ Dialogue 2

At the Chinese Restaurant

(The tourists are now at a Chinese restaurant waiting for lunch. One guest wants to know something about Chinese cuisine. The tour guide introduces the features of Chinese cuisine.)

Z: Zhang Yuan, the local guide   B: Mr. Black, the tourist

Z: OK, everyone, now we are at the a Chinese restaurant. Please wait a minute. The meals will come about 15 minutes later.

B: China has enjoyed a worldwide reputation as the kingdom of cuisine. You know, I am a lover of Chinese food, and I really want to know more about it. Zhang, while we are waiting, would you tell us something about Chinese cuisine?

Z: It is my pleasure. There is a famous Chinese old saying, "Food is god for the people." Anyone knows the meaning?

B: The food is very important?

Z: Yes, you are right. The saying means that food is the first necessity of the people, which reflects that Chinese have paid much attention to food since the ancient times. The importance of food in people's daily life in China can be seen in the way they used to send greetings to each other, "Have you eaten?" which is far away from the way people greet in Western countries and has been seen as a characteristic of Chinese culture.

B: Do all the people in China eat mantou or jiaozi?

Z: Not necessarily. Staple food in China generally includes rice, wheat, buckwheat, corn, potato, sweet potato and beans. Besides, wheaten food such as mantou (steamed bun), noodle, youtiao (deep-fried dough stick), xiaolongbao

扫码
听听力

(steamed pork-stuffed dumpling in bamboo basket), and many other local snacks are commonly seen on the table in China.

B: Wow. It is said that there are many styles of Chinese food, right?

Z: Yes, divided by region, a general feature of spicy east food, sweet south food, sour west food and salty north food can be summarized. Generally, people living in South China pay more attention to nutrition and prefer delicate and refreshing food such as rice porridge and soup. By contrast, spicy hot pot is always people's favorite in the southwest areas due to the humid and rainy climate. And people living in North China prefer wheaten food such as jiaozi, noodle, while all kinds of steamed bun, beef and mutton are most popular in northwest areas.

B: Thank you for your detailed introduction. What about the food we will take today?

Z: The dishes we take today belong to Fujian cuisine. It is one of the eight main cuisines of China. It is notable for seafood and river fish. The Fujian coastal area produces varieties of fish and different kinds of turtles and shellfish. These special products are widely used in Fujian dishes.

B: That sounds great. We like seafood very much.

Z: The most characteristic aspect of Fujian cuisine is that many dishes are served in soup. The cooking methods are stewing, boiling, braising, quick-boiling and steaming. Cutting is another important skill in Fujian cuisine. Most dishes are made of seafood, and if they are not cut in a right way, the dishes will fail to display their true flavor. Fujian dishes are slightly sweet and sour, and less salty. When a dish is less salty, it tastes more delicious. Sweetness makes a dish tastier, while sourness helps remove the seafood smell.

B: That sounds marvelous. We will have a good chance to feast our stomach today.

Z: Exactly. Now the dishes are coming. Take your time and enjoy your meal.

Useful Expressions

1. The two tables at the corner are for our group.
角落的那两张桌子是我们团预订的。

2. To make up for it, we will talk with the restaurant to arrange vegetarian dishes for you as soon as possible.
作为补偿,我们会尽快联系餐厅给你们安排素食。

3. Would you please wait in the bar for a moment and have some drinks while waiting?
你们能不能在吧台稍等一会儿,喝点东西?

4. I hope the dishes suit your taste.
希望菜品合你们的口味。

5. Staple food in China generally includes rice, wheat, buckwheat, corn, potato,

Module 3　Food and Beverage Service

sweet potato and beans.

中国的主食一般包括大米、小麦、荞麦、玉米、马铃薯、红薯和豆类。

6. Besides, wheaten food such as mantou (steamed bun), noodle, youtiao (deep-fried dough stick), xiaolongbao (steamed pork-stuffed dumpling in bamboo basket), and many other local snacks are commonly seen on the table in China.

此外,馒头、面条、油条、小笼包等面食在中国的餐桌上很常见。

7. Divided by region, a general feature of spicy east food, sweet south food, sour west food and salty north food can be summarized.

按地域划分,可以总结出东辣、南甜、西酸、北咸的特点。

8. The cooking methods are stewing, boiling, braising, quick-boiling and steaming.

烹调方法有炖、煮、焖、快煮、蒸。

Exercises

1. Match the following Chinese with the correct English versions

(1) 八大菜系　　　　　　　　　a. quick-fry
(2) 刀工　　　　　　　　　　　b. staple food
(3) 摆盘　　　　　　　　　　　c. plain-fry
(4) 清炒　　　　　　　　　　　d. steamed bun
(5) 爆炒　　　　　　　　　　　e. deep-fry
(6) 焖　　　　　　　　　　　　f. eight cuisines
(7) 油炸　　　　　　　　　　　g. layout
(8) 蒸　　　　　　　　　　　　h. cutting
(9) 馒头　　　　　　　　　　　i. deep-fried dough stick
(10) 油条　　　　　　　　　　j. steam
(11) 主食　　　　　　　　　　k. soup
(12) 汤品　　　　　　　　　　l. braise

2. Translate the following Chinese into English

(1) 中国菜非常强调色、香、味俱佳。
(2) 中国菜强调"食能养人",讲究的就是充分体现食物的营养,要荤素合理搭配。
(3) 中国菜的选材非常丰富,几乎所有能吃的东西,都可以作为中国菜的食材。
(4) 中餐的餐具,最主要的有盘、碟、筷子、碗、匙、杯、盆、勺子等。最具特点的是筷子。
(5) 几乎所有中国菜都要求食材鲜活。
(6) 鲁菜以汤为百鲜之源,讲究"清汤""奶汤"的调制。
(7) 川菜以麻辣著称,最具代表性的就是重庆火锅。
(8) 粤菜味道讲究"清、鲜、嫩、滑",追求原料的本味、清鲜味。

(9) 头盘的话，我建议您试一下今日特色——沙朗牛排，口感很棒。许多客人对它评价很高。

(10) 您可以试试我们的牛排。这是我们厨师的招牌菜，口感细腻、肉质鲜嫩。

3. Fill in the blanks with appropriate words and expressions

A: Ladies and gentlemen, while we are waiting for our dinner, I would like to say something about Chinese cuisine. OK?

B: Great. We are quite ____(1)____ in Chinese cuisine. It is said that there are eight main regional ____(2)____ in China, isn't it?

A: Yes, you are right. China covers a large territory, giving rise to a variety of regional food with different ____(3)____. Generally speaking, Chinese food can be roughly ____(4)____ into eight regional cuisines. They are Shandong cuisine, Sichuan cuisine, Guangdong cuisine, Fujian cuisine, Jiangsu cuisine, Zhejiang cuisine, Hunan cuisine and Anhui cuisine.

B: I know Sichuan food is hot and spicy. What are the main ____(5)____ of Shandong cuisine?

A: Shandong dishes are mainly quick-fried, roasted, stir-fried or deep-fried. ____(6)____ is given much emphasis in Shandong dishes. Thin soup is clear and fresh while creamy soup looks ____(7)____ and tastes strong. The dishes are mainly clear, fresh and fatty, perfect with Shandong's own famous beer, Qingdao Beer.

B: That sounds great. Shandong's most famous dish is the Sweat and Sour Carp, am I right?

A: Exactly. A truly authentic Sweet and Sour Carp must come from the Yellow River. It is really a dish you should not ____(8)____.

B: What about Guangdong food?

A: People in Northern China often say that Guangdong people will eat anything that flies ____(9)____ airplanes, anything that moves on the ground except trains, and anything that moves in the water except boats. This statement is far from the truth, but Guangdong food is one of the most diverse and richest cuisines in China. Many vegetables originate from other parts of the world. It doesn't use much spice, bringing out the natural ____(10)____ of the vegetables and meats.

B: What about Jiangsu cuisine since we are in Suzhou?

A: Jiangsu cuisine, also called Huaiyang cuisine, is popular in the lower reach of the Yangtze River. Aquatics as the main ingredients, it ____(11)____ the freshness of materials. Its carving techniques are delicate, of which the melon carving technique is especially well known. Cooking techniques ____(12)____ of stewing, braising, roasting, simmering, etc. The flavor of Huaiyang cuisine is light, fresh, sweet and with delicate elegance.

B: China is really a kingdom of delicious food. Thank you so much for your introduction.

A: It is my pleasure. Now our dishes are coming. Please enjoy your dinner.

4. Role play

Situation 1: One of your guests wants to know something about Chinese cuisine. Act as a tour guide and make a dialogue with him/her. Your dialogue will include the following points: introduce the main features of Chinese cuisine; introduce some classical Chinese cuisine; introduce some local dishes.

Situation 2: One of your guests wants to know something about Chinese breakfast. Act as a tour guide and make a dialogue with him/her, introduce some typical Chinese breakfast, and answer questions if there are any.

5. Questions & Answers

Question: What should a local guide do when taking the group to their first meal?

IV Extended Reading

Chinese Cuisine

Chinese Cuisine

Task 2   Special Meal Requirements

I Warming Up

1. Read and Match

a. fruit dish   b. Beijing Roast Duck
c. vegetarian dish   d. child meal

(1)   (2)

(3)

(4)

2. Question

What should the local guide do if the guests have special requirement about the meal?

Tips for reference:

(1) Ask about the reason if necessary.

(2) Satisfy the requirement if it is reasonable.

(3) Tell the guest in advance that the extra fee is to be covered by himself/herself.

II Situational Dialogues

➢ Dialogue 1

Having Meal by Myself

(Xiao Li, the local guide, is accompanying the guests to the restaurant. Miss Smith calls to tell that she is not feeling well and wants to have meal in her room.)

L: Xiao Li, the local guide   S: Miss Smith, the guest

L: Hi, this is Xiao Li. Who is that?

S: This is Miss Smith speaking. I have something to discuss with you.

L: Sure. What is the matter?

S: I am not feeling well. I have a headache and have no appetite. I do not want to have meal in the restaurant. I just want to have something simple and plain, like porridge or some light soup.

L: I am sorry to hear that. Do you need a doctor or shall we go to the clinic?

S: Not necessary. I am just a little tired. I haven't had a good rest in the last two days. If I have a good rest tonight, I think I will be OK tomorrow.

Module 3   Food and Beverage Service

L: I will arrange the room service for you. What about vegetable porridge? It tastes fresh and light. I will ask the waiter to prepare some light side dishes as well. I hope it will be to your taste.

S: That is good. I will take it. Thank you for your consideration.

L: It is my pleasure. One more thing, the hotel will make extra charge for the room service. The fee should be covered by yourself.

S: I understand.

L: Thank you for your understanding. I will ask the waiter to send the porridge to room 608. Am I right?

S: That is right. Please ask them to hurry.

L: OK. The porridge will be ready soon. Please wait a moment. Bye.

S: Bye.

➤ **Dialogue 2**

Requiring Meal with Local Flavor

(The guests complained that all the meals they had were of the same style with no characteristics. The tour leader requires to try meals with local flavor.)

L: Xiao Wu, the local guide   G: Mr. Grant, the tour leader

L: Good morning, Mr. Grant. You called me just now. What is the matter?

G: Some of my guests complained that all the meals we have had these days seem to be of the same style and are so monotonous. They want to try meals with local flavor. For example, Beijing Roast Duck. Can you arrange that?

L: Actually, we have arranged Beijing Roast Duck in Quan Ju De for you tonight.

G: Wow. That is exactly what we want. Thank you. I would like to know more about how Beijing Roast Duck is made and how it is served.

L: The ducks are raised for the sole purpose of making the food. Force-fed, they are kept in cages which restrain them from moving about, so as to fatten them up and make the meat comparably tender. Beijing Roast Duck is processed in several steps: first the ducks are rubbed with spices, salt and sugar, and then kept hung in the air for some time; then the ducks are roasted in an oven, or hung over the fire till they become brown with rich grease perspiring outside and have a nice odor.

G: Oh, I see. Just now, you mention Quanjude, what is it?

L: To enjoy the famous duck, the restaurant Quanjude is the best choice for you. It has multiple outlets in Beijing. The old restaurant first opened in 1860. The duck here is said to be the best in Beijing, and the service is very good as well.

G: Thank you for your introduction. Apart from Beijing Roast Duck, what about the meals in the following days? We really want to try the dishes with local

扫码
听听力

characteristics.

L: We have arranged hot pot on the third day, instant-boiled muttons on the fourth day. If you like, we can arrange one night in the snack street. You can try a variety of local snacks there. What do you think of it?

G: That will do. Thank you.

L: You are welcome. If you have any problems, please feel free to tell me. I will try my best to help you.

Useful Expressions

1. I just want to have something simple and plain, like porridge or some light soup.

我只想吃点简单清淡的东西,像稀饭或清汤。

2. The hotel will make extra charge for the room service. The fee should be covered by yourself.

酒店将额外收取客房送餐服务费。费用由您自己负担。

3. They want to try meals with local flavor.

他们想尝尝当地风味的饭菜。

4. To enjoy the famous duck, the restaurant Quan Ju De is the best choice for you. It has multiple outlets in Beijing.

全聚德餐厅是您品尝著名烤鸭的最佳选择。它在北京有多家分店。

5. We have arranged hot pot on the third day, instant-boiled muttons on the fourth day.

第三天我们安排了火锅,第四天安排了涮羊肉。

Exercises

1. Match the following Chinese with the correct English versions

（1）稀饭　　　　　　　　　a. steamed bun/bread

（2）馒头　　　　　　　　　b. stir-fried shrimps with Longjing tea leaves

（3）包子　　　　　　　　　c. local flavor

（4）地方风味　　　　　　　d. stuffed bun

（5）羊肉泡馍　　　　　　　e. porridge

（6）涮羊肉　　　　　　　　f. Lanzhou hand-pulled noodles

（7）兰州拉面　　　　　　　g. spicy hot pot

（8）酸辣汤　　　　　　　　h. Pita Bread Soaked in Lamb Soup

（9）麻辣火锅　　　　　　　i. hot and sour soup

（10）龙井虾仁　　　　　　　j. instant-boiled mutton

2. **Translate the following Chinese into English**

（1）麻辣火锅是川渝地区最有特色、也最能代表川味的一种特色小吃。

（2）我们想品尝一下你们当地的风味菜。

（3）番茄鱼是当地的特色菜,鱼肉的香嫩和番茄的酸甜相融合,口感清爽。

（4）龙井虾仁是一道最有杭州特色的杭州名菜。龙井绿茶与西湖虾仁一起制作,嫩鲜里浸透着茶特有的香味。

（5）兰州牛肉拉面有"中华第一面"之美誉。

（6）羊肉泡馍素为西北地区人民所喜爱,外宾来陕也争先品尝,以饱口福。

3. **Fill in the blanks with appropriate words and expressions**

A：OK, everyone. This is the restaurant we are going to have supper tonight. It is a typical Sichuan restaurant. I hope you will like it.

B：I only know that Sichuan cuisine is hot. Would you tell us something more about it?

A：It is my ____(1)____. Sichuan cuisine is a style of Chinese cuisine originating in Sichuan Province, which is ____(2)____ for bold flavors, particularly the pungency and spiciness resulting from liberal use of garlic and chili peppers, as well as the unique flavor of the Sichuan peppercorn.

B：Can you introduce some typical ____(3)____ in Sichuan cuisine?

A：Sure. Typical Sichuan dishes include bean curd with minced pork in chili sauce, diced chicken with peanuts and peppers, shredded pork in Sichuan style, steamed pork wrapped in lotus leaves etc. Most of them are ____(4)____ and hot.

B：That is great. I like spicy food. What are we going to eat tonight?

A：We are going to ____(5)____ hot pot today. Hot pot is the most famous and favorite dish in Chongqing. It is noted for its peppery and hot ____(6)____, scalding yet fresh and tender. People ____(7)____ around a small pot filled with flavorful and nutritious soup base. You have a choice of spicy, pure and combo for the ____(8)____. Thin sliced raw meat, fish, various bean curd products and all kinds of vegetables are boiled in the soup base. You then dip them in a little bowl of special sauce. Be careful since the spicy soup base is burning hot.

B：My mouth is almost watering. I couldn't wait to have a try.

4. **Role play**

Situation 1：Perform as a local guide in Guangdong. Your guests want to try some typical Guangdong dishes and ask for your advice.

Situation 2：Perform as a local guide in Xiamen. Your guest wants to taste some local snacks and asks for your advice.

5. **Questions & Answers**

Question：A couple of senior tourists in an inbound tour group demand that their breakfast be served in their hotel room. Is this demand reasonable? What should the tour guide do in this case?

IV Extended Reading

Chinese Snacks

Module 4
City Service

Learning Objectives

1. Learn the basic procedures and specifications of city service.
2. Introduce the bike-sharing service, currency exchange service and online tickets booking service.
3. Communicate effectively with the guests about other city service.

Case 1:

On the way to Mount Wuyi, Xiao Wang, the local guide, was informed that the site was closed because of a traffic accident.

What should Xiao Wang do to deal with the accident?

Case 2:

A tourist rented a car from a rental company in Xiamen and drove to Fujian Tulou. On the way back to Xiamen, a car accident happened. The tourist called Xiao Wang, the local guide for help.

What should Xiao Wang do?

Task 1 Public Transportation

 | Warming Up

1. Read and Match

a. subway   b. international driving license

c. taxi	d. rental agreement

(1)　　　　　　　　　　　　　　　　(2)

(3)　　　　　　　　　　　　　　　　(4)

2. Questions

Question 1：What should a tour guide do when the tourist inquires about the public transportation information?

Tips for reference：

(1) Get familiar with the transportation information of the city.

(2) Provide clear and accurate guidance to the tourists, such as where they could take a bus or take a subway.

Question 2：What should a tour guide do when the tourist wants to rent a car during the trip?

Tips for reference：

(1) Maintain the car rental information.

(2) Lead the tourist to the car rental agency.

(3) Provide necessary help.

Module 4 City Service

📖 Situational Dialogues

➤ Dialogue 1

Public Transportation

(It is free time. The tourists want to have dinner at Spoon Restaurant. Xiao Li, the local guide, tells the tour leader how to get there.)

L: Xiao Li, the local guide   G: Mr. Grant, the tour leader

G: Excuse me, Xiao Li, can you do me a favor?

L: Yes. What's the matter?

G: It is free time tonight. We want to have a dinner outside. One of my friends recommends Spoon Restaurant for us.

L: Oh, very good choice. Spoon Restaurant is one of the most popular western restaurants in Xiamen. It's famous for its comfortable environment and the decoration of coffee elements.

G: Where is the restaurant?

L: It is on the G floor of the Paragon Hotel at the intersection of Lianhua Road.

G: Could you tell me how to get there?

L: No problem. Xiamen has a very developed public transportation system. There are three ways to get to the Paragon Hotel. You can take Line 1 and get off at Lianhua Road Station. You can also take the bus to get there, such as No. 10, No. 33, No. 101, No. 116 and No. 128. In general, buses run from 6:00 in the morning to 23:00 in the evening, and it costs from 1 yuan to 3 yuan according to the distance.

G: I am afraid we will come back very late.

L: If you come back late, you can take a taxi. Taxi fare charges 8 yuan within 3 kilometers, and additional 2 yuan for every subsequent 1 kilometer. In the nighttime from 23:00 pm to 5:00 am the next day, the fare charges 9.6 yuan within 3 kilometers and additional 2.4 yuan for each subsequent kilometer. It's about 20 yuan from the Paragon Hotel to our hotel. Pay attention to your safety.

G: Oh, I see. Thanks so much for the detailed information.

L: My pleasure. If there's any problem, you can call me.

G: OK, I will.

➤ Dialogue 2

Renting a Car

(One of your tourists would like to rent a car during the trip. He inquires something about how to rent a car in Xiamen.)

Z: Zhang Yuan, the local guide   B: Mr. Black, the tourist

B: Zhang, can you do me a favor?

Z: Yes, Mr. Black, what is the matter?

B: This business trip in Xiamen is so impressive, so I am considering renting a car to have a self-driving tour with my family during the summer vocation.

Z: That's a very good idea. Now the car-rental trip is very popular.

B: Can you tell me how to rent a car in Xiamen?

Z: Yes, the procedure of renting cars in Xiamen is the same as other cities in China. Do you have international driving license?

B: Yes, I do. And I rented cars in Shanghai last year.

Z: In addition to the international driving license, you will need a guarantor and pay some deposit.

B: OK, I see. And is there anything else I should pay attention to?

Z: Choose a regular and legal car rental company. At present, there are many car rental companies in the market. You need to know in advance the models and car conditions that the rental company can provide, and then compare each of the rental forms, rental price, required documents, deposits and other specific conditions before making a decision.

B: Yes, it's not so easy to choose a rental company. And what should I pay attention to when I sign the car rental contract?

Z: When signing a contract, you should pay attention to the following points, including the gas, the daily limit of kilometers, the billing standard of exceeding the mileage, how to deal with emergencies, when and where to pick up the car, when and where to return the car, etc.

B: Thank you very much for the detailed information.

Z: My pleasure. If you need, you can call me during your self-driving tour in Xiamen. I will be very glad to be your guarantor.

B: Thank you very much.

Useful Expressions

1. Xiamen has a very developed public transportation system.
厦门的公共交通系统非常发达。

2. You can take Line 1 and get off at Lianhua Road Station.
您可以乘坐1号线,然后在莲花路站下车。

3. Taxi fare charges 8 yuan within 3 kilometers, and additional 2 yuan for every subsequent 1 kilometer.
出租车3公里以内收费8元,之后每1公里加收2元。

4. I am considering renting a car to have a self-driving tour with my family during

the summer vocation.

我考虑暑假期间租一辆车与家人进行一次自驾游。

5. In addition to the international driving license, you will need a guarantor and pay some deposit.

除了国际驾照,您还需要一个担保人并支付一定的押金。

6. You need to know in advance the models and car conditions that the rental company can provide, and then compare each of the rental forms, rental price, required documents, deposits and other specific conditions before making a decision.

您需要提前了解租车公司可以提供的车型和车况,比较每一种租车形式、租车价格、需要的文件、押金等具体情况之后再做决定。

7. When signing a contract, you should pay attention to the following points, including the gas, the daily limit of kilometers, the billing standard of exceeding the mileage, how to deal with emergencies, when and where to pick up the car, when and where to return the car, etc.

签订合同时要注意以下几点,包括油费、日限公里数、超里程计费标准、突发事件如何处理、何时何地取车、何时何地还车等。

Ⅲ Exercises

1. Match the following Chinese with the correct English versions

(1) 手动挡　　　　　　　　　　a. parking lot
(2) 保险　　　　　　　　　　　b. rental company
(3) 小型货车　　　　　　　　　c. rental agreement
(4) 停车场　　　　　　　　　　d. guarantor
(5) 地铁　　　　　　　　　　　e. manual transmission
(6) 租车公司　　　　　　　　　f. deposit
(7) 护照　　　　　　　　　　　g. passport
(8) 租车协议　　　　　　　　　h. minivan
(9) 担保人　　　　　　　　　　i. subway
(10) 押金　　　　　　　　　　　j. insurance

2. Translate the following Chinese into English

(1) 搭地铁贵吗?
(2) 最近的公交站台在哪里?
(3) 这是去市中心的地铁吗?
(4) 你有国际驾照吗?
(5) 您要租几天?
(6) 您必须出具担保人的身份证。

3. Fill in the blanks with appropriate words and expressions

A: Miss Wu, we have heard that the performance of Impressions of the West Lake is very impressive, and we would like to watch it in the evening. Could you show me the exact location of the performance?

B: No problem. It's at 82 Beishan Road, ____(1)____ to Yuefei Temple and Shangri-La Hotel, Hangzhou. As there is no direct bus to the performance place from our hotel, I suggest that you should go there ____(2)____.

A: How long will it take us to get there by taxi?

B: It is about half an hour to ____(3)____ from the hotel to the West Lake. But you'd better get there half an hour earlier, because there is always ____(4)____ jam during the show time.

A: OK, thank you for your information.

B: My pleasure. You can use Didi Car-hailing App to ____(5)____ a car and go back to the hotel. It is really a convenient way for you.

A: OK. But we don't have Didi Car-hailing ____(6)____. Can we take the bus or taxi?

B: Yes, you can take the bus or taxi directly. It'll ____(7)____ about one hour by bus and you have 10 minutes' ____(8)____ from the bus stop to the hotel. As to the taxi, sometimes you have to wait for a long time, but sometimes it will be very quick. It depends.

A: Oh, I see, thanks.

4. Role play

Situation 1: Suppose you are the local guide and one of the tourists is inquiring about how to get to the Three Lanes and Seven Alleys. Make a dialogue with your partner and your dialogue should include the following points: the city traffic of Fuzhou, the taxi service, the bus service and the subway service.

Situation 2: Suppose you are the local guide and one of your tourists is inquiring, you about how to rent a car in Fuzhou. Make a dialogue with your partner and your dialogue should include the following points: introduce the policy of renting a car, lead the tourist to the rental agency, and provide necessary help.

5. Questions & Answers

Question 1: As a local guide, how to prevent the occurrence of the traffic accident?

Question 2: As a local guide, what should you do when there is something wrong with the coach on the way to the scenic spot?

Module 4　City Service

Ⅳ Extended Reading

Xiamen Transportation

Task 2　Shared Bike

Ⅰ Warming Up

1. Read and Match

a. smart phone			b. Alipay
c. shared bike			d. account balance

(1)

(2)

(3)

(4)

2. Questions

Question 1: How to use a shared bike?

Tips for reference:

(1) download an App;

(2) have verification on the phone;

(3) scan the QR code;

(4) unlock the bike and enjoy the riding;

(5) park the bike in the appropriate place;

(6) pay the bill.

Question 2: What are the new four great inventions of China?

Tips for reference:

Alipay, shared bike, online shopping, high-speed rail.

Ⅱ Situational Dialogues

➢ Dialogue 1

How to Use a Shared Bike

(Some tourists want to ride shared bikes to travel around the city during the free time. Xiao Li, the local guide, tells them how to use a shared bike and answers relevant questions.)

L: Xiao Li, the local guide   B: guest

B: Xiao Li, it's said that travelling around Island Ring Boulevard by bike is very popular in Xiamen.

L: Yes. Island Ring Boulevard is a delicate balance of natural beauty, humanity and the spirit of sports.

B: No wonder there are lots of people who like to ride bikes along the road.

L: Yes. The best section of riding along the road is starting from Xiamen University's Baicheng, then passing Hulishan Fort, Zengcuo'an, Yefengzhai, and finally to the Convention and Exhibition Center. It's about 10 kilometers away. You can enjoy the beautiful sea view, many attractions and the snacks.

B: Wow, that is great. We plan to ride shared bikes to travel around the city during the free time. Can you tell us how to use the shared bikes?

L: Of course. First, you should download a bicycle-sharing App, such as Mobike, Coolqi, ofo, Hellobike, etc. After you download the App, you should have verification on Bike Sharing Apps.

B: Download Bike Sharing App and have verification. We get it.

L: And you can locate a bike through smart phone easily. Shared bikes can be seen in every corner of the street. Scan the QR code to unlock the bike and you can enjoy your riding.

B: How to lock the bike when we finish our riding?

L: You just park in a proper area and lock manually.

B: How to pay the fare?

L: Users can pay the fee and top up by WeChat Pay and Alipay. Mobike and ofo also accept Apple Pay. The cycling fare will be deducted from your account balance. Mobike can be used through a WeChat account without downloading the App. The fare will be deducted from your WeChat wallet.

B: That's very convenient. Thank you for your introduction.

L: It is my pleasure. Enjoy your riding.

➤ Dialogue 2

Bike-sharing Service

(On the way to the Xiamen International Conference and Exhibition Center, the tourists are interested in the shared bike along the road. Xiao Li introduces the bike-sharing system and answers relevant questions.)

L: Xiao Li, the local guide   T: tourists

L: Ladies and gentlemen, now we have come to the Island Ring Boulevard. This road is on the southeast shore of Xiamen Island. The green belt on this road is 80 to 100 meters wide. It offers local people an ideal weekend getaway.

T: There are so many bikes along the road.

L: These are shared bikes. The shared bike was first used in Holland in 1965. It was introduced in China in 2007 and it has been widely popular since 2016. With the development of the economy, shared bikes are seen everywhere in cities. It has become a popular and healthy transportation option for short-distance journey.

T: How can we use the shared bikes?

L: It's easy to operate it with our smart phone. First, we scan the QR code on the bike when we want to use them. Then when we get to our destination, we should unlock the smart lock. Finally, we pay the bill.

T: So it's popular among the local people.

L: It's popular not only among local people, but also visitors. They can ride these bikes and then have a look at the scenery around. It can save them a lot of money and the most important thing is the convenience it brings.

T: These bikes decorate the streets with different colors.

L: Yes, fleets of bikes in various colors are commonly seen in the streets, including the orange Mobike, the yellow ofo, and Hellobike in white and blue.

T: The bike-sharing service has become a new trend in China.

L: A lot of young people join the fleet to avoid the traffic jams, and also do something for environmental protection. And what is more, China shared bikes also go abroad and appear in some Western countries, such as the US, the UK, Japan and Singapore, and become a new name card of "Made in China".

T: So great. Do we have the chance to ride the shared bikes these days?

L: Tomorrow afternoon we will go to visit the Zengcuo'an. You will have some free time to enjoy yourself. You can ride the bikes.

T: That's a good idea. Thank you.

Useful Expressions

1. We plan to ride shared bikes to travel around the city center during the free time.
自由活动时我们打算骑共享单车游览市区。

2. Can you tell us how to use the shared bikes?
你能告诉我们如何使用共享单车吗？

3. You should download a bicycle-sharing App.
你要下载共享单车 App。

4. You should have verification on Bike Sharing Apps.
您必须在共享单车应用程序上进行验证。

5. You can locate a bike through smart phone.
您可以通过智能手机寻找自行车。

6. Scan the QR code to unlock the bike.
扫描二维码解锁自行车。

7. How to lock the bike when we finish our riding?
骑行结束后如何锁车？

8. Users can pay the fee and top up by WeChat Pay and Alipay.
用户可以通过微信和支付宝支付费用和充值。

9. China shared bikes also go abroad and appear in some Western countries and become a new name card of "Made in China".
中国共享单车也走出国门，成为"中国制造"的新名片。

Exercises

1. Match the following Chinese with the correct English versions

（1）共享单车　　　　　　　　　　　a. bluegogo

（2）停车　　　　　　　　　　　　　b. mobike

（3）小蓝单车　　　　　　　　　　　c. smart lock

（4）小黄车　　　　　　　　　　　　d. park

（5）摩拜单车　　　　　　　　　　　e. timer

（6）应用程序　　　　　　　　　　　f. unlock

（7）智能锁　　　　　　　　　　　　g. user

（8）计时器 h. shared bikes

（9）用户 i. App

（10）开锁 j. ofo

2. Translate the following Chinese into English

（1）街上到处都可以看到共享单车和共享电动车。

（2）您能告诉我们在哪里下车吗？

（3）我们去动物园要在哪一站转车？

（4）您可以在这站转乘 2 路车。

（5）到酒店需要多长时间？

（6）如果交通堵塞不是太严重的话大概需要 25 分钟。

（7）把车票插入旋转栅门(turnstile)上的插槽(slot)，然后推开栅门进入。

3. Fill in the blanks with appropriate words and expressions

A：Excuse me. Could you tell me ____(1)____ to get to the National History Museum?

B：Certainly, madam. It is near the Science Museum. Are you ____(2)____ with the streets around here?

A：No. I am a tour leader from China. Today I'll go to ____(3)____ the museum with some tourists.

B：I see. How would you like to go? Walking?

A：I have no idea about it at all. Is it ____(4)____ the hotel?

B：Not really. You just go straight along this street, and after 6 blocks, you will see it on your left.

A：____(5)____ will that take?

B：About 30 minutes on foot.

A：How about taking the ____(6)____?

B：It's only two stops. Do you know which train to take?

A：The A train, is it right? I just looked at the city map.

B：That's right. You ____(7)____ at the second stop, Cronwell Road, and you will see the National History Museum is opposite the stop.

A：What if I take a bus?

B：It's ____(8)____ now. The traffic is terrible. If you ____(9)____, you may get stuck in the traffic jam.

A：I see. Do you know where the nearest subway station is?

B：There is one at the corner. I'll take you there.

A：That is very kind of you. Thanks a lot.

B：Don't mention it.

4. Role play

Situation 1：Suppose you are the local guide and one of the tourists is inquiring about how to use the shared electric bike. Make a dialogue with your partner and your dialogue should include the following points: the bike-sharing service, the steps of renting a shared electric bike, safety tips.

Situation 2: Suppose you are the local guide and you are now guiding your tourist to travel around Ancient Quanzhou City by shared bike. Make a dialogue with your partner and your dialogue should include the following points: Quanzhou city introduction, bike-sharing service, city traffic in Quanzhou.

5. Questions & Answers

Question: Some tourists wish to go to church during the weekend by shared bikes. As a local guide, how to deal with this request?

IV Extended Reading

Bike-Sharing in China

Task 3 Currency Exchange

I Warming Up

1. Read and Match

a. hotel
b. currency exchange in Bank of China
c. airport exchange office
d. currencies

(1)

(2)

Module 4   City Service   055

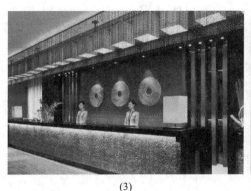
(3)

(4)

2. **Question**

Question 1: What places can you exchange the money in China?

Tips for reference:

(1) At the airport exchange office.

(2) At banks.

(3) At hotels.

(4) At exchange counter and kiosks.

Question 2: What credit cards are available in China?

Tips for reference:

Master Card, Visa Card, American Express Card, JCB card and Diners Card, etc.

Ⅱ Situational Dialogues

➢ Dialogue 1

The Currency in China

(Some tourists are inquiring the local guide about the currency in China on the way to the hotel.)

L: Xiao Li, the local guide   G: guest

G: Xiao Li, what does RMB stand for?

L: RMB is the abbreviation symbol for the Chinese word Renminbi, the Chinese currency. Renminbi is issued by the People's Bank of China. The unit of it is Yuan, Jiao and Fen.

G: What currency can be converted into RMB?

L: For the convenience of foreign guests and Hong Kong, Macao and Taiwan compatriots' consumption in China, Bank of China and other appointed banks provide foreign currency exchange business for 22 kinds of foreign currencies and foreign currency traveler's check, foreign credit card in exchange for RMB.

G: What foreign credit card is available in China?

L: Master Card, Visa Card, American Express Card, JCB card and Diners Card.

G: Can we exchange our money at the hotel? Just now I forgot to exchange some money at the airport.

L: Yes. Some hotels, restaurants or stores can also convert foreign currency into RMB.

G: What should we do if our RMB notes are not used out?

L: If the converted RMB notes are not used out, they may be converted into foreign currency within the period of validity of six months before the date of departure and then taken out of China.

G: Thanks for your introduction.

L: My pleasure.

➢ Dialogue 2

Currency Exchange Service

(After checking at the hotel, Mr. Black, one of the tourists, wants to exchange some currency at the hotel. Xiao Li, the local guide, tells Mr. Black that he can exchange the money at the front desk.)

L: Xiao Li, the local guide   B: Mr. Black, the tourist

C: the clerk at the front desk

(On the phone)

B: This is Mr. Black from Room 1203. Xiao Li, can you do me a favor?

L: Yes, what can I do for you?

B: I need to exchange some money. But I don't know which bank I should go to.

L: Don't worry. You can exchange your money at the hotel. For the convenience of the guests, providing currency exchange service is one of the national star-rated hotels evaluation standards.

B: That's great. I will go to the front desk. Thanks for your help.

L: My pleasure.

(At the front desk)

C: Good morning. How can I help you?

B: Yes. I want to change some US dollars into Chinese RMB.

C: How much is that?

B: 100 US dollars. Here you are.

C: We change foreign currencies according to today's exchange rate. 100 US dollars, an equivalent of RMB 797 yuan.

B: OK, I will take it.

C: Please fill in the exchange memo, your passport number and the total sum, and sign your name.

B: Here you are. Is that all right?

C: Yes, thanks. What denomination do you need?

B: What denomination do you have?

C: There are 100-yuan notes, 50-yuan notes, 20-yuan notes, 10-yuan notes, 5-yuan notes and 1-yuan coins.

B: Give me nine 10-yuan notes, seven 1-yuan coins, and the others are 100-yuan notes.

C: Certainly. Here is RMB 797 yuan. Please check it and keep the memo.

B: That's right. Thank you for your help.

C: Always at your service.

Useful Expressions

1. Renminbi is issued by the People's Bank of China.

人民币由中国人民银行发行。

2. Bank of China and other appointed banks provide foreign currency exchange business for 22 kinds of foreign currencies and foreign currency traveler's check, foreign credit card in exchange for RMB.

中国银行及其他外汇指定银行除受理外币旅行支票、外国信用卡兑换人民币的业务外,还受理22种外币现钞兑换业务。

3. If the converted RMB notes are not used out, they may be converted into foreign currency within the period of validity of six months before the date of departure and then taken out of China.

兑换后的人民币如未用完,可在离境前六个月有效期内兑换成外币,携带出境。

4. Providing currency exchange service is one of the national star-rated hotels evaluation standards.

提供外币兑换服务是国家星级饭店的评定标准之一。

5. Master Card, Visa Card, American Express Card, JCB card and Diners Card.

万事达卡、维萨卡、运通卡、JCB卡和大莱卡。

6. We change foreign currencies according to today's exchange rate.

我们根据今天的汇率兑换外币。

7. Please fill in the exchange memo, your passport number and the total sum, and sign your name.

请填写兑换单、护照号码和总金额,并签名。

8. What denomination do you have?

你有什么面额的?

9. There are 100-yuan notes, 50-yuan notes, 20-yuan notes, 10-yuan notes, 5-yuan notes and 1-yuan coins.

有100元、50元、20元、10元、5元纸币和1元硬币。

Ⅲ Exercises

1. Match the following Chinese with the correct English versions

（1）万事达卡　　　　　　　　　　a. Diners Card

（2）维萨卡　　　　　　　　　　　b. Euro

（3）美国运通卡　　　　　　　　　c. Master Card

（4）大莱卡　　　　　　　　　　　d. exchange rate

（5）欧元　　　　　　　　　　　　e. denomination

（6）新加坡元　　　　　　　　　　f. exchange memo

（7）面额　　　　　　　　　　　　g. American Express Card

（8）外汇兑换水单　　　　　　　　h. traveler's check

（9）汇率　　　　　　　　　　　　i. Singapore dollar

（10）旅行支票　　　　　　　　　j. Visa Card

2. Translate the following Chinese into English

（1）能否帮我把这笔钱换回到美元？

（2）我想要些旅行支票。

（3）您带着护照吗？

（4）请填写这张收据，一式两份。

（5）请填写这些单据，并签上姓名。

3. Fill in the blanks with appropriate words and expressions

A：Could you change some money for me? I need some US dollars.

B：Certainly. What kind of ＿＿＿(1)＿＿＿ have you got?

A：Chinese yuan. By the way, what is the ＿＿＿(2)＿＿＿ rate today?

B：One US dollar in cash is equivalent to 8.5 Chinese yuan.

A：How much would you like to change?

B：200000 yuan. Here you are.

A：Now would you please ＿＿＿(3)＿＿＿ this form?

B：OK. Is it all right?

A：Yes, sir. May I have a look at your ＿＿＿(4)＿＿＿?

B：Yes, here you are.

A：Thank you. (He gives it back after checking) Here you are. Please sign here on the exchange ＿＿＿(5)＿＿＿.

B: Sure. Will you please give me some one or five dollar notes?

A: Here is your money. Would you count them, and keep this exchange memo, please?

B: Oh, yes, thanks. By the way, can you tell me what I should do with the money left with me?

A: You'll have to go to the ____(6)____ of China or ____(7)____ exchange office to change it back into the RMB.

B: Thanks.

4. Role play

Situation 1: Suppose you are the local guide and one of the tourists is inquiring about how to exchange the money at Chinese bank. Make a dialogue with your partner.

Situation 2: Suppose you are the local guide and one of the tourists is inquiring about how to exchange the money at airport exchange office. Make a dialogue with your partner.

5. Questions & Answers

Question 1: Some tourists want to visit one of the houses when taking a walk in Beijing Hutong. How to deal with the request?

Question 2: Some tourists want to go swimming when visiting Baicheng Beach in Xiamen. How to deal with the request?

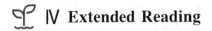 Ⅳ Extended Reading

Exchange Money in China? You Should Know These Things!

Exchange Money in China? You Should Know These Things!

Task 4   Booking Tickets

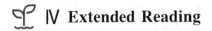 Ⅰ Warming Up

1. Read and Match

a. flight booking   b. website
c. train ticket   d. booking information

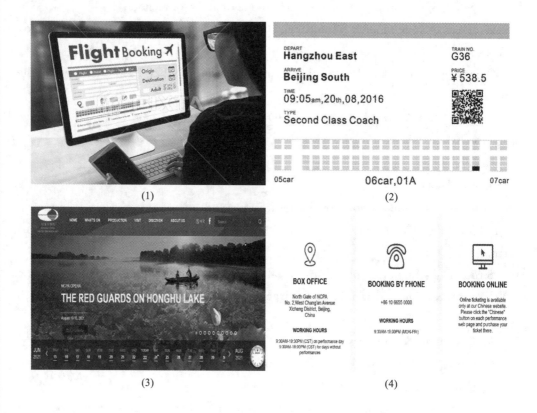

(1)　　(2)

(3)　　(4)

2. Questions

Question 1: How to book tickets from National Center for the Performing Arts?

Tips for reference:

(1) Visit the website of NCPR by Internet (on computer or mobile phone).

(2) Telephone booking.

(3) Purchase through the official authorized ticket agency of NCPR.

Question 2: How many delivery methods are there for the tickets and what are they?

Tips for reference:

No matter which method, you need to fill in the receipt information and check the performance ticket information of the purchased ticket.

(1) On-site ticket collection (online payment, bank transfer, counter settlement).

(2) Express delivery (online payment, bank transfer, and cash on delivery).

(3) Visitors who choose express delivery please keep the phone open after placing the order, and the customer service staff will communicate on the phone to confirm the delivery.

Situational Dialogues

> **Dialogue 1**

Kun Opera

(Some tourists are interested in Kun Opera and ask Xiao Li to help them book the tickets.)

L: Xiao Li, the local guide　　G: the tourists

G: Xiao Li, can you do us a favor?

L: Of course. What can I do for you?

G: It's said that Kun Opera is very popular here. We are interested in Kun Opera. Would you tell us something about it?

L: Kun Opera is one of the oldest operas in China, and it is also one of the treasures of Chinese traditional culture and art. It integrates singing, dialogue, acting, acrobatics, dancing and martial arts. It is praised as "the origin of all operas". In 2001, Kun Opera is listed as a masterpiece of "the oral and intangible heritage of humanity" by UNESCO.

G: So it has a long history.

L: Yes, Kun Opera originated in the late period of the Yuan Dynasty around the area of Kunshan City, Suzhou.

G: What are the masterpieces?

L: The masterpiece is called the *Four Dreams of Linchuan* created by Tang Xianzu, a great dramatist, praised as "Shakespeare in the East". Among the four operas, *The Peony Pavilion* is the most famous one.

G: That sounds interesting. We really want to watch a performance about it. Could you book a ticket for us?

L: Sure. There will be a performance called *The Peony Pavilion*. The program is quite influential and often performed. It's performed at the Provincial Theater at 19:00 tomorrow evening. Is it convenient for you?

G: That is good.

L: First class or second class tickets?

G: First class, please.

L: It is 500 yuan for first class. How many tickets would you like?

G: Three.

L: May I have 1500 yuan in advance?

G: Here you are.

L: I will send the ticket to your room at 5:00 pm this afternoon. Will you be staying in the room at that time?

G: Yes, I will be in the room.

L: OK. The theatre is not far from here. You can take a taxi there. It takes about 15 minutes and costs about 15 yuan.

G: That is reasonable. Thank you for your help.

L: It is my pleasure. If you have any problems, please feel free to tell me. I am always at your service. Bye.

G: Bye.

> **Dialogue 2**

Booking a Flight Ticket

(Mr. Black is reserving a flight ticket to Hangzhou on the phone.)

B: Mr. Black   R: the receptionist

R: Xiamen Airlines. What can I do for you?

B: I'd like to make a reservation to Hangzhou next week.

R: When do you want to fly?

B: Monday morning, September 12.

R: Just a moment please. Let me check whether there're seats available. I am sorry, we are all booked up for flight 802 on the morning.

B: Then, any alternatives?

R: The next available flight leaves at 12:30 Monday afternoon, September 12.

B: Er…is it a direct flight?

R: Yes, it is.

B: What about the fare for the first class?

R: One way is $176.

B: OK, I will take the 12:30 flight.

R: May I have your name and passport number, please?

B: Tom Black. T-O-M, Tom. B-L-A-C-K, Black. My passport number is EF1260892.

R: OK, Tom Black, a first class seat on flight 807 to Hangzhou, 12:30 Monday morning, September 12. Is it right, sir?

B: Right.

R: Mr. Black, do you have Xiamen Airlines App on your phone?

B: Not yet.

R: I recommend you to download Xiamen Airlines App. You can book your tickets, view your flight status anytime, anywhere, select your preferred seat in advance and check in online with ease.

B: OK, thanks.

R: With pleasure.

Useful Expressions

1. Kun Opera is one of the oldest operas in China, and it is also one of the treasures of Chinese traditional culture and art.

昆曲是中国最古老的戏曲之一,也是中国传统文化艺术的瑰宝之一。

2. It integrates singing, dialogue, acting, acrobatics, dancing and martial arts. It is praised as "the origin of all operas".

昆曲将唱、念、做、打、舞蹈、武术融为一体,被誉为"百戏之祖"。

3. In 2001, Kun Opera is listed as a masterpiece of "the oral and intangible heritage of humanity" by UNESCO.

2001 年昆曲被联合国教科文组织列为"人类口头和非物质遗产"代表作。

4. The masterpiece is called the *Four Dreams of Linchuan* created by Tang Xianzu, a great dramatist, praised as "Shakespeare in the East".

这部杰作是被称为"东方莎士比亚"的伟大剧作家汤显祖创作的《临川四梦》。

5. I'd like to make a reservation to Hangzhou next week.

我想预订下周去杭州的机票。

6. I am sorry, we are all booked up for Flight 802 on the morning.

很抱歉,802 航班早上都订满了。

7. I recommend you to download Xiamen Airlines App.

推荐您下载厦航 App。

8. You can book your tickets, view your flight status anytime, anywhere, select your preferred seat in advance and check in online with ease.

您可以随时随地预订机票、查看航班状态、提前选座,轻松地在线上办理登机手续。

 Exercises

1. Match the following Chinese with the correct English versions

(1) 软卧   a. departure city
(2) 商务舱   b. arrival city
(3) 出发地   c. concert
(4) 目的地   d. business class
(5) 无座   e. chorus
(6) 音乐会   f. soft sleeper
(7) 合唱   g. standing
(8) 交响乐   h. ballet
(9) 话剧   i. orchestra
(10) 芭蕾   j. drama

2. Translate the following Chinese into English

（1）这个周末上演什么剧？

（2）票价根据座位的不同而有所不同。

（3）您可以通过网站或者 App 轻松订票。

（4）您可以在携程网上预订酒店、航班。

（5）您可以方便享受线上线下和无线结合的一体化服务。

3. Fill in the blanks with appropriate words and expressions

A：Hello. I'm thinking about watching a Chinese traditional opera with a foreign girl. What's ____(1)____ this weekend?

B：What about *The peony pavilion*? The cast is really the best.

A：What's the performance about?

B：The story is set in the Song Dynasty. Du Liniang, the daughter of the provincial governor, studies her first love poems and ____(2)____ of meeting a young scholar in a peony pavilion in the garden. Du paints a self-portrait and asks her maid to hide it under a stone by the ____(3)____. On the eve of the traditional Mid-Autumn Festival, Du dies. Shortly after, a scholar called Liu Mengmei arrives in town. He finds Du's painting by ____(4)____ and that night sees her in a dream, where she asks him to revive her by opening her coffin. Liu does this and miraculously Du is resurrected and reunited with her parents.

A：Wonderful. How much is the ticket?

B：The price varies according to the ____(5)____. 300 yuan for the front, 200 yuan for the middle, and 50 yuan for the back. Which kind would you like?

A：Two for the front. One last thing, are there any ____(6)____ subtitles for the show?

B：Yes, we have subtitles both in Chinese and English on the big screen just beside the stage.

A：Terrific. May I stop by to get that two tickets tomorrow afternoon?

B：Sure. And our theater is located on Liberty Avenue, just opposite the biggest guitar store.

A：Thanks.

4. Role play

Situation 1：Suppose you are the local guide and one of the tourists is inquiring about how to book tickets from the NCPA (National Centre for the Performing Arts). Make a dialogue with your partner.

Situation 2：Suppose you are the local guide and some of your tourists need you to help book the tickets for the performance tonight at the NCPA (National Centre for the Performing Arts). Make a dialogue with your partner.

5. Questions & Answers

Question: What should a tour guide do if the group members have to postpone their departure to the following day because their pre-booked sleeper tickets are not available?

Ⅳ Extended Reading

FAQ for Visitors

FAQ for Visitors

Module 5
On the Way to the Scenic Spot

Learning Objectives
1. Learn the basic procedures of the services on the way to the scenic spot.
2. Narrate on the way to the scenic spot.
3. Solve incidents on the way to the scenic spot.
4. Organize games on the way to the scenic spot.

Case Introduction

Case 1:

On the way to the downtown of Quanzhou, some tourists were very interested in the Chinese antiques and asked for your advice.

What should the local guide do to deal with there quest?

Case 2:

The local tour guide explained how to make the medicinal soup of Fujian on the way to the downtown of Fuzhou. Some tourists said that they wanted to buy some traditional Chinese medicine.

What should the local tour guide do?

Task 1　Narration on Tour

 | Warming Up

1. Read and Match

a. Fujian Tulou　　　　　　　　　　　　b. white porcelain

Module 5   On the Way to the Scenic Spot

c. bodiless lacquer   d. Kulangsu

(1)   (2)

(3)   (4)

2. Questions

Question 1: As a local guide, what and how to prepare before setting out to a scenic spot?

Tips for reference:

(1) The local guide informs the time and place of meeting beforehand, forecasts the weather and reminds the tourists to wear suitable clothes and shoes.

(2) The local guide gets to the gathering place with the driver ahead of at least 10 minutes.

(3) The local guide leads the tourists to the coach.

(4) Nose count politely to insure all the tourists have got on the bus. Remind the tourists of the weather and the landform of the scenic spots.

Question 2: What should the local guide narrate on the way to the scenic spots?

Tips for reference:

(1) Offer greetings.

(2) Announce the itinerary in detail.

(3) Introduce the scenic spots briefly.

(4) Introduce the views along the way.

(5) Introduce the things that the tourists are interested in.

(6) Organize some activities.

‖ Situational Dialogues

➤ Dialogue 1

Narration on Tour

(As a local guide, Xiao Li is taking a tour group on the way to the Three Lanes and Seven Alleys. The tourists are interested in Fuzhou.)

L: Xiao Li, the local guide   T: tourists

L: Good morning, everyone. Did you have a good rest last night?

T: Oh, yes. So good.

L: I am glad to hear that. Now we are on the way to the Three Lanes and Seven Alleys, and that is called Sanfang Qixiang in Chinese. It's a must to visit in the heart of Fuzhou city. As it will take half an hour to get there, I will make a brief introduction of Fuzhou and the views on the way for you.

T: It was said that Marco Polo also paid a visit here.

L: Yes, he visited here in the 13th century. He described Fuzhou as a prosperous center of international commerce, with beautiful gardens and rich fruits. As a coastal city, Fuzhou has a comfortable environment and a mild and pleasant climate. Its average annual temperature is 21℃.

T: Yes, my impression of Fuzhou is about the weather here. Feel so comfortable.

L: Therefore, it is suitable for year-round sightseeing and tourism here. Fuzhou is a cultural city with a history of over 2000 years. It's the hometown for many celebrities. Besides, there are many handicraft industries here, such as the lacquer ware, the horn combs, and the oil-paper umbrella etc.

T: Fuzhou is a city rich in cultural tradition. I have heard that Fuzhou has an interesting nickname.

L: Yes. As you see, there are lots of banyan trees along the road. Many banyan trees were planted since the Song Dynasty, so Fuzhou got its nickname Rongcheng, which means banyan city.

T: Oh, Rongcheng. We are at Rongcheng.

L: Yes. Apart from the must-see scenery spots, Fuzhou cuisine is something you can't miss either. As one of China's eight major cuisines, Fuzhou dishes are light, giving emphasis to retaining the natural flavor of the main ingredients. One famous dish is Rouyan. The main ingredient is lean pork, which is pounded and smashed into meat paste, mixed with some starch, then stretched into a thin sheet. People use the thin sheet to wrap stuffing of minced meat. I will take you to try Rouyan when we visit the Three Lanes and Seven Alleys.

T: So amazing. I can't wait to try Rouyan.

L: We are arriving at the Three Lanes and Seven Alleys now. It is home to great men, where many famous writers and poets came from. Now please take your valuable belongings and begin our wonderful journey.

➢ Dialogue 2

On the Way to Chongwu Ancient Town

(As a local guide, Xiao Li is taking a tour group on the way to Chongwu Ancient Town and makes an introduction of Quanzhou.)

L: Xiao Li, the local guide   T: tourists

L: Ladies and gentlemen, now we are on the way to the famous Chongwu Ancient Town. It will take us an hour to get there. During the time, I'd like to introduce something about Quanzhou and its 18 sceneries. Quanzhou is located in the southeast of Fujian by the sea. It's known to the world as Zayton in ancient times. It was a busy city for ocean transportation and foreign trades, trading with more than 100 countries and regions during 10th-14th centuries.

T: So it was one of the world's major port and the starting point of the "Silk Road on the Sea", marking the golden age of ocean transportation and foreign trades.

L: Yes. It is a time-honored city of civilization and a famous hometown for overseas Chinese. As a core area and cradle of Minnan (southern Fujian) culture, Quanzhou is characterized by its distinctive and diverse cultural heritage, known as "Hometown of Traditional Operas", "City of Puppet Shows" and "City of Nanyin".

T: I heard that there are Islamic mosques here.

L: Quanzhou is called the religious museum and has created a wonder in terms of religions. There were more than nine religions in the center of this city in the past. Today, at least five religions still exist in the center of Quanzhou. People with different religious belief have lived together in harmony for hundreds of years.

T: Why do religious conflicts seldom happen in Quanzhou?

L: Everyone loves a stable and peaceful homeland. The residents are very friendly. They warmly welcome the visitors who come from far lands. Most of the people in this city have the same concept that religious belief is everyone's freedom.

T: There are many beautiful sceneries in Quanzhou.

L: Yes. Quanzhou is well endowed with beautiful scenery and natural resources, especially the 18 most beautiful sceneries, include the East and West Pagodas at the Kaiyuan Temple, the Qingjing Mosque, the statue of Lao Tze, Luoyang Bridge, the Chongwu Ancient Town, the Niumulin Forest, and Tumen Street, etc.

扫码
听听力

T: So three days is not enough for us to enjoy Quanzhou. Oh, look at that. How beautiful the women and the clothes are!

L: They are Hui'an women. For years these beautiful and bright women have been for their unique famous dresses and adornments. They wear wide-rimmed bamboo hats and wrapped headscarves. However, more and more young Hui'an women have found favor with fashionable attire such as jackets and jeans.

T: There are so many stone carvings along the road.

L: Yes. Now we are approaching Chongwu Ancient Town. It is one of the seven ancient towns in China. Nowadays it is popular with the travellers. Most people visit there for its Stone Carving Park, which can be considered as the museum of stone carving. You can leave your bags on the bus, but do not forget to take your valuable things with you. Please remember our bus number, Min C0357. Now let's get off the coach.

Useful Expressions

1. As a coastal city, Fuzhou has a comfortable environment and a mild and pleasant climate. Its average annual temperature is 21℃.

福州是一座沿海城市,环境舒适,气候宜人,年平均气温为 21℃。

2. There are many handicraft industries here, such as the lacquer ware, the horn combs, and the oil-paper umbrella etc.

福州有许多手工业,如漆器、牛角梳、油纸伞等。

3. Fuzhou dishes are light, giving emphasis to retaining the natural flavor of the main ingredients.

福州菜清淡,注重保留主要原料的天然风味。

4. The main ingredient is lean pork, which is pounded and smashed into meat paste, mixed with some starch, then stretched into a thin sheet.

主要原料是瘦肉,用木槌敲打成茸,加入淀粉,做成薄如纸的皮子,即为燕皮。

5. It's known to the world as Zayton in ancient times. It was a busy city for ocean transportation and foreign trades, trading with more than 100 countries and regions during 10th-14th centuries.

在古代,泉州被世界称为"刺桐"。10—14 世纪,这里是海上交通和对外贸易繁忙的城市,与 100 多个国家和地区进行贸易往来。

6. So it was one of the world's major port and the starting point of the "Silk Road on the Sea", marking the golden age of ocean transportation and foreign trades.

因此,它是世界主要港口之一,是"海上丝绸之路"的起点,标志着远洋运输和对外贸易的黄金时代。

7. As a core area and cradle of Minnan (southern Fujian) culture, Quanzhou is characterized by its distinctive and diverse cultural heritage, known as "Hometown of Traditional Operas", "City of Puppet Shows" and "City of Nanyin".

泉州是闽南文化的核心区和发祥地，文化遗产独特、多样，素有"戏曲之乡""木偶之城""南音之都"的美誉。

8. People with different religious belief have lived together in harmony for hundreds of years.

数百年来，不同宗教信仰的人们和谐相处。

9. Quanzhou is well endowed with beautiful scenery and natural resources, especially the 18 most beautiful sceneries, include the East and West Pagodas at the Kaiyuan Temple, the Qingjing Mosque, the statue of Lao Tze, Luoyang Bridge, the Chongwu Ancient Town, the Niumulin Forest, Tumen Street, etc.

泉州风景秀丽，自然资源得天独厚，尤以泉州十八景著称，如开元寺东西塔、清净寺、老君造像、洛阳桥、崇武古城、牛姆林、涂门街等。

10. For years these beautiful and bright women have been famous for their unique dresses and adornments. They wear wide-rimmed bamboo hats and wrapped headscarves. However, more and more young Hui'an women have found favor with fashionable attire such as jackets and jeans.

多年来，这些美丽而聪明的女性一直因其独特的服饰和装饰品而闻名。她们头戴宽边斗笠，头戴花头巾。然而，越来越多的年轻惠安女性喜欢穿夹克和牛仔裤等时尚服装。

Ⅲ Exercises

1. Match the following Chinese with the correct English versions

（1）伊斯兰教寺庙　　　　　　　　a. Hokkien
（2）石雕　　　　　　　　　　　　b. folk religion
（3）佛寺　　　　　　　　　　　　c. opera
（4）闽南话　　　　　　　　　　　d. church
（5）白瓷　　　　　　　　　　　　e. handicraft
（6）牛角梳　　　　　　　　　　　f. stone-carving
（7）民间信仰　　　　　　　　　　g. horn comb
（8）戏曲　　　　　　　　　　　　h. Buddhist monastery
（9）教堂　　　　　　　　　　　　i. white porcelain
（10）手工艺品　　　　　　　　　　j. Islamic mosque

2. Translate the following Chinese into English

（1）先生们、女士们，请注意。
（2）请各位坐好，我们马上要出发了。
（3）所有人都在车上了吗？
（4）请大家看左边的大楼。
（5）大家看到前方那栋白色的建筑了吗？

(6) 位于大家右边的就是闽江。

(7) 请大家带好贵重物品随我下车。

(8) 请大家记住我们的车牌号，我们回来时还是乘坐这辆车。

(9) 现在大家可以休息一下，欣赏下沿途的景色。

3. Fill in the blanks with appropriate words and expressions

A：Ladies and gentlemen, now we are on the ___(1)___ to Kulangsu. It will take us half an hour to get there. I'll make full ___(2)___ of the time to make a brief introduce about it. Gulang Island is located in the southwest to the Xiamen Island. The island ___(3)___ an area of 1.78 kilometers, with about 23000 permanent residents. It is about 1800 meters long and 1000 meters wide. Here you can enjoy a winding costal line, falling and rising rocks, green trees, red tiles and golden sand and buildings of various styles. Kulangsu is also named "Pearl on the East Sea" and "Garden on the Sea".

B：___(4)___ shall we stay on the island?

A：We will stay there about 3 hours.

B：Can we leave our bags on the coach?

A：Yes, you can leave your ordinary belongings on the ___(5)___. But you'd better take the ___(6)___ belongings with you, such as video cameras, purses. And please remember our flag—a blue one with white letters of CITS. Now, let's ___(7)___ the coach.

B：OK, let's go.

4. Role play

Situation 1：Suppose you are the local guide and are now on the way to Kulangsu with your tour group. Make a dialogue with your partner about the general situation of Xiamen and Kulangsu.

Situation 2：Suppose you are the local guide and are now on the way to Fujian Tulou with your tour group. Make a brief introduction of Zhangzhou and answer the tourists' questions.

5. Questions & Answers

Question 1：On the way to Kulangsu, one tourist suffers from heart attack and faint, how to deal with such case?

Question 2：On the way to Fujian Tulou, one tourist suffers from car sickness because of the bumpy mountain road. How to deal with it?

Ⅳ Extended Reading

Gongfu Tea Ceremony

Module 5   On the Way to the Scenic Spot

Task 2   Organizing Activities on the Bus

| Warming Up

1. **Read and Match**

   a. guess riddles   b. hot topics   c. sing songs   d. tell jokes

(1)

(2)

(3)

(4)

2. **Question**

As a tour guide, how to enliven the atmosphere on the bus?

Tips for reference:

Try to organize some entertainment activities for foreign tourists, such as introducing some news and hot topics, telling jokes, learning to speak Chinese or local dialect, guessing riddles, singing songs or organizing some talent shows.

Situational Dialogues

Dialogue 1

Organizing Activities on the Bus

(Xiao Li, the local guide, is on the way to the next scenic spot, and it will take about 3 hours by coach. In order to enliven the atmosphere, Xiao Li would like to organize some games. He turns to Mr. Black, the tour leader, for help.)

L: Xiao Li, local guide   B: Mr. Black, the tour leader

L: Hey, Mr. Black, could you please do me a favor?

B: Certainly. What's the matter?

L: It will take us 3 hours to get to the scenic spot. In order to enliven the atmosphere, I am going to organize some games. I need your help. The game is to learn the popular number gestures in China. Chinese people use one hand to show the ten numbers and most of the tourists feel it's unbelievable.

B: That's right. We feel puzzled about the gestures for six to ten.

L: I will show it to you. For six, the little finger and thumb are extended, other fingers closed.

B: Six, yes, I can do it. And what about seven?

L: For seven, the fingertips are all touching, pointed upwards; or just the fingertips of the thumb and first two fingers.

B: Yes, I get it.

L: For eight, the thumb and index finger are extended, and then make an "L" with other fingers closed. For nine, the index finger makes a hook with other fingers closed.

B: So interesting. And then ten?

L: The index fingers of both hands are crossed in an "X" with the palms facing in opposite directions, like this. Or the middle finger crosses an extended index finger, other fingers closed.

B: Oh, I have got it. I think I can show them how to do it.

L: I can also teach them to say some popular Chinese or organize them to sing some songs. Now I am going to explain the games to the tourists and you help me set the example for them. OK?

B: OK.

(Turning to the group)

L: Attention ladies and gentlemen, it will take us 3 hours to get to the spot, so I will make full use of the time to teach you to play some games. The game is called the popular number gestures in China. Mr. Black and I will teach you how to play the game. And after you learn it, we'll organize a competition. The winner will get some classical Chinese souvenirs as the prize. Now listen to me and I will explain the rules.

➢ Dialogue 2

Incident on the Way to the Scenic Spot

(On the way to a scenic spot, the coach suddenly breaks down. And the driver tells Xiao Li, the local guide, that there is a mechanic failure. Xiao Li organizes some activities while they are waiting.)

L: Xiao Li, the local guide   B: Mr. Black, the tour leader

L: Hello, Mr. Black, there seems to something wrong with our coach. We have to stop for a while.

B: I have felt it. What exactly is that? I hope it is not serious.

L: The driver heard some noise from the left front tire. He had checked it and found there is a mechanic failure.

B: So can he repair it?

L: Don't worry. Our driver has many years of driving experience. He said it's a minor problem and can be fixed in about half an hour. If so, it won't be too late for us to arrive at the scenic spot this morning, but our lunch might be delayed half an hour.

B: OK. How to spend the half an hour?

L: Let's play a game called "the tour guide says".

B: What's the game about?

L: It is related to people's quick reaction. First, we choose a host to act as a tour guide and the host will lead everyone to play the game. He sends out some password and others should judge if it's valid or invalid. If it's valid, people need to perform the password. If it is invalid, people can remain their original state.

B: How to judge the password is valid or invalid?

L: The password with the four words "the tour guide says" is valid, or it is invalid. For example, when you hear "the tour guide says raise your right hand", it is valid. You should raise your right hand. When you hear "raise your left hand", it is invalid because it is without the words "the tour guide says".

B: OK, I see.

L: And one tip for the game. The game's password is mainly based on actions and voices, such as raising the left or the right hand, clapping hands once or twice, coughing once, etc.

B: It seems easy to play the game.

L: Yes, not difficult. So everyone can take part in it actively. The key is the pace of game. At the beginning we can play it leisurely and then speed up our pace gradually. For example, send a series of passwords once.

B: As a punishment, the tourists who fail to perform an action can tell some jokes or sing songs for others.

L: Good idea. So now let's begin our game.

B: OK.

Useful Expressions

1. In order to enliven the atmosphere, Xiao Li would like to organize some games.

为了活跃气氛,小李准备组织一些游戏。

2. He had checked it and found there is a mechanic failure.

司机检查了一下大巴,发现出了点机械故障。

3. Chinese people use one hand to show the ten numbers and most of the tourists feel it's unbelievable.

中国人用一只手表示十个数字,大多数游客都觉得不可思议。

4. I can also teach them to say some popular Chinese or organize them to sing some songs.

我也可以教他们说一些流行的中文或者组织他们唱歌。

5. It won't be too late for us to arrive at the scenic spot this morning, but our lunch might be delayed half an hour.

今天早上我们不会太晚到达景区,但我们的午餐可能会推迟半个小时。

6. First, we choose a host to act as a tour guide and the host will lead everyone to play the game.

首先,我们选择一个主持人做导游,然后由这个主持人带领大家玩游戏。

7. He sends out some password and others should judge if it's valid or invalid. If it's valid, people need to perform the password. If it is invalid, people can remain their original state.

他发出一些指令,其他人应判断指令是否有效。如果是有效的,人们需要执行指令。如果是无效的,人们可以保持原来的状态。

8. The key is the pace of game. At the beginning we can play it leisurely and then speed up our pace gradually.

游戏的关键是节奏。一开始我们可以慢慢地玩,然后逐渐加快节奏。

 **Exercises**

1. Match the following Chinese with the correct English versions

(1) 笑话   a. document

Module 5 On the Way to the Scenic Spot

(2) 娱乐活动　　　　　　　b. personal belongings
(3) 谜语　　　　　　　　　c. entertainment
(4) 事故　　　　　　　　　d. joke
(5) 证件　　　　　　　　　e. activity
(6) 普通话　　　　　　　　f. carsick
(7) 个人物品　　　　　　　g. symptom
(8) 症状　　　　　　　　　h. accident
(9) 活动　　　　　　　　　i. riddle
(10) 晕车　　　　　　　　 j. Mandarin

2. Translate the following Chinese into English

(1) 中山路不仅仅是一条商业街，更是厦门的休闲、娱乐、美食中心。
(2) 中山路沿线的建筑大多是维多利亚时代和中国传统建筑相结合的"骑楼"（一种两层楼的建筑）。
(3) 鼓浪屿以海滩、曲折的小巷和多姿多彩的建筑而闻名。
(4) 胡里山炮台建筑保留了明代和清代军事风格的鲜明特色。
(5) 南普陀寺是一座非常著名的佛教寺庙，始建于唐代。

3. Fill in the blanks with appropriate words and expressions

A：Hey Mr. Smith, could you please do me a ___(1)___ ?

B：Certainly. What's the matter?

A：It will take us 3 hours to get to the scenic spot. In order to ___(2)___ the atmosphere, I am going to organize some games. I need you to help me organize it. The first game's name is called "Obvious Sevens & Hidden Sevens". Here is the ___(3)___ : Our group members are going to count numbers, when they confront the "obvious sevens", which are seven, seventeen, twenty-seven, thirty-seven and so on, they have to pat their legs; when they confront the "hidden sevens", which are fourteen, twenty-one, twenty-eight, thirty-five and so on, they have to pass the numbers and speak out the following ones, such as fifteen, twenty-two, twenty-nine, thirty-six etc. The one who is the last to make mistake will be the ___(4)___ .

B：OK, I got it. Pat legs for ___(5)___ sevens and pass directly for ___(6)___ sevens. So what do you want me to do?

A：I would like you to explain it to your group members and cheer them up. You can ask a few ones to set examples.

B：No problem.

4. Role play

Situation 1：It will take 2 hours to get to the destination. You organize some activities on the bus with your tour leader.

Situation 2：It's the rush hour and your coach encounters a traffic jam. In order to kill the time, you teach your tourists to say some Minnan dialect.

5. Questions & Answers

Question: On the way to the scenic spot, what information should be introduced about the scenic spot?

Ⅳ Extended Reading

Travelling in Zhangzhou

Task 3　Reminding Before Getting off the Coach

Ⅰ Warming Up

1. Read and Match

a. tourist center　　b. parking lot　　c. valuable belongings　　d. tour flag

(1)

(2)

(3)

(4)

2. Questions

Question 1: How to introduce the views along the way?

Tips for reference:

(1) Choose the representative views along the way; the narration should be the same pace with the sight.

(2) Remember that the tourists' direction is opposite to that of the tour guide.

(3) Answer the tourists' questions.

Question 2: What should the local guide remind the tourists before getting off the coach?

Tips for reference:

(1) Remind the tourists to take their valuable belongings with them.

(2) Inform the tourists of the time spending in the scenic spot.

(3) Inform the tourists of the time and place of meeting after visiting.

(4) Remind the tourist to remember the model, color, bus number and the parking place of the coach.

(5) Remind the tourist to remember the feature of the tour group's flag.

(6) Introduce the tour route in front of the tour map of the scenic spot.

‖ Situational Dialogues

Reminding Before Getting off the Coach

(Xiao Li, the local guide, is arriving at the scenic spot with the tourists. Xiao Li is reminding them of some details before getting off the coach.)

L: Xiao Li, the local guide   G: guest

L: Ladies and gentlemen, attention, please. We are arriving at the Confucian Temple. We'll spend one hour here. Now it's 9:00 and we'll meet at the gate of the Confucian Temple at 10:00. Our coach will wait for us at the parking lot, which is two minutes' walk from the gate. Our coach is blue and the bus number is Min C1367, please remember it.

G: Can we leave our bags on the bus?

L: Yes, you can leave your bags on the bus, but do remember to take your valuable belongings with you. Our flag is blue with white letters C&D. After getting off the coach, please get together in front of the tour map of the scenic spot first. I will introduce our travel route briefly. OK, let's get off the bus to explore the Confucian Temple.

G: OK, let's go.

Useful Expressions

1. Now it's 9:00 and we'll meet at the gate of the Confucian Temple at 10:00.
现在是 9:00,我们 10:00 在文庙大门口集合。

2. The bus will wait for us at the parking lot.
大巴会在停车场等我们。

3. You can leave your bags on the bus, but do remember to take your valuable belongings with you.
你可以把你的东西留在大巴车上,但贵重物品一定要随身携带。

4. Our coach is blue and the bus number is Min C1367.
我们的车牌号是闽 C1367,蓝色的车。

5. Our flag is blue with white letters C&D.
我们的导游旗是蓝色的,上面有白色的字母 C&D。

6. After getting off the coach, please get together in front of the tour map of the scenic spot first.
下车后,请先在景区的旅游地图前集合下。

III Exercises

1. Match the following Chinese with the correct English versions

(1) 才艺展示   a. Fahrenheit temperature
(2) 集合时间   b. Celsius temperature
(3) 娱乐活动   c. scenic spot
(4) 自由活动   d. talent show
(5) 华氏度   e. entertainment activity
(6) 摄氏度   f. free activity
(7) 停车场   g. peak season
(8) 景区   h. parking lot
(9) 集合地点   i. gathering time
(10) 旺季   j. gathering place

2. Translate the following Chinese into English

(1) 大家记得带上自己的贵重物品。
(2) 我们的游览时间是两小时。
(3) 12 点的时候请大家回到我们待会下车的地方。
(4) 我们的导游旗是蓝色三角形的,上面有白色的英文字母 C&D。
(5) 我们的车牌号是闽 D3625,车身是白色的。

3. Fill in the blanks with appropriate words and expressions

Now, we are arriving at Fujian Tulou. Before getting ____(1)____ the coach, I have some tips for you. First, after arriving at the scenic spot, we will ____(2)____

Module 5 On the Way to the Scenic Spot

to the scenic bus and it's the peak season, so please follow me after getting off the coach. Second, the weather here is hot and humid and there are many mosquitoes, so you'd better ___(3)___ anti-mosquito supplies. Third, according to the weather forecast it will be rainy, so please remember to bring your ___(4)___. Last, in order to provide tourists with a safe, healthy, civilized and harmonious tourism environment, please abide by the epidemic prevention and requirements of the scenic spot. When entering the scenic spot, please wear a ___(5)___, keep a safe ___(6)___ and take body ___(7)___.

4. Role play

Situation 1: Now the tour group is arriving at Tumen Street. Work as a local guide and give some reminding to your tour group before getting off the coach.

Situation 2: Now the tour group is arriving at Zengcuo'an Village. Work as a local guide and give some reminding to your tour group before getting off the coach.

5. Questions & Answers

Question 1: On the way to the scenic spot, what information should be introduced about the scenic spot?

Question 2: On the way to the scenic spot, what should be announced about the itinerary?

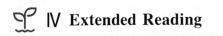 Extended Reading

The Belt and Road Initiative

The Belt and Road Initiative

Module 6
Visiting Scenic Spot

Learning Objectives

1. Master the procedure of service on sightseeing.
2. Introduce the characteristics and cultural elements of different scenic spots.
3. Explore the cultural elements of city tour, natural landscapes and cultural landscapes.
4. Answer the tourist questions about scenic spots.

Case Introduction

Xiao Wang, the local guide was guiding his tour group in Tianluokeng Tulou Cluster. Suddenly one of the tourists was stung by a bee.

What should the local tour guide do?

Task 1 Brief Introduction of a Scenic Spot

| Warming Up

1. Read and Match

a. the Site of Deji Gate
b. the Confucian Temple
c. the sites of Dehua Kilns
d. the East and West Pagodas

Module 6　Visiting Scenic Spot

(1)　　　　　　　　(2)

(3)　　　　　　　　(4)

2. Questions

Question 1: As a tour guide, how to introduce Chinese city to your tourists?

Tips for reference:

(1) Be familiar with the city and the surroundings, such as local history, culture, population, location, administrative areas, weather, cuisine, architecture, etc.

(2) Get more information about the tour group, such as their jobs, interests, etc.

(3) Explain the significant features of the city in simple and vivid language in an entertaining way.

Question 2: What should a tour guide do to give a good cultural sightseeing for the tourists?

Tips for reference:

(1) Have an in-depth understanding and knowledge of the culture.

(2) Be familiar with the travel route.

(3) Master the methods of introducing the cultural landscape.

(4) Use the skills of proper guiding and vivid explanation.

(5) Answer the tourists' questions actively.

Situational Dialogues

Dialogue 1

Travel in Quanzhou

(The tour group will go to visit the Emporium of the World in Song-Yuan China. The tourists want to know something more about it.)

L: Xiao Li, the local guide   G: Mr. Grant, the tour leader

L: Ladies and gentlemen, according to the itinerary, today we'll go to visit the sites of Deji Gate, the Kaiyuan Temple and Anping Bridge, which are all the component of the Emporium of the World in Song-Yuan China in Quanzhou. Song-Yuan Quanzhou presents a prosperous picture and symbolic relationship among ports, city and hinterland. The 22 component sites reflect the maritime trade structure and the multi-cultural social structure of Song-Yuan Quanzhou.

G: What are the 22 component sites?

L: They include administrative buildings, religious buildings and statues, cultural memorial sites, production sites of ceramics and transportation network, such as the maritime trade office, the statue of Lao Tze, the site of Deji Gate, the Confucian Temple, Qingjing Mosque, Luoyang Bridge, Shihu Dock, etc.

G: Will we have chance to visit the statue of Lao Tze?

L: Yes. Tomorrow we will go to Mount Qingyuan, where the statue of Lao Tze is located. The statue is 5.63 meters high, 6.85 meters thick and 8.01 meters wide. There is a very interesting proverb in Quanzhou about the statue, which means that if you can touch the nose of Lao Tze, you can live to 120 years old; if you can touch the eyes, you can live to 160 years old.

G: So interesting. I am eager to enjoy the magic power of Lao Tze.

L: It's worth your visit tomorrow. And today our first stop is Anping Bridge. It is China's longest existing cross-sea stone beam bridge.

G: I have heard about the bridge. Can you tell us more about it?

L: It was first built in 1128 AD and was completed in 1152 AD. It was combined the efforts of monks, merchants, government officials and locals. The bridge runs roughly 2255 meters from east to west, so is also known as Five Li Bridge due to its length, which is around five li (one "li" measures around 500 meters). There are 360 stone step piers in rectangular, pointed boat-shape and bicuspid boat-shape styles.

G: So cool. I can't wait to have a look at it.

L: We are arriving at Anping Bridge. I will tell you more detailed information about it at site.

G: Thank you.

> Dialogue 2

On the Way to the Tiger Hill Scenic Spot

(The tour group is on the way to the Tiger Hill Scenic Spot. The tourists want to know more about it.)

Z: Zhang Yuan, the local guide   B: Mr. Black, the tour leader

Z: Ladies and gentlemen, welcome to Suzhou, a city of great beauty.

B: We feel so excited. We often hear the saying that "In heaven there is paradise, on earth there are Suzhou and Hangzhou".

Z: Yes, that proverb goes popular all among the whole country. Suzhou is also called Venice of the East. Suzhou is world-famous especially for its landscaped gardens. There are about 150 gardens in Suzhou. Some of them are more than 1000 years old. Now we are on the way to Tiger Hill Scenic Spot. Tiger Hill is 34 meters in height and about 5 kilometers from Suzhou downtown. It's famous for its natural beauty and historical sites. So it is a must see for tourists.

B: Tiger Hill? Why is it called this name? Are there tigers on the hill?

Z: Not really. There is a story behind it. In the Spring and Autumn Period, this area was ruled by the king of the State of Wu. One of its famous kings was called He Lv. After the death of King He Lv, his son King Fu Chai buried him on the hill which was previously his pleasant resort. A legend says that three days after the burial of King He Lv, a white tiger appeared crouching on the hill to guard the king's final resting place.

B: What an interesting story!

Z: The Tiger Hill (or Huqiu) enjoys a reputation as "the first scenic spot in the State of Wu", for Suzhou was once the capital of the State of Wu during the Spring and Autumn Period. With a history of more than 2500 years, the Tiger Hill has been known as the No. 1 Sight of Suzhou.

B: What are the main attractions there?

Z: The famous attractions are Yunyan Pagoda, Sword Pond, Mountain Villa, and Sword-Testing Rock. The Yunyan Pagoda has been leaning since its completion in 959-961 AD.

B: Just like the Leaning Tower of Pisa?

Z: Yes, it's also called the Leaning Tower of Pisa of the East. It was constructed earlier and taller than the Leaning Tower of Pisa. It leans to the north by about 3.5 degrees. The tower was partially repaired in 1981 by the local government.

B: What about the Sword Pond?

Z: It's a small rectangular pond. He Lv was a famous warrior and sword collector. The Sword Pond is said to hold his treasured swords in its watery depths. A treasure of some 3000 swords is believed to have been buried here. This site is not excavated because the Leaning Pagoda's foundations rest on the site.

B: Oh, so Sword-Testing Rock is a rock to test the sharpness of sword.

Z: That's right. OK, we are arriving at Tiger Hill. Please take your personal belongings and follow me.

Useful Expressions

1. Song-Yuan Quanzhou presents a prosperous picture and symbolic relationship among ports, city and hinterland.

宋元泉州呈现出港口、城市和腹地之间的繁荣景象和联动关系。

2. The 22 component sites reflect the maritime trade structure and the multi-cultural social structure of Song-Yuan Quanzhou.

22个遗产点体现了宋元泉州的海外贸易体系与多元社会结构。

3. They include administrative buildings, religious buildings and statues, cultural memorial sites, production sites of ceramics and transportation network.

22个遗产点包括行政管理机构、宗教建筑和造像、文化纪念地、陶瓷和冶铁生产基地,以及水陆交通网络。

4. The statue is 5.63 meters high, 6.85 meters thick and 8.01 meters wide.

雕像高5.63米,厚6.85米,宽8.01米。

5. It is China's longest existing cross-sea stone beam bridge.

安平桥是中国现存最长的跨海梁式石桥。

6. There are 360 stone step piers in rectangular, pointed boat-shape and bicuspid boat-shape styles.

共有石砌桥墩360座,有长方形、单尖船形、双尖船形等式样。

7. In heaven there is paradise, on earth there are Suzhou and Hangzhou.

上有天堂,下有苏杭。

8. A legend says that three days after the burial of King He Lv, a white tiger appeared crouching on the hill to guard the king's final resting place.

传说在吴王阖闾下葬三天后,一只白虎蹲伏在山上,守护着吴王的安息之地。

9. The Yunyan Pagoda is also called the Leaning Tower of Pisa of the East.

云岩寺塔又被称为"东方比萨斜塔"。

Exercises

1. Match the following Chinese with the correct English versions

(1) 行政区域划分   a. population

Module 6　Visiting Scenic Spot

(2) 县　　　　　　　　　　　　b. area
(3) 餐饮　　　　　　　　　　　c. geographic location
(4) 县级市　　　　　　　　　　d. administrative division
(5) 夜生活　　　　　　　　　　e. district
(6) 国内生产总值　　　　　　　f. county
(7) 区　　　　　　　　　　　　g. nightlife
(8) 面积　　　　　　　　　　　h. dinning
(9) 人口　　　　　　　　　　　i. county-level city
(10) 地理位置　　　　　　　　 j. GDP

2. **Translate the following Chinese into English**

(1) 这座寺庙的历史可以追溯到500年前。
(2) 这座桥建于20世纪初。
(3) 鼓浪屿建筑的重要性是什么？
(4) 跟其他塔比起来，东西塔有什么特别之处？
(5) 三明冬无严寒，夏无酷暑，一年四季都很适合旅游。

3. **Fill in the blanks with appropriate words and expressions**

A：Why is Xiamen called "garden on the sea"?

B：There is a proverb about Xiamen here："The city is on the ___(1)___, the sea is in the city." Xiamen borders the East China Sea and faces Penghu and Taiwan Islands. It's connected with the mainland by the Gaoji Seawall and Xiamen Bridge. There is another name about the city, "Egret Island", do you know why?

A：I don't know. Tell me more about it.

B：It's said that hundreds of thousands of egrets used to ___(2)___ on the island. This is due to the beautiful natural scenery, the fresh air and the clean environment.

A：It's said that Xiamen used to be ___(3)___ Amoy.

B：Yes. Foreigners in Xiamen used to call it Amoy because they could not pronounce the South Fujian dialect word. It ___(4)___ like amen spoken through one's nose.

A：What's the climate here?

B：It's a subtropical monsoon climate with mild weather all year. So it's an ideal ___(5)___ destination.

A：Can you recommend some scenic spots for us?

B：The popular scenic spots include Kulangsu, Wanshi Botanical Garden, Nanputuo Temple, Jimei School Village, Xiamen University and so on.

A：Thank you for your information.

B：My pleasure.

4. Role play

Situation 1: Suppose you are the local guide and one of the tourists is inquiring about Jimei School Village. Make a dialogue with your partner.

Situation 2: Suppose you are the local guide and one of your tourists is inquiring you about Xiamen University. Make a dialogue with your partner.

5. Questions & Answers

Question 1: If the guest is bitten by a poisonous snake in the scenic spot, what should the tour guide do?

Question 2: One of the tourists suffers from heat stroke while climbing the mountain. What should the tour guide do?

Ⅳ Extended Reading

Fujian Travel Guide

Task 2　A Visit to Fujian Tulou

Ⅰ Warming Up

1. Read and Match

a. Hegui Lou　　　　　　　　b. Yunshuiyao Ancient Town
c. Dadi Tulou Cluster　　　　d. Chengqi Lou

(1)

(2)

(3)

(4)

2. Questions

Question 1: When was Fujian Tulou included in the World Heritage List?

Tips for reference:

On July 6, 2008, Fujian Tulou was officially included in the World Heritage List at the 32nd World Heritage Conference held in Quebec City, Canada.

Question 2: What is Fujian Tulou composed of?

Tips for reference:

Fujian Tulou is composed of 46 Tulou in Yongding District of Longyan, Nanjing Country and Hua'an Country of Zhangzhou, Fujian Province. They are Chuxi Tulou Cluster, Hongkeng Tulou Cluster, Gaobei Tulou Cluster and Yanxiang Lou, Zhenfu Lou, Tianluokeng Tulou Cluster, Hekeng Tulou Cluster and Huaiyuan Lou, Hegui Lou, and Dadi Tulou Cluster.

‖ Situational Dialogues

➢ Dialogue 1

A Visit to Tianluokeng Tulou Cluster

(Xiao Li, the local guide, is visiting Tianluokeng Tulou Cluster with his tour group at the upper viewing platform.)

L: Xiao Li, the local guide   T: the tourists

L: Ladies and gentlemen, our first stop of the Tulou trip today is the Tianluokeng Tulou Cluster. Now let's go up to the upper viewing platform to appreciate its unique charm. Now we are on the viewing platform overlooking the cluster. It is located halfway up the mountain. It consists of five Tulou buildings, one square building in the center and four round ones around it.

T: So that is "Four Dishes and One Soup" that people often speak of.

L: Yes, the Tianluokeng Tulou Cluster is also called "Four Dishes and One Soup". The square building at the center is Buyun Lou, that is, Reach-the-Cloud-Building. Built in 1796, the three-floor building covers an area of 1050 square meters.

T: How many rooms are there in Buyun Lou?

L: There are 26 rooms on each floor, four sets of stairs, and a go-around corridor in front of the rooms. The round Tulou to the right is Zhenchang Lou. Zhenchang Lou was built in 1930. It is also a three-floor Tulou with the same number of rooms as Buyun Lou.

T: What's the oval one?

L: The oval Tulou to the left is Wenchang Lou, built in 1966. It's larger than Buyun Lou. It is also three-floor, but with more rooms. A well is built in the yard. The earthen wall of the first floor is 1.2 meters thick, which makes it strong enough to fend off bullets. The nearest round building is Hechang Lou, first built around 600 years ago. There are 22 rooms on each of the three floors. It used to be a square building. In the 1930s, bandits burned it down. In 1953 it was rebuilt in the present round shape. The one to its left is Ruiyun Lou, built in 1936. It is almost the same as Buyun Lou in size, the number of floors, rooms and structure.

T: They are so amazing.

L: You'll have 15 minutes for taking photos. The second column is the best place to take photos. Please be careful. Thank you.

T: Can we go inside to feel their mystery?

L: Yes, I will take you to visit each Tulou one by one and explain their special feature to you. And you can explore the local people's life there.

T: That's good.

(Xiao Li guides the tourists to visit the inside of Tulou.)

L: Now we are at the courtyard of Tulou. In the middle of the earthen house is an open-air courtyard, toward which all the doors and windows are facing. All the rooms are neatly arranged around the courtyard like the inside of an orange. There is a well in the courtyard. The first floor usually consists of kitchens, dining halls, hallways and staircases. Our next stop of the Tulou trip is Yuchang Lou. It's only 5 minutes ride from Tianluokeng. Now you can have 20 minutes to take some pictures.

➢ Dialogue 2

Visit Yuchang Lou

(Xiao Li, the local guide, is visiting Tianluokeng Tulou Cluster with his tour group at the upper viewing platform.)

L: **Xiao Li, the local guide**　　T: **the tourists**

L: Here we are at Yuchang Lou. Built in 1308, Yuchang Lou is the oldest Tulou

among the existent Tulou.

T: It looks larger than other Tulou.

L: Yes. This round building has five floors with 54 rooms on each. Five clans pooled money to build the big house.

T: What's the round building in the center? It's different from Tianluokeng cluster.

L: The round building in the center of the courtyard is used as the public activity center. Inside it is the ceremonial hall, where weddings and funerals are held.

T: What's the shape? Does it have some special meaning?

L: The floor of the hall is covered with cobblestones in the pattern of the five elements of metal, wood, water, fire and earth, an expression loaded with rich culture in Chinese architecture. Look up there, have you found something special?

T: Oh, the pillars are leaning.

L: Yes, that's the most mystical. The wooden pillars on the third, fourth and fifth floors are leaning left or right, so the building got a nickname "the leaning building". It's said when this building was built, the carpenters, in order to show his superior techniques, leaned the pillars by applying the principles of structural mechanics.

T: Can we go upstairs?

L: I'm afraid not. For the sake of safety, now visitors in large groups are not allowed to crowd into the building. Well, I will show you something really peculiar in Yuchang Lou. Please follow me to the kitchens.

T: What peculiar?

L: Look at the well. Each of the 25 kitchens on the ground floor at the back half of the circle has a private water-well. This is the only Tulou in Fujian with such convenient water supply.

T: There must be something different with other tulou. Just now in Tianluokeng, there is only a well in the courtyard.

L: The underground springs happen to run under the kitchens and it's not deep from the surface of the ground. So people dig wells in the kitchen and they can easily scoop the water in the indoor wells. It never dries or overflows, and tastes fresh and sweet all the year round.

T: Oh, that's very convenient.

L: Well, so much for Yuchang Lou. You can walk around by yourself and we'll meet outside the building in 20 minutes. Thank you.

Useful Expressions

1. It consists of five Tulou buildings, one square building in the center and four round ones around it.

田螺坑土楼群由五座土楼组成，中间是一座方形土楼，周围是四座圆形土楼。

2. Built in 1796, the three-floor building covers an area of 1050 square meters.

步云楼建于 1796 年，3 层楼，占地面积 1050 平方米。

3. There are 26 rooms on each floor, four sets of stairs, and a go-around corridor in front of the rooms.

每层有 26 个房间，4 组楼梯，1 个通廊。

4. The first floor usually consists of kitchens, dining halls, hallways and staircases.

一楼通常由厨房、餐厅、走廊和楼梯组成。

5. The floor of the hall is covered with cobblestones in the pattern of the five elements of metal, wood, water, fire and earth, an expression loaded with rich culture in Chinese architecture.

地面铺满鹅卵石，呈现"金、木、水、火、土"五行图案，富有中国建筑文化气息。

6. It never dries or overflows, and tastes fresh and sweet all the year round.

井水永不干涸，永不溢出，常年鲜甜可口。

Ⅲ Exercises

1. Match the following Chinese with the correct English versions

（1）地　　　　　　　　　　　　a. couplet
（2）防火　　　　　　　　　　　b. ancestral hall
（3）楼梯　　　　　　　　　　　c. the Eight Trigrams
（4）仓库　　　　　　　　　　　d. heaven
（5）祖堂　　　　　　　　　　　e. earth
（6）对联　　　　　　　　　　　f. human
（7）八卦　　　　　　　　　　　g. staircase
（8）厨房　　　　　　　　　　　h. kitchen
（9）天　　　　　　　　　　　　i. granary
（10）人　　　　　　　　　　　 j. fireproof

2. Translate the following Chinese into English

（1）接下来我带领大家参观素有"土楼之王"之称的承启楼。
（2）承启楼坐落于福建龙岩高北村，已有 300 多年的历史。
（3）承启楼外圈 4 层，高 16.4 米，每层 72 个房间。
（4）一层是厨房和餐厅，二楼是仓库，三楼、四楼是卧室。
（5）祖堂位于中央的内环，是楼内居民举行重大仪式的地方。

3. Fill in the blanks with appropriate words and expressions

A：Now we are in front of the Eryi Lou. It ＿＿＿(1)＿＿＿ a reputation of being the "No. 1 Round Tulou in China". It was first ＿＿＿(2)＿＿＿ in 1740 and the whole construction took 30 years. It was built to protect the people from bandits and ___(3)___ animals.

B: What does Eryi mean?

A: The name "Eryi" in Chinese is from *the Book of Songs*, the earliest general collection of ancient Chinese poems. It means a ___(4)___ between male and female, husband and wife, inside and outside, the old and the young. It also means a harmony with the environment we live in.

B: It seems the building is fortified.

A: Yes, as you see. The outer wall is 16 meters high. On the top floor some lookout windows and gun-ports are equipped. The thick wall base is ___(5)___ of five-meter granite ___(6)___. Have you noticed the holes in the wall?

B: Yes. What are they for?

A: These holes serve as doorbells. Please follow me inside to discover its mystery.

4. Role play

Situation 1: Suppose you are the local guide and the tourists are inquiring about how to build a tulou in the mountainous area. Make a dialogue with your partner and your dialogue should include the following points: the distribution, the scale, the building materials, the functions.

Situation 2: Suppose you are the local guide and you are visiting Eryi Lou with your tour group. Make a dialogue with your partner and your dialogue should include the following points: the history, the paintings and murals, the structures and the drainage system.

5. Questions & Answers

Question 1: What introduction should be made on the way back from the scenic spot?

Question 2: What are the basic guiding methods while taking the tour group to enjoy the scenery?

Ⅳ Extended Reading

Yongding Hakka Tulou Cluster

Module 7
Shopping and Entertainment

Learning Objectives

1. Learn the basic procedures and specifications of shopping and entertainment service.
2. Help tourists choose local specialties.
3. Recommend entertainment activities to tourists.
4. Introduce relevant laws and regulations related to shopping and entertainment.

Case Introduction

Case 1:

Mr. Baker wanted to buy some handicrafts. He asked the tour guide Xiao Wang for suggestions.

How should Xiao Wang recommend handicrafts to Mr. Baker?

Case 2:

Mr. Baker and his parents wanted to go to the theater to watch Peking Opera. They asked the tour guide Xiao Wang for help.

How should Xiao Wang arrange the activities for Mr. Baker?

Task 1　The Four Treasures of the Study

 ｜ Warming Up

1. Read and Match

a. Chinese brush　　b. inkstick　　c. Xuan paper　　d. inkstone

Module 7　Shopping and Entertainment

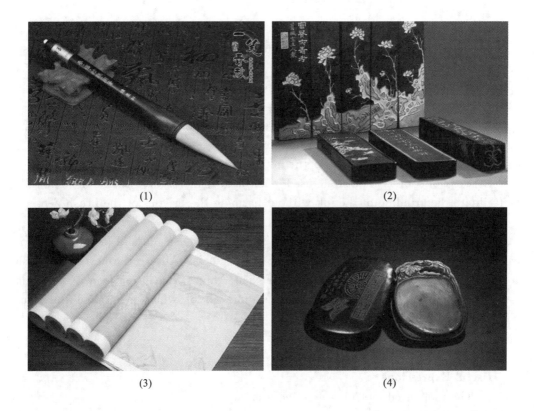

(1)　(2)　(3)　(4)

2. Question

What is considered a good shopping tour?

Tips for reference:

(1) Tourists can enjoy a good shopping experience.

(2) Tourists are satisfied with the purchase.

(3) While shopping, there's no pressure to purchase.

‖ Situational Dialogue

Introducing the Four Treasures of the Study

(As a local guide, Xiao Li is talking with Jane, the tourist, about the Four Treasures of the Study.)

　　L: **Xiao Li, the local guide**　　J: **Jane, the tourist**

L: Jane, how is your calligraphy practice going?

J: Just so so. Everything goes wrong.

L: Why is that?

J: The brush doesn't write well, the ink is smelly, the paper is not good.

L: Where did you get these?

J: The store at the corner of the street.

L: No wonder. The tools used by Chinese are very dainty.

扫码
听听力

J: What do you mean?

L: Good brushes are soft, flexible, absorbent and produce bold, vigorous lines.

J: How about the ink?

L: It should be pure, solid black in color, without murkiness or roughness.

J: I see. Then the paper?

L: An ideal paper must be able to absorb ink quickly and hold it well. The surface of paper is neither very firm nor smooth.

J: Any special requirement for the ink stone?

L: Yes, of course. The stone used must be of relatively fine whetstone materials to facilitate the grinding of the ink without harming the bristles of the brush pen.

J: I didn't know these before.

L: It doesn't matter. You can go to Rongbaozhai, an old and famous shop for calligraphy and paintings, and buy a set of these tools. All are the best, the brush from Xuancheng Anhui, the ink from Shexian Anhui, the paper from Xuancheng Anhui and the ink stone from Shexian Anhui, all of which are called the Four Treasures of the Study.

J: Thank you. Sharp tools make good work.

Useful Expressions

1. The tools used by Chinese are very dainty.

中国人使用的工具非常精致。

2. Good brushes are soft, flexible, absorbent and produce bold, vigorous lines.

好的毛笔柔软、有弹性、吸水性强,能画出粗犷有力的线条。

3. It should be pure, solid black in color, without murkiness or roughness.

它应该是纯正的、纯黑的,不模糊也不粗糙。

4. The stone used must be of relatively fine whetstone materials to facilitate the grinding of the ink without harming the bristles of the brush pen.

使用的石头必须是相对优质的磨石材料,有助于研磨,而不损害毛笔的鬃毛。

5. All are the best, the brush from Xuancheng Anhui, the paper from Xuancheng Anhui Anhui and the inkstone from Shexian Anhui, all of which are called the Four Treasures of the Study.

所有(器物)都是最好的,宣笔、徽墨、宣纸、歙砚,被誉为"文房四宝"。

Exercises

1. Match the following Chinese with the correct English versions

(1) 有力的;精力充沛的   a. absorbent

(2) 促进;帮助;使容易   b. bold

(3) 能吸收的   c. vigorous

(4) 研磨、磨碎   d. facilitate

(5) 加粗的   e. grinding

Module 7 Shopping and Entertainment

2. Translate the following Chinese into English

（1）难怪中国人使用的工具非常讲究。
（2）好的毛笔柔软、有弹性、吸收力强,能画出粗犷有力的线条。
（3）它应该是纯正的、纯黑的,不模糊也不粗糙。
（4）理想的纸要能够快速吸墨而且墨迹不易渲染开。纸的表面不能太硬也不能太光滑。
（5）制作砚台的石头必须是相对优质的磨石材料,有助于研磨,而不损害毛笔的鬃毛。
（6）工欲善其事,必先利其器。

3. Fill in the blanks with appropriate words and expressions

A：___(1)___ did you get these?
B：The store at the ___(2)___ of the street.
A：___(3)___ do you think of this Chinese brush?
B：Oh, it looks pretty nice.
A：How about the ink?
B：It seems pure, solid black in ___(4)___. You are good in picking things.
A：I didn't know these before. Thanks to Xiao Wang, he told me a lot about the Four Treasures of the Study.
B：What a lot of things Xiao Wang knows! He is a tour guide with ___(5)___ experience.

4. Role play

Situation：Suppose you are the tour guide, one of your guests, Mr. Baker wants to buy some handicrafts at a local specialties store and asks for your advice. Make a short dialogue with your partner.

5. Questions & Answers

Question：What should the guide do when tourists want to go shopping?

Ⅳ Extended Reading

The Four Treasures of The Study

The Four Treasures of The Study

Task 2 Chinese Painting

Ⅰ Warming Up

1. Read and Match

a. landscape painting   b. ink-and-wash painting
c. figure painting   d. flower-and-bird painting

(1)　　　　　　　　　　　　(2)

(3)　　　　　　　　　　　　(4)

2. Question

What advice will the local guide give to tourists before a shopping expedition?

Tips for reference:

(1) Give them a friendly reminder (take care of their personal belongings including passports and valuables).

(2) Recommend unique gifts and souvenirs honestly.

(3) Suggest that they ask for formal receipts for major purchases.

(4) Suggest that they compare the price of items with that of similar ones at home to see whether it is worth buying and try to bargain.

(5) Announce an appointed time and place for regrouping.

II Situational Dialogue

Introducing Chinese Painting

(The group leader Tom is talking with the tourist, Jane about Chinese Painting.)

T: Tom, the group leader　　J: Jane, the tourist

T: Jane, your cup is so special with that painting.

J: It's Chinese painting. I bought it in the antique market.

T: Why don't they paint on paper?

J: They do that too. Chinese painting is just always closely related to the other crafts, from pottery to the decorations used on the bronzes and carved jade.

T: Do you have a Chinese painting on paper?

J: Yes, I bought a counterfeit of the famous *Spring Outing*. It's in my bedroom.

T: It looks beautiful and it makes me feel happy.

J: That's why I bought it. The enchanting spring scene with people enjoying popular activities, the waterfall behind the bridge, near slopes and distant mountains all make me pleasant.

T: What a magic painting!

J: Actually, all the excellent Chinese paintings must be infused with imagination and soul.

T: Wow, you know it so well.

J: I learned all these from the local guide Xiao Li.

Useful Expressions

1. I bought it in the antique market.
我在古董市场买的。

2. Chinese painting is just always closely related to the other crafts, from pottery to the decorations used on the bronzes and carved jade.
从陶器到青铜器、玉雕上的装饰,中国画总是与其他工艺密切相关。

3. The enchanting spring scene with people enjoying popular activities, the waterfall behind the bridge, near slopes and distant mountains all make me pleasant.
明媚的春光、尽情玩乐的人们、桥后瀑布、近坡远山,都让我心旷神怡。

4. Actually, all the excellent Chinese paintings must be infused with imagination and soul.
实际上,所有优秀的中国画都要融入想象力和灵魂。

Exercises

1. Match the following Chinese with the correct English versions

(1) 创新　　　　　　　　　a. engrave
(2) 雕刻　　　　　　　　　b. depiction
(3) 壁画　　　　　　　　　c. decoration
(4) 精致的;细致的　　　　d. genre
(5) 描述、叙述　　　　　　e. exquisite
(6) 装饰品　　　　　　　　f. mural
(7) 类型　　　　　　　　　g. innovation

2. Translate the following Chinese into English

(1) 从陶瓷到青铜器和玉雕上的装饰,中国画总是与其他工艺密切相关。

(2) 明媚的春光、尽情玩乐的人们、桥后瀑布、近坡远山,都让我心旷神怡。

(3) 事实上,优秀的中国画应该融入想象力和灵魂。

(4) 公元 4 世纪时,山水画就已经形成了自己独立的表现形式。

(5) 在水墨画里,只用墨水就可以层次分明地表现出明与暗、浓与淡之间的平衡。

3. Fill in the blanks with appropriate words and expressions

A: Good morning, madam. Can I ____(1)____ you?

B: Yes, thank you. I am especially ____(2)____ in traditional Chinese paintings. Do you have any good ones?

A: Yes, we do. Do you ____(3)____ landscape or figure paintings?

B: That one with beautiful lady seems good.

A: You've made a good ____(4)____. The lady's name is Xishi; she was one of the four most famous ____(5)____ in ancient China.

B: It's really very nice. ____(6)____ is it?

A: 270 yuan.

B: I will ____(7)____ it. Here is 300 yuan.

A: Here's the ____(8)____. Thank you, madam. Have a nice stay.

4. Role play

Situation: One tourist wants to buy something for his family, but it is hard for him to decide. He asks the advice of the local guide. Make a dialogue with your partner.

5. Questions & Answers

Question: What should the local guide do when some tourists want to buy antiques?

Ⅳ Extended Reading

The Art of Ink — Chinese Painting

Task 3　Introducing Local Specialties

Ⅰ Warming Up

1. Read and Match

a. Chinese tea　　　　　　　　　　　　b. silk

Module 7   Shopping and Entertainment

c. Beijing Roast Duck   d. Chinese knot

(1)   (2)

(3)   (4)

2. Question

What should the local guide do on a shopping tour?

Tips for reference:

(1) Don't stay away from tourists in case they need help.

(2) Don't hover and give them space but be nearby.

(3) Never get yourself involved in bargain.

(4) If something unpleasant happens, try to solve the problem in the interests of the tourists.

Ⅱ Situational Dialogues

> **Dialogue 1**

Talking about Chinese Knot

(The tour guide, Tom is talking with the tourist, Jane about Chinese knot.)

T: Tom, the tour guide   J: Jane, the tourist

J: Tom, what's that on the wall? I didn't see it the last time I came.

T: It's a Chinese knot. I got it in a store at a street corner yesterday and made it a wall decoration.

J: It seems nice. It's symmetrical and all the circles are linked with one another.

T: Can you believe that it is woven separately from one piece of thread?

J: Impossible! How can one piece of thread form such a complicated pattern? How smart the Chinese are!

T: The endless variations and elegant patterns help Chinese knot win the favor of many foreigners.

J: I want one too.

T: You can get in that store over there. You know what? I am looking for the materials and tutorial to prepare learning.

J: The learning must be difficult.

T: Actually, the knot-tying methods are fixed and it's easy to learn.

J: Is that so?

T: Yes, it is. But the tightening can determine the degree of tension in a knot, the length of loops and the smoothness and orderliness of the lines.

J: I see. It's similar to tie a tie. The methods are fixed and the most difficult and important part is to tidy up.

T: Yes. You are smart enough to learn this, I think.

> **Dialogue 2**

Talking about Chinese Silk

(The tour guide, Xiao Cheng is talking with the tourist, Jane about Chinese silk.)

C: Xiao Cheng, the tour guide   J: Jane, the tourist

J: Xiao Cheng, I have heard that there is a busy silk market near People's Square.

C: Yes, it is in the northeast corner of the square, about 6 minutes' walk from here. That is a great place to pick up some real silk products. The handmade silk carpets made here are high value products and all are done by hand through complicated process. From the silkworms to the final products, it will take many complicated processes to weave these beautiful carpets.

J: I really want to go there. Can you show me there?

C: My pleasure. Later we will have an hour's free time, and I will show you there.

J: Thank you so much.

(At the silk market)

C: OK, here we are at the silk market. Silk has a long history in China. It's said

Module 7 Shopping and Entertainment

that the sericulture has been found out by the Chinese about 5000 years ago. Chinese silk is famous for its excellent quality, exquisite designs and colors, and rich cultural connotation. Thousands of years ago, silk spread to Europe along the ancient Silk Road, bringing not only gorgeous costumes and ornaments, but also the ancient and splendid civilization of the East. Since then, silk has almost become the symbol of Oriental civilization.

J: Oh, yes, China is indeed a kingdom of silk. Look at this, how beautiful and delicate this silk carving is. It suits my study well. It is just what I am looking for. I will take it.

C: You really have good taste.

Useful Expressions

1. It's symmetrical and all the circles are linked with one another.
它是对称的，所有的圆都是相互连接的。

2. How can one piece of thread form such a complicated pattern?
一根线怎么能形成如此复杂的图案？

3. The endless variations and elegant patterns help Chinese knot win the favor of many foreigners.
无尽的变化和优雅的图案让中国结赢得了许多外国人的青睐。

4. From the silkworms to the final products, it will take many complicated processes to weave these beautiful carpets.
从蚕丝到最终产品，编织这些美丽的地毯需要许多复杂的步骤。

5. It's said that the sericulture has been found out by the Chinese about 5000 years ago.
据说养蚕是中国人在大约5000年前发现的。

6. Thousands of years ago, silk spread to Europe along the ancient Silk Road, bringing not only gorgeous costumes and ornaments, but also the ancient and splendid civilization of the East.
数千年前，丝绸沿着古老的丝绸之路传到欧洲，不仅带去了华丽的服饰和饰物，也带去了古老灿烂的东方文明。

Exercises

1. Match the following Chinese with the correct English versions

(1) 织布机   a. thread
(2) 服装   b. cord
(3) 线   c. waistband
(4) 切片   d. fragrance

(5) 缎带　　　　　　　　　　e. cocoon
(6) 腰带　　　　　　　　　　f. ribbon
(7) 浸泡　　　　　　　　　　g. loom
(8) 绳索　　　　　　　　　　h. garment
(9) 茧　　　　　　　　　　　i. process
(10) 加工　　　　　　　　　　j. steep
(11) 香味　　　　　　　　　　k. fermentation
(12) 发酵　　　　　　　　　　l. slice

2. Translate the following Chinese into English

(1) 它是对称的,而且所有的圆环都环环相扣。

(2) 无穷的变化和优雅的图案使中国结赢得了很多外国人的喜爱。

(3) 抽紧这一步骤决定了结的松紧程度、圆环长度和绳子之间的平滑有序。

(4) 据说大约五千年前中国人发现了养蚕。

(5) 中国丝绸以其优良的品质、精美的花色和丰富的文化内涵而闻名。

3. Fill in the blanks with appropriate words and expressions

A：＿＿(1)＿＿ you like to have a look at this picture on the wall? Don't you think it's special?

B：Yes, it's ＿＿(2)＿＿ from other paintings. What is it made of?

A：It's a shell picture ＿＿(3)＿＿ of seashells.

B：You are kidding. Can seashells be made ＿＿(4)＿＿ a picture? That would be too challenging.

A：It is really made of seashells. First, the shells are selected and carved. And the craftsman draws a design on a piece of board and arranges the shells on it. Nearly all the colors are ＿＿(5)＿＿ on it.

B：It's unbelievable! The craftsmen's ＿＿(6)＿＿ are superb.

4. Role play

Situation：A customer is shopping in a souvenir shop and has no idea about what to take. He asks the advice of the tour guide. Make a dialogue with your partner based on the above situation.

5. Questions & Answers

Question：If the tourist has bought the fake products, how does the tour guide help to settle the matter?

Ⅳ Extended Reading

Creative Chinese Knots

Task 4 Recreation Activities

| Warming Up

1. **Read and Match**

   a. billiards room
   b. fitness center
   c. bowling room
   d. exercise bicycle

(1)　(2)　(3)　(4)

2. **Question**

What kind of services will local guide provide for entertainment program?

Tips for reference:

(1) Try to learn something about the program and give a brief introduction to the program.

(2) Tell tourists the meeting time and place.

(3) Help with seating the tourists.

(4) Remind tourists to take care of themselves and their personal belongings.

(5) On the way back, review the program and answer questions if there is any.

Ⅱ Situational Dialogues

➢ Dialogue 1

The Recreational Center

(Alice wants to enjoy herself at the recreational center and inquires the tour guide, Xiao Huang, for information.)

A：Alice, the tourist　　H：Xiao Huang, the tour guide

A：Xiao Huang, could you spare me some minutes?

H：Sure, Alice. Go ahead.

A：I want to do some exercise and relax myself today. Could you tell me what facilities you have here in the hotel?

H：Well, you can enjoy yourself at the recreational center. There is a well-equipped gymnasium with all the latest recreational sports apparatus such as exercise bicycle, barbells and wall bars. And we have the billiards room and bowling center.

A：That sounds very interesting.

H：Then we have two excellent saunas. By the way, there's a free supply of towels and Finnish sauna soap.

A：Very good. And what about swimming?

H：Yes, you can have a dip in the heated swimming pool which contains special salt in the water to stimulate the skin. The water is very clean and the hotel changes it every other day. You can also borrow swimming trunks free of charge.

A：Oh, good. I've left mine at home.

H：And afterwards, you can relax with beer or soft drinks and some pastries in the after-sauna room where there is a large open fireplace with birch logs.

A：That is exactly what I want.

H：Besides, if you like dancing, you can enjoy yourself in our modern dance hall.

A：Oh, I don't like disco. It's too noisy.

H：Well, we have all kinds of music. You can try waltz or tango if you like.

A：That's a good idea. How about outdoor activities?

H：We have a nine-hole golf course or if you prefer you can water-ski on the lake or hire a rowing boat if you feel energetic.

A：Do you have any tennis courts?

H：Oh yes. You can also play badminton. Rackets and balls are available at a

Module 7　Shopping and Entertainment

small charge. And if that is not enough, there is always croquet on the lawn.

A: Wonderful. Thanks a lot.

Dialogue 2

The Indoor Swimming Pool

(Alice wants to swim in the indoor swimming pool with her friends and asks the local guide, Xiao Huang for information.)

A: Alice, the tourist　　H: Xiao Huang, the local guide

H: Good morning, Alice. You called me just now. What is the matter?

A: Good morning. My friends and I would like to go swimming today and I want to have a look at the indoor swimming pool here. Will you please show me there?

H: I am glad to do that. This way, please.

(In the indoor swimming pool)

H: Here we are. Please put these covers over your shoes. They are beside the pool. This is the indoor swimming pool. It features artificial waves and is the biggest indoor pool in the area. They make waves at regular in thermals.

A: How often do they make waves in the pool?

H: Usually every half an hour at night from 21:00 to 24:00. It depends. If there are many people here swimming, they will make the interval time shorter. The waves create a lift as high as 1.2 meters.

A: I see. The environment is quite nice, including palm trees, waterfall, rockery, delicate bridge over the joining part of the bigger pool and smaller pool. I like here. What about the water temperature?

H: The water and room temperature stays 28℃ all year. Besides, there is a hot spring massage pool over there. The temperature of the massage pool is 39℃.

A: That is great! How deep is the pool?

H: Its depth is from 1 meter to 1.8 meters. You can swim in the shallow areas if you want.

A: But you see, I am not so good at swimming. Are there any coaches here? I need a woman coach.

H: There is a man coach at the moment. There are lifeguards as well. There will be a woman coach if you make an appointment in advance.

A: Good. May I know the business hours?

H: It's from 8:00 am to 12:00 pm.

A: Then I will be here at 8:00 am with my friends. Thank you for your help. Oh, one more thing, are there any swimming suits for sale? I did not take my swimming suit with me.

H: Yes, would you like to have a look?

导游英语

A: Yes, can you show me the way?
H: No problem. This way, please.

Useful Expressions

1. Could you tell me what facilities you have here in the hotel?
你能告诉我酒店里有什么设施吗?

2. You can enjoy yourself at the recreational center.
您可以在娱乐中心玩得开心。

3. Yes, you can have a dip in the heated swimming pool which contains special salt in the water to stimulate the skin.
是的,你可以在加热的游泳池里泡一泡。游泳池的水中含有一种特殊的盐,可以激活肌肤。

4. And afterward, you can relax with beer or soft drinks and some pastries in the after-sauna room where there is a large open fireplace with birch logs.
之后,你可以在桑拿室享用啤酒或软饮料和一些糕点。那里有一个巨大的开放式壁炉,壁炉里有桦木原木。

5. How often do you make waves in the pool?
你们多久在游泳池里制造一次波浪?

6. Its depth is from 1 meter to 1.8 meters. You can swim in the shallow areas if you want.
深度为1米至1.8米。如果你愿意,你可以在浅水区游泳。

7. May I know the business hours?
请问营业时间是几点?

8. Are there any swimming suits for sale?
有泳衣出售吗?

 Exercises

1. Match the following Chinese with the correct English versions

(1) 门球　　　　　　　　　　a. gymnasium
(2) 滑水　　　　　　　　　　b. apparatus
(3) 网球　　　　　　　　　　c. barbells
(4) 健身房　　　　　　　　　d. wall bars
(5) 羽毛球　　　　　　　　　e. water-ski
(6) 器械　　　　　　　　　　f. badminton
(7) 肋木　　　　　　　　　　g. tennis
(8) 杠铃　　　　　　　　　　h. goalball

2. Translate the following Chinese into English

（1）我们有一座装备完善的健身馆，里面有各种各样最新的健身器械，比如供锻炼用的自行车、举重用的杠铃及肋木等。

（2）如果您愿意，您可以跳华尔兹或探戈。

（3）球拍和球都低价出租。

（4）它以人工海浪为特色，是该地区最大的室内游泳池。

（5）环境相当不错，有棕榈树、瀑布、假山，大水池和小水池的连接部分有精致的桥。

（6）如果您事先预约，会有女教练。

3. Fill in the blanks with appropriate words and expressions

A：Anything particular you'd like to do this evening?

B：I don't know. Is there ___(1)___ interesting to do in the hotel?

A：Sure. There is a musical fountain performance in the discotheque near the lobby. People can enjoy the beautiful fountains while ___(2)___ to the wonderful music.

B：Mm, sounds ___(3)___.

A：There are various computer games in the recreation center.

B：And do they have a ___(4)___ center here?

A：Yes, they have one. It's on the second floor.

B：What ___(5)___ do they have?

A：Massage and sauna. Apart from that, they also have facilities like a very big swimming pool, a gym, a billiards room, a bowling room…

B：That's great! Bowling is my favorite. I must go and enjoy ___(6)___. Is it open now?

A：It's 19:10. Yes, it's open now.

B：Super! Thank you for your information.

4. Role play

Situation：A group of American tourists would like to explore the wonderful night life in Xiamen. The tour guide takes them to a local night club and introduces the facilities and activities inside. They have a great time there. Make a dialogue with your partner based on the above situation.

5. Questions & Answers

Question：If the group asks to change the theatrical performance in the itinerary to another show, how will the local guide deal with it?

Ⅳ Extended Reading

Fun Things to Do

Module 8
Seeing the Tour Group off

Learning Objectives

1. Learn the basic procedures and specifications of service before departure.
2. Help the tourists check out of a hotel.
3. Make a farewell speech.
4. Deal with unexpected situations, such as tourist missing, traffic accident, passport missing, etc.

Case Introduction

Xiao Wang's tour group will return to their own country after breakfast. When they checked out, the hotel clerk found that the blanket of one room had been spoiled and claimed for damage. The local guide Xiao Wang went to the room and found there were a lot of vomit on the blanket. The tourist who lived in the room admitted that he had spoiled the blanket in the early morning. It was about three hours away from the flight's takeoff, the local guide asked all the tourists to wait 30 minutes for the settlement of the matter. Some of the other tourists were dissatisfied with the arrangement.

How should Xiao Wang deal with the accident?

Module 8　Seeing the Tour Group off

Task 1　Preparation for Seeing Off Tourists

Warming Up

1. Read and Match

a. weather condition　　　　　　　b. bullet train ticket
c. currency exchange　　　　　　　d. E-ticket itinerary

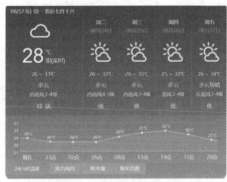

(1)

(2)

(3)　　　　　　　　　　　　　　　　(4)

2. Question

What preparations is local guide supposed to make for seeing off the tourists?
Tips for reference:

(1) confirm the departure time.
(2) check the travel tickets.
(3) prepare evaluation forms.
(4) get to know the weather condition.
(5) get to know the traffic condition.

(6) contact the coach driver.

(7) contact the hotel.

(8) communicate with the tour leader.

(9) inform the guests of Chinese currency exchange.

(10) prepare a farewell speech.

Ⅱ Situational Dialogues

➢ Dialogue 1

Double Checking the Amount of Luggage

(The local guide Xiao Wang is talking with tour leader Mr. Chen about luggage packing before leaving.)

W: Xiao Wang, the local guide   C: Mr. Chen, the tour leader

W: Mr. Chen, since we are going to leave early tomorrow morning, we should have the luggage checked out tonight. Would you please inform the group members to have their bags packed and put them outside their doors? Then the bellman will collect and carry them to the lobby.

C: Sure, no problem. Shall we meet on the 18th floor five minutes before 22:30 tonight? We will be there together to double check the amount of the luggage.

W: Certainly. You're very considerate.

(At 10:30 pm, on the 18th floor where the tour group is staying)

C: We've got 32 pieces of luggage altogether.

W: Let me see. Oh, this one has no lock on it. It's Mr. Ding's, I think. According to the regulations of the airline, all bags must be locked except the carry-on luggage. Otherwise, they will not be accepted.

C: I will tell Mr. Ding to lock it.

(The bag has been locked)

W: Everything is fine, Mr. Chen. We can hand over the luggage to the bellboy now.

C: Yes, certainly.

➢ Dialogue 2

Asking the Bellboy to Take the Luggage Downstairs

(The local guide Xiao Wang calls the bell captain's desk to pick up the luggage of the tourists.)

A: Xiao Wang, the local guide   B: the tour leader   C: bell captain

Module 8 Seeing the Tour Group off

C: This is the bell captain's desk. How may I help you?

A: Yes. We are going to check out early tomorrow morning. Could you pick up our luggage now, please?

C: Certainly, ma'am. May I have your room number, please?

A: Of course. It's on the 18th floor. Room 1801 to Room 1810, Room 1821 to Room 1826. 16 rooms altogether.

C: All right, ma'am.

(A few minutes later)

C: Good evening, sir. I've come for your baggage.

B: Thank you. Please carry our luggage down to the lobby. There are 32 pieces altogether.

C: Are there any valuables or anything breakable in them?

B: No.

C: This is your claim tag, sir. We will keep your luggage at the Locker Room. Could you pick it up there tomorrow morning, please?

B: Certainly, thank you very much.

C: It is our pleasure to serve you.

Useful Expressions

1. We will be there together to double check the amount of the luggage.
我们会一起去检查行李的数量。

2. You're very considerate.
你考虑得很周到。

3. Are there any valuables or anything breakable in them?
里面有贵重物品或易碎物品吗?

4. We'll keep your luggage at the Locker Room.
我们会把你们的行李放在寄存间。

Exercises

1. Match the following Chinese with the correct English versions

(1) 叫醒服务　　　　　a. departure time
(2) 退房时间　　　　　b. morning call
(3) 出发时间　　　　　c. gathering time
(4) 集合时间　　　　　d. coach number
(5) 大巴车号　　　　　e. check-out time

2. Translate the following Chinese into English

(1) 请通知团队客人把行李打包好,并放在他们的房门外面,好吗?

(2) 行李员将收集行李并把行李拿到大堂。

(3) 我们将在那里会合,核实行李数量。

(4) 根据航空公司的规定,所有箱包必须上锁,手提行李除外。

(5) 我们现在可以把行李交给行李员了。

(6) 请你现在帮我们拿行李,好吗?

(7) 请把行李拿到大堂。

(8) 我们会把你们的行李寄存在寄存间。

3. Fill in the blanks with appropriate words and expressions

A: Good evening. Mike.

B: Good evening. Xiao Wang. Have a seat, please.

A: Thanks. How time ____(1)____ ! Tomorrow, you'll leave for London.

B: Yeah. Thank you very much for everything you've done for us.

A: You are welcome. Thank you for your ____(2)____ and understanding.

B: I'm happy to make a good friend like you. We'll gather at 7:30 am tomorrow, right?

A: Yeah. The plane ____(3)____ at 11:30 am After everyone checks out, we will gather at the lobby. I have informed the Front Office of a ____(4)____ call at 6:20 am.

B: That's OK. I have told all the members to check and keep their passports and luggage well.

A: You are always considerate. The ____(5)____ is still AH8822.

B: Yes. I hope one day you'll go to London, and then I'll show you around my city.

A: Sure. Thanks. I am looking forward to it.

4. Role play

Situation: Suppose you are the tour guide. The tour group is going to leave at 10 am tomorrow. You need to inform the tour leader of the departure time, the weather condition, morning call, etc.

5. Questions & Answers

Question: What should the local guide do to help tourists check out of the hotel?

Ⅳ Extended Reading

Preparation for Seeing off

Module 8   Seeing the Tour Group off

Task 2 Check out of the Hotel

Warming Up

1. Read and Match

a. check out   b. luggage cart   c. payment   d. bill

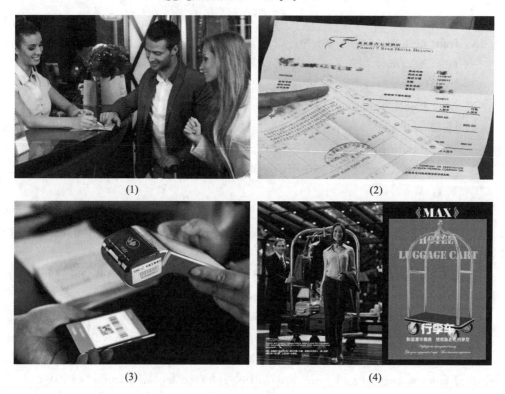

(1)   (2)

(3)   (4)

2. Question

What will the local guide do when you find a tourist missing in the hotel before departure?

Tips for reference:

(1) Wait for another 10-15 minutes and look for the tourist in all the places he/she might go to, such as a coffee shop, souvenir shop, cashier's desk, business center, bookstore, etc.

(2) If you still fail to find him/her, call the office and leave a message for him/

her at the hotel with your cell phone number.

(3) If there is still no news about the missing tourist before the group boards the plane/ship/train, call the office again. Report the case to the police if necessary.

(4) Keep a record afterwards.

II Situational Dialogues

➤ Dialogue 1

Settling the Accommodation Bill

(The tour leader Mr. Chen is settling the accommodation bill at the front desk.)

A: front desk cashier   B: Mr. Chen, the tour leader

A: Good morning. How can I help you?

B: I'd like to check out for our group.

A: May I have your room cards, please?

B: Here you are. My name is Chen Dong, the tour leader from ABC Travel Service. We stay in Room 1515 to Room 1518, 4 rooms altogether.

A: Yes, Mr. Chen. You came here three days ago on December 6, didn't you?

B: Yes, Miss.

A: Just a moment, please. I will draw up your bill for you. Your bill totals 880 dollars, Mr. Chen. Would you like to check it? The telephone charge for Room 1516 hasn't been paid yet.

B: Yes. Telephone charges will be paid individually. Maybe the guest in Room 1516 forgot to clear his bill. Just a minute, please. I will inform him.

A: Thank you, Mr. Chen. Would you please sign your name on the bill?

B: Certainly. Here you are. I paid 100 euros as deposit at check in with my credit card.

A: Yes. Since you had no extra charge during your stay, nothing will be deducted from your card and your card will be released within a couple of days.

(After a while)

A: Thank you. Mr. Chen. Here is your receipt. Hope you've enjoyed your stay in our hotel.

B: Thank you for your service.

➤ Dialogue 2

Briefing on the Departure Schedule

(The local guide Xiao Wang is briefing on the departure schedule before leaving.)

A: the local guide   B: the tour leader   C: the whole group   D: cashier

Module 8 Seeing the Tour Group off

A: Good morning, everyone. We are going to check out this morning. Is everybody here? And is everybody's luggage ready?

C: Yes.

A: Thank you for being so punctual. The bellmen will take your luggage to the coach. Ten minutes later, we'll meet at the coffee shop. Breakfast is to be served at 6:30. After the breakfast, let's meet on the bus. We will set off to the airport at 7:00. The departure time of the flight is 10 o'clock this morning. Is this schedule all right?

C: Yes, thank you.

A: (To the tour leader) Shall we go to the front desk to check out?

B: Certainly.

(At the front desk)

D: Good morning, are you checking out?

A: Yes, our rooms are 601, 602, 603, 604, 605 and 606.

D: Here is your bill. Please have a check. The total amount including the meal charge is 3000 dollars. Is that right?

A: Yes. I think so.

D: Would you please sign your name on the bill?

A: Certainly. Here you are.

D: Thank you. Here is your receipt. Have a nice day.

Useful Expressions

1. Hope you've enjoyed your stay in our hotel.
希望您在我们酒店住得愉快。
2. We are going to check out this morning.
我们今天上午结账离店。
3. Is everybody here?
大家都到了吗?
4. And is everybody's luggage ready?
行李都准备好了吗?
5. Would you please sign your name on the bill?
请您在账单上签名好吗?
6. Here is your receipt.
这是您的收款收据。

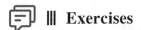 **Exercises**

1. Match the following Chinese with the correct English versions

(1) 收据　　　　　　　　　　　a. deposit

（2）准时的　　　　　　　　　　　b．deduct

（3）扣除　　　　　　　　　　　　c．release

（4）解除　　　　　　　　　　　　d．punctual

（5）押金　　　　　　　　　　　　e．receipt

2．Translate the following Chinese into English

（1）含餐费的总额是3000美元。

（2）您的账单总额是880美元。

（3）电话费将单独支付。

（4）我用信用卡支付了100欧元的押金。

（5）不会从卡中扣钱，您的信用卡将在几天内解除冻结。

3．Fill in the blanks with appropriate words and expressions

A：Good morning. What can I do for you?

B：Good morning. We'd like to ＿＿＿(1)＿＿＿. China International Travel Service. Room 3011 to 3015.

A：Have you got all the ＿＿＿(2)＿＿＿ cards?

B：Yes. Here you are.

A：Thank you. Has all the luggage been ＿＿＿(3)＿＿＿ of the rooms?

B：Yes. All the bags have already been ＿＿＿(4)＿＿＿ onto the shuttle bus.

A：OK. Wait a minute, please, (after a while) Here is the bill, Miss. Please check it. And if there are no mistakes, ＿＿＿(5)＿＿＿ here.

B：OK. (Signs the bill) Here you are.

A：OK. Thank you. Hope you all have a good journey.

B：Thank you. Goodbye.

4．Role play

Situation：Suppose you are a tour leader. Your group members will check out and leave for Xi'an today. Make a short dialogue with your partner.

5．Questions & Answers

Question：What should the local guide do if there is a delay in sending off tourists?

Ⅳ Extended Reading

How to Check out of the Hotel

Module 8 Seeing the Tour Group off

Task 3 Making a Farewell Speech

Warming Up

1. Read and Match

a. visa

b. evaluation forms

c. prohibited articles

d. customs declaration form

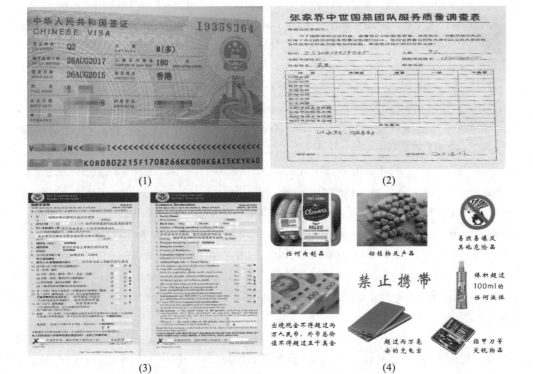

(1)   (2)

(3)   (4)

2. Question

What will the local guide do if the group has to end the tour ahead of schedule due to certain reasons?

Tips for reference：

(1) If the decision is made in your city, inform the travel company through your office, so they are able to cancel the rest of the trip in time.

(2) Inform the tour leader and try to get his support.

(3) Inform some tourists who have high prestige in the group and try to win their support.

(4) With the help of these people, inform the group and try to win support of the group.

(5) Try your best to show people as many highlights as possible in the program within the time limit.

(6) Follow the instructions of the office and make the tour a good ending.

Ⅱ Situational Dialogues

Farewell Speech

(The local guide Janet Jin is addressing a farewell speech to the tour group.)

J: Janet Jin, the local guide   D: Daniel Black, the group leader   T: tourists

D: Attention please, everybody. Please wait a moment. We'll check out in a while. Please recheck your belongings to make sure we've left nothing in the hotel.

J: Good morning, ladies and gentlemen. Your current visit to Beijing is drawing to a close. I would like to say a few words before you leave. Although I am not a speechmaker, there is an old Chinese saying, "It is a good banquet that must come to an end" and I think you can more or less guess what it means. I really hate to say goodbye to all of you, but I have to do so. It has been a wonderful experience for me to accompany you during your stay here. We have visited many wonderful places in Beijing, and I hope it will be a nice memory for you. If there is anything you are not satisfied with my job, please do tell me so that I can do better in the future. And I'd like to take this opportunity to thank you all for your understanding and cooperation. I sincerely hope that you'll come to visit China again. I hope to see you again in the future and to be your guide again. Once more, thank you for your cooperation and support. Bon voyage.

(On behalf of the tour group, Daniel Black is expressing gratitude to Janet Jin.)

D: Thank you very much, Miss Jin. On behalf of the whole group, I'd like to express our heartfelt gratitude to you for your efforts and excellent services. We certainly have had a wonderful time in the past 5 days and will always hold dear this unforgettable trip. I hope we can see each other again.

(They've arrived at the airport. Janet is reminding the tourists to take care of their belongings and documents they need for going through airport security check.)

J: Here we are at the airport. Please get your passports, air tickets, and 90 yuan for the departure tax ready. And now, please recheck your personal belongings to make sure you have nothing left on the coach.

(Janet Jin leads the tour group to the airport quarantine zone. Janet is telling the group leader, Daniel Black how to go through the airport security check.)

J: Daniel, I am afraid I have to say goodbye to you. I am not allowed to enter the quarantine zone. I suggest that you collect the plane tickets, passports and 90 yuan for airport departure tax first, and then go to check in for the flight. The clerks there will tell you how to go through the airport security check.

D: I will. You have been always so considerate.

(To the tour group)

J: Ladies and gentlemen, I have to say goodbye to you here. Then, Daniel will help you go through the airport controls. Please remember: if you have some remaining RMB, please change them back to US dollars after a while, and the clerk will tell you where the exchange desk is. Hope to meet you again. Have a pleasant trip. Bye.

T: Thank you. Bye.

Useful Expressions

1. Please recheck your belongings to make sure you have nothing left on the coach.

请再次检查您的物品,确保您没有任何东西落在车上。

2. On behalf of the whole group, I'd like to express our heartfelt gratitude to you for your efforts and excellent services.

我代表旅游团对您的努力和优质服务表示衷心的感谢。

3. We certainly have had a wonderful time in the past 5 days and will always hold dear this unforgettable trip.

在过去的5天里,我们的确度过了一段美好的时光,我们将永远珍视这段难忘的旅程。

4. Please get your passports, air tickets, and 90 yuan for the departure tax ready.

请准备好护照、机票和90元的离境税。

5. Please remember: if you have some remaining RMB, please change them back to US dollars after a while, and the clerk will tell you where the exchange desk is.

请记住:如果您还有剩余的人民币,请过一会儿把它们换回美元,工作人员会告诉您兑换台在哪里。

Exercises

1. Match the following Chinese with the correct English versions

(1) 送别　　　　　　　　a. common aspiration

(2) 共同努力　　　　　　b. mutual understanding

(3) 出境签证　　　　　　c. cooperative efforts

(4) 共同愿望　　　　　　　　　　　d. exit visa

(5) 相互理解　　　　　　　　　　　e. see off

2. Translate the following Chinese into English

(1) 天下没有不散的筵席。

(2) 我希望它会成为您美好的回忆。

(3) 如果您对我的工作有什么不满意的地方，请一定告诉我，以便我将来能做得更好。

(4) 我愿借此机会感谢各位的理解与配合。

3. Fill in the blanks with appropriate words and expressions

A：Good morning! Are you sure there is nothing ＿＿(1)＿＿?

B：Yeah, I am sure. What is the ＿＿(2)＿＿ of my flight?

A：It is 11 o'clock this morning.

B：Then, we don't have to be in a ＿＿(3)＿＿.

A：Well, I think we should start earlier. It may take some time on the way. There are always many ＿＿(4)＿＿ in this city. Besides, we should arrive at the airport one hour before the plane takes off so that we have time to go ＿＿(5)＿＿ the customs.

B：In that case, let's go a little bit earlier.

A：It's a pity you are leaving. I hope you will ＿＿(6)＿＿ to China again.

B：I will. Before I came, my knowledge about China mainly came from travel books and TV programs, many of which are quite stereotyped. After a trip in China, I've got a better ＿＿(7)＿＿ of China and Chinese culture, and I'm quite happy about the trip.

A：I'm glad you have enjoyed your stay in China.

T：You've been very considerate and helpful. I'd like to express my ＿＿(8)＿＿ gratitude to you.

B：It has been my pleasure to help you.

A：Everything I've seen here has left a deep ＿＿(9)＿＿ on me. I'll never forget my stay here in China. Thank you again for all the trouble you've taken, you're a very good guide.

B：Thank you for your compliment. Have a ＿＿(10)＿＿ journey home.

4. Role play

Situation：Suppose you are a tour guide, make a farewell speech to the tourists.

5. Questions & Answers

Question：What should be included in a farewell speech?

Ⅳ Extended Reading

A Farewell Speech

Module 8　Seeing the Tour Group off

Task 4　At the Airport

Warming Up

1. Read and Match

a. self-service
b. boarding gate
c. boarding pass
d. baggage check in

(1)

(2)

(3)

(4)

2. Question

When should the local guide arrive at the airport with a departing group? When should a group arrive at the railway station to await a departure?

Tips for reference:

Two hours in advance of the scheduled departure time for international flights; one hour and a half for domestic flights and 45 minutes before the train leaves.

Situational Dialogues

➤ Dialogue 1

Seeing off the Guests at the Airport

(The local guide Li Min is seeing off the guests at the airport.)

L: Li Min, the local guide   M: Mr. Black, the group leader

L: Here we're now at the airport. Could you please wait a few minutes for me? I am going to get your boarding passes and baggage claim tags.

M: OK. We'll wait right here.

(Li Min comes back)

L: Sorry to have kept you waiting. Here are your passports, boarding passes and baggage claim tags. You can check them now.

M: They all look fine. Thanks a lot.

L: Shall we go to the security check now?

M: OK. Let's go.

L: Here we are. These are the airport security channels you have to proceed through. Now please have your passports and boarding passes ready.

M: Thank you for all your help, Li Min.

L: It's been my pleasure. Have a wonderful flight and hope to see you again.

Guests(together): Bye.

➤ Dialogue 2

Saying Goodbye

(The local guide Li Tao has come to the airport to see the tourist Mrs. Abraham off.)

L: Li Tao, the local guide   A: Mrs. Abraham, the tourist

A: Time really flies! The time has come for us to say goodbye.

L: I feel very sad to see you go.

A: I will come again. I won't forget your kind help during my stay here.

L: We've enjoyed your stay here, too. It's hard to leave an old friend, but I am sure we will meet again.

A: You are welcome to come and visit us in the United States.

L: I hope so. Don't forget to contact me as soon as you get home. You have my email address and telephone number, don't you?

A: Sure. I will keep in touch with you. You know, China is such a large country with such a long history and such a rich culture that I think my brief visit can hardly do it justice. There are still so many places I would like to visit and so many things I would like to see. I will definitely come back.

L: Good. Don't forget to say hello to your family and friends.

A: I won't. Thank you again for all the trouble you have taken. Now I have to say goodbye to you.

L: OK, see you again soon.

Useful Expressions

1. Here are your passports, boarding passes and baggage claim tags.

这是你们的护照、登机牌和行李认领牌。

2. Shall we go to the security check now?

我们现在去安检吗?

3. These are the airport security channels you have to proceed through.

这些是您要通过的机场安全通道。

4. You know, China is such a large country with such a long history and such a rich culture that I think my brief visit can hardly do it justice.

您知道,中国是一个有着悠久历史和丰富文化的大国,我认为我的短暂访问还无法对其做出全面的评价。

5. Don't forget to say hello to your family and friends.

别忘了代我向您的家人和朋友问好。

Exercises

1. Match the following Chinese with the correct English versions

(1) 赞美   a. impression
(2) 超重   b. compliment
(3) 多才多艺的   c. appreciation
(4) 印象   d. overweight
(5) 感激   e. versatile

2. Translate the following Chinese into English

(1) 您喜欢什么样的座位,是靠窗的还是靠通道的?

(2) 我们要在飞机起飞前一个小时抵达机场,以便有足够的时间办理海关手续及其他手续。

(3) 我诚恳地希望你们对我及我们旅行社的服务提出宝贵的意见和建议。

(4) 请允许我代表我们旅行社及以我个人的名义向你们表示衷心的感谢。感谢你们的大力支持与合作。

(5) 我确信,今后的合作和不断的交往能使我们两国人民更亲近,并促进世界和平。

3. Fill in the blanks with appropriate words and expressions

A: Are you sure nothing is left ____(1)____ ?

B: Yeah, I'm sure.

A: How time flies! You've been in China for half a month. It seems as if it were only yesterday when I went to meet you at the airport. And now you're leaving.

B: Yeah, it has been a most ____(2)____ experience for us.

A: What's your impression of China now?

B: Well, It's definitely different from what we had heard before we came. You know, before we came, our knowledge about China mainly came from books and TV programs, many of which were quite stereotyped. I think I have a much better understanding of China and Chinese culture now. The more I know about China, the ____(3)____ I want to learn.

A: I'm glad you have ____(4)____ your stay in China.

B: You have been a great help to us along the way, Mr. Wang. We'd like to express our heartfelt ____(5)____ to you. Your companionship and consideration have made our trip most fruitful. Here, this is for you, as a going-away token.

G: Wow! So lovely! Thank you very much. It's a great pleasure for me to be your guide.

B: Well, it's time to board the plane. Thank you for everything.

G: Goodbye and happy landing.

4. Role play

Situation 1: Suppose you are a tour leader. The group members are at the airport. A tour guide helps you to check in at the airport. Make a short dialogue with your partner.

Situation 2: Suppose you are a tour guide. You go to the airport with the tour leader and the group members. After arriving at the airport, you first go to get the boarding passes, the baggage claim tags and passports. Make a short dialogue with your partner.

5. Questions & Answers

Question: What does the local guide need to do after the group leaves?

IV Extended Reading

Beijing Daxing International Airport

Module 9
Handling Emergencies

Learning Objectives

1. Master the basic procedures and specifications of handling emergencies.
2. Master the standard requirements of handling emergencies.
3. Make precautions and pre-arrangements for diminishing the possible danger.
4. Deal with unexpected situations, such as passport loss, traffic accidents, sudden illnesses, etc.

Case 1:

An old tourist had a heart attack, and another tourist, the old tourist's son, advised the local guide to allow his father to take the medicine that the patient had prepared beforehand.

What should the local guide do?

Case 2:

The local guide Mr. Zhao's tour group had finished the tour in Tibet. But one of the tourists had been hospitalized due to altitude sickness, and he was not allowed to leave the hospital when the tour group had to leave China.

What should the local guide do?

Task 1　Certificate Loss

Warming Up

1. Read and Match

a. embassy　　　　　　　　b. Lost and Found
c. consulate　　　　　　　 d. Public Security Bureau

(1)　　　　　　　　　　　　　(2)
(3)　　　　　　　　　　　　　(4)

2. Question

Passport is essential and vital for outbound tour. What if it got lost for a foreign tourist during the visit in China?

Tips for reference:

(1) Report to the local travel agency.

(2) Get the written testimonial.

(3) Go to the local Public Security Bureau.

Module 9 Handling Emergencies

(4) Go to the embassy of one's own country or the Consulate General in China together with valid testimonials and photo.

(5) Apply for the new passport.

(6) Apply for a new visa from the Office of Entry and Exit.

Situational Dialogues

➢ Dialogue 1

Passport Loss

(Jane, the tourist, hasn't found her passport. Tom, the tour leader, is helping her to find her passport.)

T: Tom, the tour leader　　J: Jane, the tourist　　F: Jane's friend, the tourist

J: I think I'm down on my luck!

T: What's the matter, Jane?

J: My passport! I lost my passport! I distinctly remember putting it in the inside pocket of my jacket, but it's not there anymore. Everything is in a mess these days. God!

T: Don't panic. Are you sure you lost it?

J: I'm positive about it. I've checked everywhere.

T: No matter it was lost or stolen, you should go immediately to the embassy.

J: But the problem remains that I don't have a passport, how can I get into the embassy?

T: Have you made a copy of your passport? I believe the travel service told you to make a photocopy of the passport in case of emergency, didn't they?

J: Yeah, they did! I do have a copy somewhere in my luggage. Let me find it and then directly go to the embassy. What do you say?

T: It sounds like a good plan. Hopefully they will issue you a replacement. I will accompany you to the embassy if you want.

J: You are most understanding! But what about my visa?

T: I don't think that will be a problem. You had a tourist visa to begin with. The local Public Security Bureau will reissue your visa if you have the replacement of your passport.

J: That's all solved then.

F: Hey, Jane, what's up? Are you going somewhere?

J: I was looking for my passport the whole morning!

F: I took it out to make a copy of it just in case. Here you are, darling!

扫码
听听力

J: You almost frightened me to death.

T: False alarm!

➢ Dialogue 2

Reapplying for a Passport

(The local guide tells the tourist how to reapply for a passport.)

L: the tour leader　　F: Frank, the local guide　　T: the tourist

L: Frank, Mr. Ma has got a trouble. His passport was perhaps lost.

F: I'm sorry to hear that.

T: I remember putting it in the pocket of my suit, but it's not there anymore.

L: Please check once more. Are you sure you lost it?

T: I'm sure it was lost. I've checked everywhere.

F: In this case, we should first go to my travel agency to get a proof for the loss. And then, with the proof, we will go to the police station to have a certificate. Finally, with the certificate and a few of your photos, we'll go to the Chinese Embassy to apply for a replacement of the passport.

T: What about my visa?

F: I don't think that will be a problem. You had a tourist visa to begin with. The local Public Security Bureau will reissue your visa if you have the replacement of your passport.

T: You can help us with it, can't you, Frank?

F: Certainly. I will accompany you to get all these documents.

T: You are most helpful. Thank you so much.

F: Don't mention it. Shall we go?

T: Let's go.

Useful Expressions

1. I remember putting it in the pocket of my suit, but it's not there anymore.

我记得我把它放在了衣服口袋里,但它不在那。

2. Have you made a copy of your passport?

你准备护照复印件了吗?

3. I will accompany you to the embassy if you want.

如果您需要,我会陪您去大使馆。

4. Finally, with the certificate and a few of your photos, we'll go to the Chinese Embassy to apply for a replacement of the passport.

最后,带着证明和您的几张照片,我们将去中国大使馆申请更换护照。

Module 9　Handling Emergencies

💬 Exercises

1. Match the following Chinese with the correct English versions

(1) 复印件　　　　　a. bureau
(2) 证书　　　　　　b. photocopy
(3) 国籍　　　　　　c. certificate
(4) 文件　　　　　　d. nationality
(5) 局;所　　　　　 e. document

2. Translate the following Chinese into English

(1) 如果您更换了护照,当地公安局将重新为您签发签证。
(2) 请问我什么时候能拿回护照?
(3) 他可以在我们营业时间的任何时候来。
(4) 我们应该先到我的旅行社去拿遗失证明。
(5) 有了这个证明,我们就去派出所开个证明。

3. Fill in the blanks with appropriate words and expressions

A: What's wrong with you, Judy?

B: My handbag is missing. There is much money in it. And my passport is in it, too.

A: Then, you have to apply for a new ____(1)____ from your embassy in Beijing. You also need to apply for new ____(2)____ from Exit and Entry unit of China.

B: Beijing is too far. How could I get there to apply for my passport?

A: Don't worry. I'll take you to the police station first, then to your consulate general here. You can apply for a new passport.

B: Thank you very much. You have been always helpful.

A: Don't ____(3)____ it. Is there anything ____(4)____ that is bothering you?

B: I also lost my credit card.

A: It is urgent. You should call your credit card company immediately to ____(5)____ the loss.

B: Oh. It is a bad day for me today. I lost all my belongings.

A: It is not the end of the world. My travel service will try to help you to get all documents ready.

B: Thank you very much.

A: You are ____(6)____.

4. Role play

Situation: Suppose you're a tour guide. A foreign tourist has lost her passport. Make a short dialogue with your partner.

5. **Questions & Answers**

Question: If a tourist can't locate his/her passport, what kind of help can the local guide offer?

IV Extended Reading

Nipping in the Bud vs. Lending a Helpful Hand

Task 2　Personal Property Loss

I Warming Up

1. Read and Match

a. handbag　　　b. jewelry　　　c. camera　　　d. watch

(1)　　　　　　　　　　　　(2)

(3)　　　　　　　　　　　　(4)

2. Question

How will the local guide handle the loss of luggage at the port of entry?

Tips for reference:

(1) Make sure that the tourist has filled out the airline's missing luggage form and has the name of the airline person in charge and his/her contacting telephone number.

(2) Inform the tourist that you will keep in contact with the airline while he/she is in your city.

(3) Help the tourist get things that are needed before the luggage is located (such as small items of daily necessities).

(4) If the missing luggage fails to show up before the group leaves your city, inform the travel company or the next stop of tracing the luggage.

Situational Dialogues

➢ Dialogue 1

Dealing with Loss and Theft

(At the train station, one tourist loses her bag. She is asking the local guide, Miss Wang, for help.)

T: the tourist   W: Miss Wang, the local guide

T: Oh, Miss Wang. You must help me.

W: Calm down, first. Tell me what happened.

T: Yes. I think I left my bag in the ladies' room. I went back there but I couldn't find it.

W: What was in your bag?

T: Everything. My purse, camera, passport and a map of Hangzhou.

W: Oh, that's too bad. Did you have a lot of money in the bag?

T: Luckily, there was only 20 euros or so in my purse. But my passport, driver's license and 2 credit cards were all in there.

W: Have you been to the Lost and Found Desk first?

T: Yes, I have, but in vain.

W: I suggest reporting your loss to the police, too.

T: I see. Is there a police station nearby?

W: There is one on the second floor. I will go with you.

T: That is very kind of you. Let's go now.

W: By the way, don't forget to contact your credit card companies and report the

扫码
听听力

loss of your cards as soon as possible.

T: That's right. Thanks a million for reminding me.

➢ Dialogue 2

Help Tourists with Lost Luggage

(Li Hua is a new tour guide. He is now asking Wang Fang, an experienced guide about dealing with emergencies.)

L: Li Hua   W: Wang Fang

L: Miss Wang, if some of my guests fail to claim their luggage at the airport but others have been waiting impatiently, what should I do?

W: That happens sometimes. Although you are not responsible for the lost luggage, you should help them look for the luggage as a local guide. You should take them to the Lost and Found Office to register the lost luggage. With their boarding pass and luggage tags in hand, they could specify the number of luggage and exterior characteristics. Then they will be asked to leave their phone number for further contact. Meanwhile, you may leave your phone number to the clerks there. If the luggage is found, they can contact you as well.

L: I see. It is a good idea to leave my phone number to the clerks.

W: Yes. Then you should leave the phone number of the travel agency so that they may contact the travel agency if you are visiting another city. Meanwhile, you should write down the address and phone number of the airline office and those of the Lost and Found Office at the airport so that you can keep in touch with them wherever you travel.

L: Oh, yes. What else should I do to help the guests before their luggage is found?

W: You should tell your guests to buy some daily necessities, and submit the receipt to the airline company for reimbursement later.

L: Miss Wang, if the luggage is still missing and they have to leave Xiamen, what should I do then?

W: You should ask your guests to inform the airline company of the address and phone number of the next stop of their trip, or you may help them to lodge a claim against the airline company.

L: Oh, I see. Your suggestions are really helpful as these things happen sometimes. Thank you very much.

W: You are welcome.

Useful Expressions

1. But my passport, driver's license and 2 credit cards were all in there.

Module 9　Handling Emergencies

但我的护照、驾驶执照和两张信用卡都在里面。

2．Then you should leave the phone number of the travel agency so that they may contact the travel agency if you are visiting another city.

然后你应该留下旅行社的电话号码，以便他们在你访问其他城市时可以联系旅行社。

3．Meanwhile, you should write down the address and phone number of the airline office and those of the Lost and Found Office at the airport so that you can keep in touch with them wherever you travel.

同时，你应该写下航空公司办公室和机场失物招领处的地址和电话号码，这样无论你在哪里旅行都能与他们保持联系。

4．You should ask your guests to inform the airline company of the address and phone number of the next stop of their trip, or you may help them to lodge a claim against the airline company.

你应该让你的客人告诉航空公司他们旅行的下一站的地址和电话号码，或者你可以帮助他们向航空公司提出索赔。

Ⅲ Exercises

1．Match the following Chinese with the correct English versions

（1）提交收据　　　　　　a．claim the luggage
（2）领取行李　　　　　　b．exterior characteristic
（3）保持联系　　　　　　c．further contact
（4）外部特征　　　　　　d．submit receipt
（5）进一步联系　　　　　e．lodge a claim
（6）提出索赔　　　　　　f．keep in touch

2．Translate the following Chinese into English

（1）我建议您向警方报案。
（2）别忘了联系您的信用卡公司，并尽快挂失您的信用卡。
（3）你应该带他们去失物招领处登记遗失的行李。
（4）他们手上的登机牌和行李牌可以说明行李的数量和外部特征。
（5）你应该记下航空公司和机场失物招领处的地址和电话号码，以便随时取得联系。

3．Fill in the blanks with appropriate words and expressions

A：I don't remember where I left my bag.
B：What's ＿＿＿(1)＿＿＿ the bag?
A：Well. I had my digital camera, passport, wallet and a Rome guidebook.
B：What does the bag look ＿＿＿(2)＿＿＿?
A：It is a big, black bag with my name tag on it. Please ＿＿＿(3)＿＿＿ me at this number if you find it.
B：OK. No problem.

A: When can I expect to ____(4)____ you?

B: If the bag is found, I will call you as soon as possible.

A: Thank you. I await your call.

4. Role play

Situation 1: Suppose you're a tour guide. A foreign tourist has lost her purse. Make a short dialogue with your partner.

Situation 2: Suppose you're a tour guide. A tourist, Mr. Li, tells you that he lost his bag. Make a short dialogue with your partner.

5. Questions & Answers

Question: How to handle the loss of personal belongings?

Ⅳ Extended Reading

Common Travel Disasters

Task 3   Dealing with Sudden Illnesses

Ⅰ Warming Up

1. Read and Match

a. capsule   b. ointment   c. bandage   d. aspirin

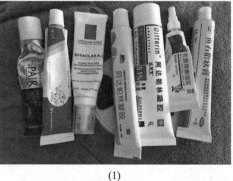

(1)   (2)

Module 9 Handling Emergencies

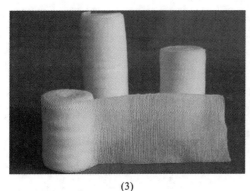
(3)

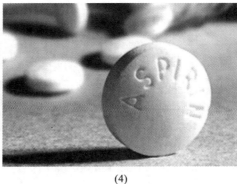
(4)

2. Question

How to help sick tourists properly during the travel?

Tips for reference:

(1) Show concern for the tourist's health and offer help.

(2) Lead the patient to see a doctor.

(3) Visit the patient properly.

Ⅱ Situational Dialogues

➢ Dialogue 1

Accompany Tourist to See a Doctor

(When having breakfast, Janet Jin, the local guide, notices a tourist, Mr. Smith looks very weak. Janet shows concern for him and offers help.)

J: Janet Jin, the local guide   S: Mr. Smith, the tourist

C: Mr. Chen, the waiter   L: Mr. Lee, the doctor

J: Excuse me, Mr. Smith. But you look a bit pale today. Are you all right?

S: No. I have a stomachache and loose bowels.

J: I'm sorry to hear that. Shall I send for a doctor?

S: No, thank you. I think I can pull through.

J: Then I hope you will get well soon.

(That afternoon is the time for free activity. The group leader Daniel Black tells Janet that Mr. Smith's condition is worsening. Janet hurries to help him. A waiter, Mr. Chen wants to offer his medicine to Smith.)

C: I have some medicine for loose bowels. Shall I give it to Mr. Smith?

J: (to Mr. Chen) No, thank you, Mr. Smith had better go to see a doctor.

(Janet leads Smith to the hospital by taxi. Janet assists Mr. Smith to register and pay.)

J: Mr. Smith, the registration fee is 10 yuan.

S: Here you are. Thank you.

J: Mr. Smith, let's sit here and wait to see a doctor.

L: What is the trouble?

S: I have a terrible stomachache and loose bowels.

L: How long have you suffered from this?

S: About 12 hours.

L: Did you eat something bad?

S: I ate some ice-cream last night.

L: Do you have a temperature?

S: Yes. I am running a fever.

L: I will get your stool tested first. Here, take this slip and give it to the technician at the lab. She will tell you what to do. When the result comes out, just bring it back to me.

(After a while, Janet and Mr. Smith return with the result. The doctor says Mr. Smith has got acute gastroenteritis and prescribes him some medicine.)

S: How do I take the medicine?

L: Take 4 tablets at a time and 3 times a day. Take one of these capsules every 6 hours, but do not exceed 4 in 24 hours. And try to drink more boiled water.

S: Thank you.

L: My pleasure.

➢ Dialogue 2

How to Deal with Different Disease

(Li Hua is a new tour guide. He is now asking Wang Fang, an experienced guide, about dealing with emergencies during traveling.)

L: Li Hua   W: Wang Fang

L: Miss Wang, sometimes our tourists suffer from some diseases during the trip. How should I help them?

W: What do you mean?

L: For example, one of the tourists suffers a heart attack. What should I do? Can I give him my medicine?

W: No. You mustn't give him your own medicine because you are not a doctor. What you should do is to have the patient lie down and raise his leg slightly up. If the patient has medicine with him, you can help him take it. Meanwhile, you should call for an ambulance and take the patient to a nearby hospital as soon as possible.

L: I see. Yes, since it is very urgent, I should send him to the hospital as quickly as possible. But if the tourist suddenly falls down and has his leg fractured, what should I do?

W: If there is bleeding, you should first stop the bleeding by using your fingers, palm or fist to press the blood vessel above the wound. Then you should wrap a tourniquet tightly above the wound, place thick dressing on the wound and bind it tightly with a bandage. Before binding, you should rinse the wound first, then wrap it up gently and tie the knot away from the wound. Finally, you should put the fractured limb in a splint made of any available material to fix the joint and avoid moving the fractured limb.

L: OK. I will follow your advice in case they are injured during the trip. Miss Wang, since it is very hot here in Hainan, if one of my tourists gets sunstroke, what should I do to help him?

W: As you said, it is hot here and it is easy for people to get sunstroke. You should know the symptoms of sunstroke and offer correct method to help them.

L: What are the symptoms of sunstroke then?

W: The symptoms include excessive sweating, thirst, dizziness, ringing in the ears and nausea. The patient may also vomit and develop a fever.

L: How should I help them?

W: If the tourist feels sick, you should help him to rest in a cool and breezy place, unbutton his collar and unfasten his belt. If possible, give him some salty water. If he develops a fever, you may bathe his body with cold water and help him to drink some water. When he feels better, you should encourage him to have a rest. But if he suffers from serious sunstroke, you should send him to the nearest hospital after the first aid.

L: Yes. Thank you very much, Miss Wang. You are really knowledgeable and helpful.

W: You are welcome. I hope you can deal with the emergencies better.

L: I will try my best.

Useful Expressions

1. I will get your stool tested first. Here, take this slip and give it to the technician at the lab. She will tell you what to do.

我先给您做粪便检查。您拿着这张纸条,交给实验室的技术人员。她会告诉您怎么做。

2. Take 4 tablets at a time and 3 times a day.

每次服用 4 片药片,每天服用 3 次。

3. Take one of these capsules every 6 hours, but do not exceed 4 in 24 hours.

这种胶囊,每 6 小时服用一粒,但在 24 小时内服用不得超过 4 粒。

4. What you should do is to have the patient lie down and raise his leg slightly up.

你应该做的是让患者躺下,稍微抬起腿。

5. But if the tourist suddenly falls down and has his leg fractured, what should I do?

但是,如果游客突然摔倒,腿部骨折,我该怎么办?

6. The symptoms include excessive sweating, thirst, dizziness, ringing in the ears and nausea. The patient may also vomit and develop a fever.

症状包括过度出汗、口渴、头晕、耳鸣和恶心。患者也可能呕吐并发烧。

Ⅲ Exercises

1. Match the following Chinese with the correct English versions

（1）腹泻　　　　　　　　a. stomachache
（2）心脏病　　　　　　　b. loose bowels
（3）骨折　　　　　　　　c. heart attack
（4）中暑　　　　　　　　d. fracture
（5）胃痛　　　　　　　　e. sunstroke

2. Translate the following Chinese into English

（1）我胃痛得厉害,还拉肚子。
（2）你这种症状持续多久了?
（3）因为你不是医生,不能给他吃你自己的药。
（4）你应该叫救护车尽快把病人送到附近的医院。
（5）包扎之前,你应该先清洗伤口,然后轻轻地把伤处包起来,在伤口以外的位置打结。
（6）你应该带他到凉爽通风的地方休息,解开他的衣领和腰带。

3. Fill in the blanks with appropriate words and expressions

A：Good afternoon. What seems to be the problem, Mr. Liang?

B：Afternoon, doctor. I'm not feeling well at all. I have a headache and sore throat. Besides, I've been coughing a lot.

A：How long have you had these ＿＿(1)＿＿?

B：Since last weekend, about 4 days already.

A：Let me check your ＿＿(2)＿＿. 38.5℃. That's a bit high. So you have a ＿＿(3)＿＿ too.

B：What do you think it is?

A：Not sure yet. Do you have a stuffy nose?

B：No, but my nose runs a lot.

A：I see. It looks like you have a flu. I will write you a prescription. Are you allergic to ＿＿(4)＿＿?

B：I don't think so. Does the drug have any ＿＿(5)＿＿ effects?

A：You will feel a bit ＿＿(6)＿＿ for a few hours after you take the medicine, which is fine, because what you need now is sleep.

B：OK. How do I take the medicine?

A：Don't worry. Just take the prescription to the pharmacy. The pharmacist will give you ＿＿(7)＿＿ instructions on that.

Module 9　Handling Emergencies　　141

B: Thanks a lot.

A: Not at all. Have a good rest for a few days, and drink lots of liquids. I'm sure you'll be feeling a lot better soon.

4. Role play

Situation 1: Suppose you're a tour guide. Xiao Ming, a tourist, sprains his ankle during the trip. Make a short dialogue with your partner.

Situation 2: Lily, the local guide, and Mr. White, the tour leader, are talking about one group member's illness. Make a short conversation with your partner.

5. Questions & Answers

Question: How will you deal with someone who is seriously ill?

IV Extended Reading

How to Deal with Tourists' Diarrhea

How to Deal with Tourists' Diarrhea

Task 4　Tourists Missing

I Warming Up

1. Read and Match

a. navigation map　　　　b. guide map

c. scenic spots signs　　　d. Tourist Service Center

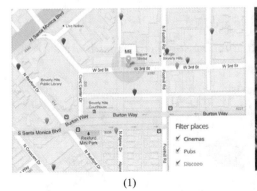
(1)

(2)

(3)

(4)

2. Question

What should the local guide do in order to prevent tourists from getting lost?

Tips for reference:

(1) Before they start their journey, tell them about the itinerary of the day, including the places of sightseeing and the places of meeting.

(2) Ask them to remember the bus number, the parking place and the departure time each time when arriving at a tourist spot.

(3) During the journey, count them from time to time.

(4) During the time for free sightseeing or shopping, remind the tourists not to go too far and the time of departure.

(5) Tell the tourists your phone number and take down their phone numbers in case they get lost.

Ⅱ Situational Dialogues

➢ Dialogue 1

When Tourists are Lost

(The local guide and the tour leader are looking for the missing tourists.)

G: the local guide　　L: the tour leader　　D: the doorkeeper

Y: the young tourist　　O: the old tourists

G: Mr. Chen, do you like the National Park?

L: Yes. It is a nice place. The scenery is splendid. We've enjoyed it very much.

G: I am very glad to hear that. Shall we go back to the hotel?

L: Yes. I think so.

G: Is everybody on the bus?

Y: I am afraid not. Mr. and Mrs. Huang, the elderly couple sitting in front of me are not here.

G: Probably they are left behind in the park. There are three entrances in the park. Would you please go to the side entrance and ask some tourists to go with me to the back entrance?

L: All right.

(To the doorkeeper of the side entrance)

L: Excuse me, sir. We are looking for an old couple. Did you see them here?

D: What did they look like?

L: The old man is tall and thin, wearing a black jacket and brown trousers and the old lady is short and fat, wearing a yellow blouse and a light blue skirt.

D: They have been here five minutes ago. They said they were looking for the back entrance but went the wrong way.

L: Where did they go?

D: They took the left path to the back entrance.

(At the back entrance)

G: Thank God. I find you at last. We were looking for you everywhere.

O: We are terribly sorry. The view here is so splendid. We were lost in it and failed to catch up with the group. Somebody told us that we could find the exit this way, but perhaps we turned the wrong way and came to the side entrance.

G: It is my fault. I haven't taken care of you. I do apologize for it.

O: That's all right. You are always so considerate.

G: Don't mention it. Mind your step, Mr. and Mrs. Huang.

➤ Dialogue 2

Handling with the Lost Tourists

(Li Hua is a new tour guide. He is now asking Wang Fang, an experienced guide about dealing with emergencies during traveling.)

L: Li Hua, a new tour guide   W: Wang Fang, an experienced guide

L: Miss Wang, may I ask you some questions about how to deal with some emergencies during traveling as an English tour guide?

W: Certainly.

L: If two of my guests get lost at a tourist spot, what should I do?

W: First, you should make sure when and where other guests saw them last time, and then try to look for them.

L: But how should I deal with other guests?

W: You may ask them to take a rest on the bus and the bus driver will take care of them. Then you should look for the missing tourists along the route.

L: If I cannot find them, what should I do then?

扫码
听听力

W: If you fail to find them, you should report to the local police station and ask for help.

L: Oh, I see. After I find them, what should I do then?

W: After they are found, you should make an apology if you are to blame; if the tourists are to blame, you should remind them not to travel alone again graciously. Don't criticize them.

L: OK. What should I do in order to prevent such kind of situation?

W: Before they start their journey, you should tell them about the itinerary of the day, including the places of sightseeing and the places of meeting. In this way, they may go to the meeting places by themselves if they get lost. Remember, each time when you arrive at a tourist spot, you should ask them to remember the bus number, the parking place and the departure time.

L: So it is extremely important to remind the guests from time to time.

W: Yes. Meanwhile, during the journey, you should count the number of tourists from time to time. During the time for free sightseeing or shopping, you should remind them not to go too far and keep in mind the time of departure. In my opinion, it is important to tell them your phone number and you should take down their phone numbers in case they get lost.

L: Yes, it is important to remember each other's phone number. If they get lost, we can still contact with each other.

W: Yes, exactly.

L: If they want to have an individual sightseeing, what should I do?

W: Normally, you should ask them to follow the group and you should arrange everything according to the schedule.

L: OK, I see. Thank you very much. Your advice is very helpful. I think I can deal with this situation well now.

W: You are welcome.

Useful Expressions

1. Is everybody on the bus?

大家都在车上吗？

2. First, you should make sure when and where other guests saw them last time, and then try to look for them.

首先，你应该确定其他客人在何时何地看到他们，然后试着寻找他们。

3. After the guests are found, you should make an apology if you are to blame; if the tourists are to blame, you should remind them not to travel alone again graciously. Don't criticize them.

当找回客人后，如果是你的责任，你应该道歉；如果游客自己走失，你应该委婉地提醒他们不要再独自行动了。不要批评他们。

Module 9 Handling Emergencies

4. During the time for free sightseeing or shopping, you should remind them not to go too far and keep in mind the time of departure.

在自由观光或购物期间,你应该提醒他们不要走得太远,记住出发时间。

Ⅲ Exercises

1. Match the following Chinese with the correct English versions

(1) 集合地点　　　　　　　a. catch up with
(2) 赶上　　　　　　　　　b. mind your step
(3) 走路当心　　　　　　　c. blame
(4) 责备　　　　　　　　　d. remind
(5) 提醒　　　　　　　　　e. criticize
(6) 批评　　　　　　　　　f. prevent
(7) 防止　　　　　　　　　g. place of meeting

2. Translate the following Chinese into English

(1) 坐在我前面的老夫妻黄先生和黄太太不在。
(2) 你去侧门,然后叫几个游客跟我一起去后门好吗?
(3) 老大爷又高又瘦,穿着黑色的夹克和棕色的裤子,老太太又矮又胖,穿着黄色的衬衫和浅蓝色的裙子。
(4) 我们沉浸其中,没能跟上旅行团。
(5) 你应该沿着来的路线寻找丢失的游客。
(6) 你应该委婉地提醒他们下次不要单独出行。
(7) 每到达一个旅游景点,你应该让他们记住车牌号、停车的地方和发车时间。

3. Fill in the blanks with appropriate words and expressions

A: Excuse me, sir. Could you do me a ＿＿＿(1)＿＿＿?

B: Sure. What's the problem?

A: I came here with my group. But I can't ＿＿＿(2)＿＿＿ them now. They have left without my notice while I was taking pictures.

B: How long have you been here?

A: I'm not sure. Perhaps one and a half hours.

B: In that case, your group maybe has left for their bus. Do you know the name of your local guide? I'm quite ＿＿＿(3)＿＿＿ with many of them.

A: Yes. Frank is our ＿＿＿(4)＿＿＿.

B: Frank just went by here a couple of minutes ago in the direction to the ＿＿＿(5)＿＿＿. He can't go fast with his group. I'm sure you can ＿＿＿(6)＿＿＿ him soon.

A: Thank you ever so much, sir. I'm afraid I must go now.

4. Role play

Situation: Suppose you're a tour guide. Xiao Ming, a tourist, is missing during the trip. Make a short dialogue with your partner.

5. Questions & Answers

Question：If the tourists get lost at the tourist spot, what should the local guide do?

IV Extended Reading

If the Tourists Get Lost While Going out

Task 5 Dealing with Emergencies En Route

I Warming Up

1. Read and Match

a. No tossing   b. Caution vehicle   c. No burning   d. No touching

(1)

(2)

(3)

(4)

2. Question

In case of fire, how can a tour guide react properly?

Tips for reference:

(1) Keep calm.

(2) Call 119 immediately.

(3) Notify all the tourists and the tour leader.

(4) Help with the evacuation.

II Situational Dialogues

➤ Dialogue 1

Dealing with a Traffic Accident

(Li Hua, a new guide is now asking Wang Fang, an experienced guide, about how to deal with a traffic accident.)

L: Li Hua, a new guide   W: Wang Fang, an experienced guide

L: Miss Wang, during the trip, we have to travel from one place to another. If there is a traffic accident, what should I do?

W: That happens sometimes due to some reasons. If traffic accident happens, you should first rescue the injured immediately. You should stay calm and lead your guests to a safe distance from the accident.

L: If there is bleeding, what should I do?

W: You should help them stop bleeding and bandage up the wounded, then you should send them to the hospital as soon as possible.

L: Do I have to report to the travel agency?

W: Yes. You should report to the traffic police and the travel agency as soon as possible. If there are heavy casualties, you should call for an ambulance and report immediately to the traffic police for help and rescue.

L: Do I need to stay at the accident site before the police come?

W: Yes, and it is important to protect the accident site for further investigation.

L: After the accident, what should I do?

W: If the accident is not serious, you may console the tourists and continue the trip as planned.

L: Do I need to write a report after the accident?

W: Yes. You should submit a written report about the accident to the travel agency. You should give detailed description of the time, place, causes, sequence of events and process of handling the accident, tourists' feedback and the account of those responsible for the accident.

L: Yes, these details are really important. Thank you very much, Miss Wang.

W: You are welcome.

➢ Dialogue 2

When There Is Fire Alarm

(The local guide is helping the tourist to flee from the fire.)

M: Martin, the tour guide   P: Peter, the tourist   H: the housekeeper

M: Peter, wake up! Wake up!

P: What's the matter, Martin? It's in the middle of the night.

M: Listen, there is a fire alarm.

P: Oh my God. I can hear it now.

M: Hurry up! Look at the hotel's fire escape plan. Let's take the stairs over there to an open place. Take a wet towel if possible.

P: Shall we take the elevator to get down? Anyway, it goes much faster.

M: Never use any electrical equipment during a fire. It is really dangerous.

H: Ladies and gentlemen, please don't panic. It is not a big fire. Someone was smoking in the room.

P: Thank goodness. Fortunately, this is just a false alarm. Martin, can you tell me more about what we can do when fire happens?

M: Sure. You should keep calm and warn everyone in the house about the danger. It is most important to be calm and act fast when there is a fire.

P: What can we do then?

M: You'd better get out of the house as quickly as you can. Once you are out of the house, stay out. Do not go back into the house for any reason.

P: When should we call the firefighters, when the fire breaks out or when we get out of the house?

M: When you get out of the firing house, call 119 and let the skilled firefighters put the fire out at once. Don't try to put out the fire by yourself. That can be very dangerous.

P: Thank you very much for your advice. I've learned a lot from it.

Useful Expressions

1. You should help them stop bleeding and bandage up the wounded, then you should send them to the hospital as soon as possible.

你应该帮他们止血，给伤员包扎，然后尽快送他们去医院。

2. If there are heavy casualties, you should call for an ambulance and report immediately to the traffic police for help and rescue.

如果有重大伤亡，你应该叫救护车，并立即向交警报告，寻求帮助和救援。

3. You should give detailed description of the time, place, causes, sequence of events and process of handling accident, tourists' feedback and the account of those responsible for the accident.

你应该详细描述事故发生的时间、地点、原因、事件顺序和处理过程、游客的反馈和事故责任人的描述。

4. Hurry up! Look at the hotel's fire escape plan. Let's take the stairs over there to an open place. Take a wet towel if possible.

快点！看看酒店的逃生平面图。我们从那边的楼梯走到一个开阔的地方。如果可能的话，拿一条湿毛巾。

5. You'd better get out of the house as quickly as you can.

你最好尽快离开这所房子。

6. Once you are out of the house, stay out. Do not go back into the house for any reason.

一旦你逃出，就待在外面。无论什么原因，都不要回到房子里去。

7. When you get out of the firing house, call 119 and let the skilled firefighters put the fire out at once. Don't try to put out the fire by yourself.

当你走出火场时，立即拨打119，让熟练的消防员将火扑灭。不要试图自己灭火。

Ⅲ Exercises

1. Match the following Chinese with the correct English versions

(1) 救护车　　　　　　　a. casualty
(2) 事故现场　　　　　　b. ambulance
(3) 调查　　　　　　　　c. accident site
(4) 火警　　　　　　　　d. investigation
(5) 消防队员　　　　　　e. fire alarm
(6) 伤亡人员　　　　　　f. firefighter

2. Translate the following Chinese into English

(1) 如果发生交通事故，首先应立即抢救受伤人员。
(2) 你应该保持冷静，把客人带到离事故现场较远的安全的地方。
(3) 保护事故现场对于后续调查很重要。
(4) 当发生火灾时，不要使用任何电器设备。
(5) 当发生火灾时，最重要的是保持冷静并迅速采取行动。
(6) 不要试图自己把火扑灭。

3. Fill in the blanks with appropriate words and expressions

A: Hello, this is 119. What can I do for you?
B: Yes. We had a traffic ＿＿＿(1)＿＿＿ and some of us were badly ＿＿＿(2)＿＿＿.

A: Where are you?

B: We are on the Zhongshan Road.

A: Stay where you are. The police will arrive soon.

(After the policemen come)

C: What happened here?

B: We had a traffic accident. A car hit our car from behind and ran away.

C: Did you stop at a ＿＿(3)＿＿ light?

B: Yes. I'm pretty sure that I did not ＿＿(4)＿＿ any law.

C: I see. Did you see the car's ＿＿(5)＿＿?

B: I'm sorry. I was in too much shock. But I think it was a white BMW.

C: May I see your driver's ＿＿(6)＿＿?

B: Sure. Here you are. I'm a tourist from America.

C: Good. Is anyone injured?

B: I'm OK, but my friend broke his arm.

C: We'll call an ambulance right now.

4. Role play

Situation: Suppose you're a tour guide. Your group has a car accident. Make a short dialogue with your partner.

5. Questions & Answers

Question: What should a local guide do in case of a traffic accident?

Ⅳ Extended Reading

Basic First Aid

Basic First Aid

PART Ⅱ Scenic Spots Interpretations

Module 10
Tour of Famous Mountains

Learning Objectives
1. Master the vocabulary and sentence patterns of the tour of famous mountains.
2. Describe the mountain scenery to the tourists.
3. Explore the cultural elements of mountain scenery.
4. Summarize the main features of mountain scenery.

Task 1 A Trip to Mount Taishan

Read and Match

a. Dai Temple
b. Doumu Palace
c. Eighteen Bends
d. Jade Emperor Peak

(1)

(2)

(3)　　　　　　　　　　　　(4)

Situational Dialogue

A Trip to Mount Taishan

(As a local guide, Xiao Li is guiding the guests to Mount Taishan. He introduces Mount Taishan on the way and answers relevant questions.)

L: Xiao Li, the local guide　　S: Ms. Sadie, the tourist

L: Ladies and gentlemen, we are now on the way to Mount Taishan. Now let me give you an introduction of Mount Taishan. Have you ever heard of Mount Taishan?

S: Yes, it is said that Mount Taishan is the first of the Five Sacred Mountains in China. What makes it so special?

L: Mount Taishan is a perfect example of mountain resort that embodies natural scenery and cultural heritage. Mount Taishan was included in the UNESCO World Heritage List in 1987. Located in the central part of Shandong Province, Mount Taishan is also named Eastern Mountain. As you know, the east is the place where the sun rises. The ancients thought it was the place where everything originated and the spring began. The east became the source of life, hope and an auspicious symbol. The ancient ancestors often regarded the magnificent Mount Taishan as gods, and worshipped the mountain gods to pray for the smooth weather, which was essential in agricultural society. So Mount Taishan became the auspicious mountain and the house of gods in the birthplace of all things.

S: I see. Its significance is related to its geological location. Right?

L: That is only partly the reason. The emperors, who regarded themselves as "son of heaven", regarded Mount Taishan as a symbol of national unity and power. In order to thank the heavenly gods for giving the grace, many emperors went to Mount Taishan to offer sacrifice. It is said that 72 emperors of different dynasties made pilgrimages here. It was believed that their rule were consolidated with the help of the divine power of Mount Taishan, which made the sacred status of Mount Taishan to an unprecedented extent.

S: That sounds interesting. Is it very high?

L: The actual altitude of Mount Taishan is not too high. Mount Taishan is 1545 meters above sea level and it is only the third among the Five Sacred Mountains. Mount Taishan rises in the east of the North China Plain, above the Qilu Plain, adjacent to the vast sea in the east and the Yellow River in the west. The relative height difference between Mount Taishan and the plain and hills is 1300 meters, which makes it very high in vision. The mountain ranges stretch for more than 100 kilometers, covering an area of 426 square kilometers. Its broad base produces a sense of stability, and its large and concentrated shape produces a sense of massiness, which is of great prestige of "calming the earth without shaking". So there are some Chinese words related to Mount Taishan, which means "as stable as Mount Taishan" and "as heavy as Mount Taishan". These are the reflection of its natural characteristics on people's psychology.

S: What can we see in Mount Taishan?

L: Mount Taishan has been regarded as "the cliff carving museum in China". It has attracted a large number of cultural celebrities, scholars and poets of all ages. They have visited the mountain, written poems and articles, and left a wealth of cultural treasures. From the foot of the mountain to the top, there are more than 2200 carved stones. The large scale and the number of works, the continuity of the times, the exquisite style and art, and the ingenious landscape construction are unparalleled in the world. You can also appreciate ancient buildings and structures.

S: I remember there is a Dai Temple, right?

L: Yes, Dai Temple is the place where emperors stayed and offered their sacrifices. Its design has been a replica of the imperial palace, which makes it one out of three extant structures in China with the features of an imperial palace. The other two are the Forbidden City and the Confucian Temple in Qufu.

S: Wow, we will have a good chance to feast our eyes. What is the peak of Mount Taishan?

L: The Jade Emperor Peak is the top of Mount Taishan. The plaque on the shrine shows that the ancient emperors burnt firewood here to worship the gods of mountains and rivers. In front of the hall, there is a summit stone that marks the highest point of Mount Taishan.

S: The view must be fantastic. One of my friends said it's an unforgettable experience to see the rising sun in the east on the top of Mount Taishan.

L: Yes, indeed. But it is too late to see the rising sun today, but we can see the Yellow River Jade Belt.

S: What is the Yellow River Jade Belt?

L: Seen from the top of Mount Taishan, the Yellow River is inlaid in the Central Plains of China, just like a jade belt, while Mount Taishan is like the buckle on the belt, which firmly ties the jade belt.

S: The view is bound to be fantastic.

L: Yes, it is really worth your visit. Now, we have arrived at the parking lot. Please take your belongings and get off with me.

Useful Expressions

1. Mount Taishan is a perfect example of the kind of mountain resort that embodies natural scenery and cultural heritage.

泰山是自然风光和文化遗产融为一体的名胜典范。

2. The emperors, who regarded themselves as "son of heaven", regarded Mount Taishan as a symbol of national unity and power. In order to thank the heaveny gods for giving the grace, many emperors went to Mount Taishan to offer sacrifice.

皇帝视自己为"天子",把泰山视为国家统一和权力的象征。为了感谢天神的恩赐,许多帝王都到泰山祭祀封禅。

3. It was believed that their rule were consolidated with the help of the divine power of Mount Taishan, which made the sacred status of Mount Taishan to an unprecedented extent.

人们认为帝王借助泰山神力巩固统治,使泰山的神圣地位达到前所未有的高度。

4. Mount Taishan was included in the UNESCO World Heritage List in 1987.

泰山于1987年被联合国教科文组织列入《世界遗产名录》。

5. Mount Taishan has been regarded as "the cliff carving museum in China".

泰山被誉为"中国摩崖雕刻博物馆"。

6. It has attracted a large number of cultural celebrities, scholars and poets of all ages. They have visited the mountain, wrote poems and articles, and left a wealth of cultural treasures.

泰山吸引了众多的文化名人,历代诗人墨客纷至沓来,他们朝山览胜,赋诗撰文,留下了丰富的文化瑰宝。

7. The large scale and the number of works, the continuity of the times, the exquisite style and art, and the ingenious landscape construction are unparalleled in the world.

作品规模之大、数量之多、时代之延续、风格和艺术之精湛、景观营造之巧妙,是世界上无与伦比的。

8. The Jade Emperor Peak is the top of Mount Taishan.

玉皇顶是泰山主峰之巅。

Module 10 Tour of Famous Mountains

Exercises

1. Match the following Chinese with the correct English versions

(1) 五岳之首　　　　　　a. cultural treasure
(2) 文化瑰宝　　　　　　b. cliff carving
(3) 玉皇顶　　　　　　　c. offer sacrifice to heaven and earth
(4) 摩崖雕刻　　　　　　d. the World Heritage List
(5)《世界遗产名录》　　　e. as stable as Mount Taishan
(6) 极顶石　　　　　　　f. the first of the Five Sacred Mountains in China
(7) 祭祀封禅　　　　　　g. Dai Temple
(8) 稳如泰山　　　　　　h. cultural celebrities and scholars
(9) 岱庙　　　　　　　　i. the Jade Emperor Peak
(10) 文人雅客　　　　　　j. summit stone

2. Translate the following Chinese into English

(1) 泰山位于山东省中部，为五岳之首。
(2) 泰山已成为中国山岳风景的代表，自然景观与人文景观融为一体。
(3) 泰山于1987年被列入《世界遗产名录》，是我国第一个世界自然与文化双遗产。
(4) 历朝历代帝王不断在泰山祭祀封禅，在泰山上建庙，刻石题字。
(5) 古代的文人雅士纷纷前来泰山游历，作诗记文。
(6) 泰山宏大的山体上留下了20余处古建筑群，2200余处碑碣石刻。
(7) 泰山日出是岱顶奇观之一，也是泰山的重要标志。
(8) 泰山风景区以泰山日出、云海玉盘、晚霞夕照和黄河金带四景最为出名。

3. Fill in the blanks with appropriate words and expressions

　　In ancient times, one of the biggest wishes for an ＿＿＿(1)＿＿＿ to do on ascending to the throne was to climb Mount Taishan and ＿＿＿(2)＿＿＿ to heaven and earth or their ancestors. It was said that 72 emperors of different ＿＿＿(3)＿＿＿ made pilgrimages here in Mount Taishan. These special ceremonies and sacrifices earned the mountain widespread fame. In addition, many poets and literary ＿＿＿(4)＿＿＿ also visited the mountain to gain inspiration. The grandiose temples, the numerous stone inscriptions and stone tablets are the best testaments to these visits. Mount Taishan also played an important ＿＿＿(5)＿＿＿ in the development of Buddhism and Taoism.
　　East route is ＿＿＿(6)＿＿＿ to be the Imperial Route（泰山御道）because the emperors all took this way to make sacrifices. With elegant natural scenery, palaces, stone inscriptions are also scattered along the winding path. People set off ＿＿＿(7)＿＿＿ Dai Temple, and then you will see Dai Zong Archway（岱宗坊）, Doumu Palace（斗母宫）, Red Gate Palace（红门宫）, Jing Shi Valley（经石峪）, and Eighteen Bends（十八盘）, etc. Dai Temple is the place where emperors stayed and offered their sacrifices. The temple was ＿＿＿(8)＿＿＿ in the Han Dynasty and expanded in the

Tang and Song Dynasties. After several renovations, it has become the biggest and most complete temple on Mount Taishan. It is said there are 6666 steps along this route and it ____(9)____ about four hours at an average to reach the ____(10)____. This classical route is an ideal ____(11)____ for most people.

The west route is made ____(12)____ of two parts. One ____(13)____ is the highroad from the Heaven and Earth Square to Mid-heaven Gate（中天门）. The other part is the cable way from Mid-heaven Gate to the top of the mountain. This route is well ____(14)____ with modern facilities and is the most fashionable way to reach Jade Emperor Peak. Attractions concentrated on this route are Heaven and Earth Square（天地广场）, Black Dragon Pool, Tomb of General Feng Yuxiang and Celestial Street（天街）, etc.

4. Role play

Situation: Suppose you are the local guide and are now guiding the guests to visit Mount Taishan. Make introductions and answer relevant questions.

Ⅳ Extended Reading

Sacrificial Rites at Mount Taishan

Task 2　A Trip to Mount Huangshan

Ⅰ Read and Match

a. Sea of Clouds　　　　　　　　b. Guest-greeting Pine
c. Monkey Gazing at the Sea　　　d. Lotus Peak

(1)

(2)

Module 10 Tour of Famous Mountains

(3)   (4)

‖ Situational Dialogues

A Trip to Mount Huangshan

(As a local guide, Xiao Li is guiding the guests to Mount Huangshan. He introduces Mount Huangshan on the way and answers relevant questions.)

L: Xiao Li, the local guide   S: Ms. Sara, the tourist

L: Ladies and gentlemen, we are now on the way to Mount Huangshan. Anyone knows the origin of the name of the mountain?

S: I know Huang means yellow color in Chinese. Does it have anything to do with the yellow color?

L: Let me tell you in detail. Mount Huangshan was called the Black Mountain before the Tang Dynasty in China because the rocks on the mountain were green and black. Legend has it that the Yellow Emperor, the ancestor of Chinese nationality, came here to collect medicine and make pills after he completed the unification of the Central Plains and created Chinese civilization. He bathed in hot springs, thus becoming immortal. Li Longji (685-762 AD), the famous emperor of the Tang Dynasty, believed this statement very much. He issued an imperial edict and renamed the mountain to be Mount Huangshan, meaning the mountain of the Yellow Emperor. Since then, Huangshan has been the name until now.

S: That sounds interesting. So today we are visiting the mountain of the Yellow Emperor. It is said that there are four wonders in Mount Huangshan. What are they exactly?

L: Yes, Mount Huangshan is famous for its strange-shaped pines, spectacular rocks, sea of clouds and hot springs. The pines in Mount Huangshan are notable for its extremely tenacious vitality. Generally speaking, soil can produce grass, wood and crops, while the pines in Huangshan grow from the hard granite rock. There are pine trees everywhere in Huangshan, lush and vibrant in long peaks, cliffs, and deep valleys. For thousands of years, they have been bursting out of the rock, deeply rooted in the rock cracks, not afraid of barren drought, wind, rain or snow. Secondly, the Huangshan pines are also strange in its unique natural shape. Each pine tree has unique beauty in appearance and charm. According to their different forms and charm, people give them appropriate names, such as Guest-greeting Pine, Black Tiger Pine, Dragon Claw Pine, Sea Exploration Pine and so on.

S: Terrific. What about the strange stones?

L: There are spectacular rocks everywhere in Mount Huangshan. The appearance of these rocks is very different. Some of them are of human shape, some look like particular objects, while some reflect myths, legends and historical stories. Among the 121 famous stones, some famous stones are "Flying Stone", "Playing Chess by Cactus", "Magpie Climbing Plum", "Monkey Gazing at the Sea" and so on. Some grotesque stones will change in different views of position and angles, giving more charm to the scenery.

S: The third wonder is the sea of clouds. But clouds can be seen in many famous mountains.

L: Indeed. But none of them can be so spectacular and myriad as the sea of clouds in Mount Huangshan. Mount Huangshan has another name called Yellow Sea. In the Ming Dynasty about 400 years ago, a famous historian named Pan Zhiheng lived in Huangshan for decades, and wrote a large volume of 60 books named *Huangshan Mountain Chronicle*, which is also called the *Yellow Sea*. The names of some scenic spots, hotels and many landscapes in Mount Huangshan are related to this special "sea". If some landscapes are viewed in the clouds, they will be more charming.

S: That is marvelous. I couldn't wait to see it.

L: Finally, let me introduce the hot spring. The hot spring we often talk about and visit is the hot spring of Huangshan Hotel. The water temperature keeps at 42 degrees all year round, the water quality is good, and contains minerals beneficial to human body, which has certain medical value. It has certain curative effect on skin disease, rheumatism and digestive system diseases.

S: Could we have a hot spring bath in Huangshan Hotel?

L: Surely you could. We will stay in Huangshan Hotel tonight and you can enjoy the hot spring bath freely.

S: That is marvelous. Thank you so much.

Useful Expressions

1. Mount Huangshan is famous for its strange-shaped pines, spectacular rocks, sea of clouds and hot springs.

黄山以奇松、怪石、云海、温泉"四绝"闻名于世。

Module 10 Tour of Famous Mountains

2. The pines in Mount Huangshan are notable for its extremely tenacious vitality. Generally speaking, soil can produce grass, wood and crops, while the pines in Huangshan grow from the hard granite rock.

黄山奇松以无比顽强的生命力而闻名。一般来说,凡有土的地方就能长出草木和庄稼,而黄山松则是从坚硬的花岗岩石里长出来的。

3. There are spectacular rocks everywhere in Mount Huangshan. The appearance of these rocks is very different. Some of them are of human shape, some look like particular objects, while some reflect myths, legends and historical stories.

在黄山,到处都可以看到奇形怪状的岩石,这些怪石的模样千差万别,有的像人,有的像物,有的反映了某些神话传说和历史故事。

4. Clouds can be seen in many famous mountains, but none of them can be so spectacular and myriad as the sea of clouds in Mount Huangshan.

虽然在中国其他名山也能看到云海,但没有一个能比得上黄山云海那样壮观和变幻无穷。

5. The water temperature keeps at 42 degrees all year round, the water quality is good, and contains minerals beneficial to human body, which has certain medical value.

这里的水,水温常年保持在42℃左右,水质良好,并含有对人体有益的矿物质,有一定的医疗价值。

Exercises

1. Match the following Chinese with the correct English versions

(1) 奇松   a. Sea of Clouds
(2) 怪石   b. Bright Summit
(3) 云海   c. Flying Stone
(4) 温泉   d. strange-shaped pines
(5) 迎客松   e. Lotus Peak
(6) 飞来石   f. Dragon Claw Pine
(7) 龙爪松   g. spectacular rocks
(8) 莲花峰   h. Tiandu Peak
(9) 天都峰   i. hot springs
(10) 光明顶   j. Guest-greeting Pine

2. Translate the following Chinese into English

(1) 黄山位于安徽省南部,面积约1200平方千米。
(2) 1990年,黄山被列入《世界文化与自然遗产名录》。
(3) 黄山的美,首先就美在它的奇峰。这里群峰竞秀,峰峰称奇。
(4) 80多座山峰的海拔高度绝大多数都在千米以上,其中莲花峰最高(1864米),

光明顶次之(1860 米),天都峰第三(1810 米)。

(5) 迎客松是黄山奇松的代表。

(6) 在黄山到处都可以看到奇形怪状的岩石。

(7) 除了"四绝",黄山的瀑布、日出和晚霞也是十分壮观和美丽的。

(8) 黄山不仅雄伟壮丽,而且资源丰富,动物种类繁多。

3. Fill in the blanks with appropriate words and expressions

Mount Huangshan, often described as the "loveliest mountain of China", has played an important ____(1)____ in the history of art and literature in China since the Tang Dynasty around the 8th century, when a legend dated from the year 747 described the mountain as the place of discovery of the long-sought elixir of immortality. This ____(2)____ gave Mount Huangshan its name and assured its place in Chinese history.

____(3)____ in southern Anhui Province, Mount Huangshan covers an area of 1200 square kilometers. Its landscape features "four ____(4)____" of strange-shaped pines, spectacular rocks, sea of clouds and hot springs.

Mount Huangshan ____(5)____ 72 peaks, more than 1000 meters above sea level, with three main peaks rising majestically. They are both fascinating and dangerously steep. Cliffs, stone forests, stone pillars, stone blocks and egg-shaped stones form the unique granite geomorphological scenery.

The ____(6)____ on the mountain are tall and have fascinating shapes. The famous Guest-greeting Pine (1500 years old) and See-guest-off Pine have become a ____(7)____ of being faithful, unyielding and hospitable. More than 200 days each year on Mount Huangshan are misty and cloudy. The vapors coagulate to form a sea of ____(8)____. As the clouds cloak the mountain, they give a feeling of being in fairyland. Mount Huangshan has more than 400 famous scenic attractions, of which 140 have been developed and opened to tourists.

In 1990, Mount Huangshan went on both the World Cultural and Natural ____(9)____ List.

4. Role play

Situation: Suppose you are the local guide and are now guiding the guests to visit Mount Huangshan. Make introductions and answer relevant questions.

Ⅳ Extended Reading

Four Seasons in Mount Huangshan

Module 10　Tour of Famous Mountains

Task 3　A Trip to Mount Wuyi

I　Read and Match

a. the Nine-bend Stream　　b. Hanging Coffin
c. the King Peak　　　　　　d. the Maidens Peak

(1)　　　　　　　　(2)

(3)　　　　　　　　(4)

II　Situational Dialogue

A Trip to Mount Wuyi

(As a local guide, Xiao Li is guiding the guests to Mount Wuyi. He introduces Mount Wuyi on the way and answers relevant questions.)

L: Xiao Li, the local guide　　G: Mr. Gipson, the tourist

扫码
听听力

L: Ladies and gentlemen, today we will visit Mount Wuyi, the landmark attraction in Fujian Province. It has been called the No. 1 mountain in Fujian Province and is of typical Danxia landform.

G: Why is it called Mount Wuyi? Does it have any special meaning?

L: Yes, the name of Mount Wuyi comes from a legend. It is said that in ancient times an old man named Peng Zu lived and cultivated himself on the peak of the mountain. At that time, the flood flooded everywhere and people lived on the edge of starvation. Peng Wu and Peng Yi, two sons of Peng Zu, led people to dig rivers, regulate watercourses and dredge floods. After Peng Wu and Peng Yi died, people named the Mount Wuyi in memory of the two brothers.

G: Oh, that is a moving story.

L: The first scenic spot we arrived at is the Jiuqu Stream (the Nine-bend Stream). The soul of the beauty of Wuyi Scenic spot lies in this Nine-bend Stream. This stream originates from the foot of Huanggang Peak, the main peak of Mount Wuyi. It passes through the whole scenic spot from the west to the east. Covering an area of 8.5 square kilometers, with a total length of 9.5 kilometers, the stream turns into nine curves and gives rise to different sceneries. Now we are going to take a bamboo raft and go boating on the Jiuqu Stream. Everyone, please get on the raft one by one. Be careful.

(Xiao Li points to the stone along the way)

L: Now, please look at the stone on the right. It is the most typical stone spectacle in Mount Wuyi. There are two vertical joints on the peak wall that divide the column into three pieces of rock with increasing height, just like the three sisters standing together, so it is called Maidens Peak. The stone on the left is the King Peak. It is 530 meters above sea level and looks like a giant pillar of heaven, with unique majesty of a king. That is how it gets its name.

G: What are the boat-like woods hanging on the cliff?

L: These are hanging coffins. Like sky burial and water burial, hanging coffin burial was an ancient form of funeral. The coffins were placed in natural or man-made caves tens to hundreds of meters away from the water surface, and some were directly placed on the suspended wooden piles. After carbon 14 determination, some coffins have been well preserved for more than 3000 years.

G: Why were the coffins placed on the cliff?

L: There are many opinions about why the coffin was placed on the cliff. Some people think that this is to protect the body of the dead from wild animals. Some people think that this is the embodiment of the ancient mountain worship consciousness, in order to make the ghosts of the dead more convenient to ascend to heaven. Because of their admiration for the mountains, they put the dead in the place closest to the God, so that they would not be disturbed by the world, so as to better protect the future generations. Another opinion is that the boat was an indispensable tool in the life of the ancient Yue minority people, and putting the dead into the boat-shaped coffin was respect for the dead.

G: That is singular.

L: Now we are approaching the Narrow Strip of Sky. It is the strangest cave in Mount Wuyi. The Narrow Strip of Sky is in fact a crack in the middle of the mountain, just like a sharp axe. It is about 100 meters long and less than 90 centimeters wide. The narrowest part is only 50 centimeters.

G: This is indeed the miracle of nature.

Useful Expressions

1. Peng Wu and Peng Yi, two sons of Peng Zu, led people to dig rivers, regulate watercourses and dredge floods. After Peng Wu and Peng Yi died, people named the Mount Wuyi in memory of the two brothers.

彭祖的两个儿子彭武、彭夷带领人们开河、整治河道、疏通洪水。彭武和彭夷去世后，人们给这座山取名为武夷山，以纪念两兄弟。

2. There are two vertical joints on the peak wall that divide the column into three pieces of rock with increasing height, just like the three sisters standing together, so it is called "Maidens Peak".

峰壁有两条垂直节理将柱状体分成高度递增的三块削岩，宛如比肩俏立的三姐妹一般，所以被人们称为"玉女峰"。

3. The coffins were placed in natural or man-made caves tens to hundreds of meters away from the water surface, and some were directly placed on the suspended wooden piles.

棺材放置在距水面数十米至数百米的天然或人造洞穴中，有的直接放置在悬挂的木桩上。

4. Some people think that this is the embodiment of the ancient mountain worship consciousness, in order to make the ghosts of the dead more convenient to ascend to heaven.

有人认为这是古代山岳崇拜意识的体现，是为了让亡灵更方便升天。

5. The Narrow Strip of Sky is in fact a crack in the middle of the mountain, just like a sharp axe.

"一线天"其实是山中央的一条裂缝，就像一把锋利的斧子。

Exercises

1. Match the following Chinese with the correct English versions

(1) 九曲溪　　　　　　　　　a. the Narrow Strip of Sky

(2) 一线天　　　　　　　　　b. bamboo raft

(3) 玉女峰　　　　　　　　　c. Wuyi Rock Tea

(4) 大王峰　　　　　　　　　d. the Nine-bend Stream

(5) 悬棺　　　　　　　　　　e. natural reserve

(6) 竹筏　　　　　　　　　　f. hanging coffins

(7) 漂流　　　　　　　　　　g. Maidens Peak

(8) 丹霞地貌　　　　　　　　h. drift

(9) 武夷岩茶　　　　　　　　i. Danxia landform

(10) 自然保护区　　　　　　　j. King Peak

2. Translate the following Chinese into English

(1) 武夷山位于福建省武夷山市南郊,总面积999.75平方千米,是中国著名的风景旅游区和避暑胜地。

(2) 武夷山自然保护区,是地球同纬度地区保护最好、物种最丰富的生态系统,拥有2527种植物物种,近5000种野生动物。

(3) 中外生物学家把武夷山称为"鸟类天堂""蛇的王国""昆虫世界"。

(4) 武夷山有高悬崖壁数千年不朽的船棺18处,有书院遗址35处,有堪称中国古书法艺术宝库的历代摩崖石刻450多方。

(5) 武夷山被考古学家认为是悬棺葬俗的发祥地,其实物是研究我国先秦历史和已消逝的古闽族文化的极为珍贵的资料。

(6) 武夷山也是中国古代朱子理学的摇篮。

(7) 武夷岩茶产于武夷山,茶树生长在岩缝之中。武夷岩茶具有绿茶之清香、红茶之甘醇,是中国乌龙茶中之极品。

(8) 武夷山于1999年12月被联合国教科文组织列入《世界遗产名录》,成为全人类共同的财富。

3. Fill in the blanks with appropriate words and expressions

Mount Wuyi Scenic Spot is ＿＿＿(1)＿＿＿ in Wuyishan City, northwest of Fujian Province about 15 kilometers south of the urban area, with an area of about 999.75 square kilometers. There is a typical Danxia ＿＿＿(2)＿＿＿. With hundreds of millions of years' nature's uncanny workmanship, it is ＿＿＿(3)＿＿＿ for beautiful scenery.

Mount Wuyi is also a famous historical and cultural mountain. It is also the cradle of ancient Chinese Neo Confucianism. As a theory, Neo Confucianism once occupied a dominant position in East and Southeast Asian countries for many centuries, and ＿＿＿(4)＿＿＿ a large part of the world in philosophy and politics. Zhu Xi, a famous Neo Confucianist and educator in Song Dynasty, had a close ＿＿＿(5)＿＿＿ with Mount Wuyi in his life. In his 71 years' life, he ＿＿＿(6)＿＿＿ more than 40 years in Northern Fujian and Wuyishan City. He set ＿＿＿(7)＿＿＿ an academy to teach disciples and wrote books, which made Wuyishan the cultural ＿＿＿(8)＿＿＿ of Southeast China. When he toured Jiuqu Stream with his friends, he wrote a seven-line poem, *Jiuqu Folk Song*. This poem, written in the form of folk song, is the first panoramic masterpiece to ___(9)___ the scenery along the Nine-bend Stream and reveals the beauty of Mount Wuyi. Later, there are no less than 2000 hymns written by literati and scholars in different ___(10)___. There are more than 400 inscriptions on the cliffs. These rich cultural and historical relics also add to the ___(11)___ of the famous mountain.

4. Role play

Situation: Suppose you are the local guide and are now guiding the guests to visit Mount Wuyi. Make introductions and answer relevant questions.

IV Extended Reading

Mount Wuyi

Mount Wuyi

Module 11
Tour of Water Landscape

Learning Objectives

1. Master the vocabulary and sentence patterns of the tour of famous water landscape.
2. Describe the water scenery to the tourists.
3. Explore the cultural elements of the famous water landscape.
4. Summarize the main features of the famous water landscape.

Task 1　A Trip to the Three Gorges of the Yangtze River

Read and Match

a. Qutang Gorge　　　　　　b. Wu Gorge
c. Xiling Gorge　　　　　　d. Three Gorges Dam

(1)

(2)

Module 11 Tour of Water Landscape

(3)   (4)

📖 ‖ Situational Dialogue

A Trip to the Three Gorges of the Yangtze River

(As a local guide, Xiao Li is guiding the guests to the Three Gorges of the Yangtze River. He introduces the scenery on the way and answers relevant questions.)

L: Xiao Li, the local guide   S: Ms. Sadie, the tourist

L: Ladies and gentlemen, starting from Chaotianmen, we begin our trip to the Three Gorges. There is a popular saying, "If you don't go to the Three Gorges, you can't say you have visited the Yangtze River." At the beginning of our trip to the Three Gorges, let me give you a brief introduction of the Yangtze River. The Yangtze River originates from the southwest of Tanggula Mountain in Qinghai Province and flows through 11 provinces and cities. From west to east, it flows across the hinterland of China and finally into the East China Sea. With a total length of 6300 kilometers, it is the longest river in China and the third longest river in the world, third only to the Nile and the Amazon River. It breeds the ancient civilization of the Chinese nation, and integrates with mountains to form the magnificent Three Gorges of the Yangtze River.

S: What are the Three Gorges?

L: With a total length of 193 kilometers, the Three Gorges of the Yangtze River are composed of Qutang Gorge, Wu Gorge and Xiling Gorge. Dear friends, we are now entering Qutang Gorge, the first gorge of the Three Gorges. Qutang Gorge has a total length of 8 kilometers and is famous for its imposing majesty. As you see, at the entrance of the canyon, there are two young cliffs opposite each other, forming a natural gate. This is called Kuimen. The mighty Yangtze River passes through here. Due to the sudden narrowing of the river, the flow of the river is like ten thousand horses galloping through. Because of the precipitous location and numerous mountains on both sides, the Yangtze River has become a thin strip here. Looking up, you can only see a line of clouds and sky, but looking down, you can see rough waves.

S: The view is really magnificent.

L: Now we are at the deep and beautiful Wu Gorge. It is 45 kilometers long and notable for its beauty. Although there are many beautiful sceneries in Wu Gorge, the most eye-catching one is the twelve peaks of Wushan.

S: That peak shapes like a girl. Is that the famous Goddess Peak?

L: Exactly. There is a legend behind it. A long time ago, there were twelve dragons in the Three Gorges, which did harm to the people. When Yao Ji, the youngest daughter of the Heaven Queen, knew about it and made great efforts to kill the dragons with her sisters. They were also attracted by the beautiful scenery of the Three Gorges, so they became the twelve peaks of Wushan to guard the Three Gorges. These are the most prominent aspects of the scenery of Wu Gorge. Among the twelve, the Goddess Peak is the highest and most notable.

S: Now I know why some people compare Wu Gorge to a "circuitous landscape gallery".

L: Yes, you are right.

(After some time)

L: As you can see, the surface of the river has suddenly become open, and we are now in the last gorge in the Three Gorges, Xiling Gorge. With a total length of 76 kilometers, Xiling Gorge is the longest gorge in the Three Gorges. It is known for the turbulence and the rapidity of the water flow. It used to be very dangerous to boat in the river. Boatmen in the past had been fighting the torrent here for generations. When boatmen sailed into the Xiling Gorge, the ships were often broken on the rocks, the corpses were floating all over the river. Everyone, have you noticed that tower? There is a white bone tower on the green beach, which was specially used to pile up the corpses of the dead boatmen.

S: Oh, that is terrible. But now it seems the boat is very stable.

L: With the construction of the Three Gorges Dam, all that misery has become history. Now it is very stable to sail on the river. Well, dear friends, that's all I'm going to tell you today. Now it is free time and you can appreciate the beauty of the gorges as you like.

Useful Expressions

1. The Yangtze River originates from the southwest of Tanggula Mountain in Qinghai Province and flows through 11 provinces and cities. From west to east, it flows across the hinterland of China and finally into the East China Sea.

长江发源于青海省唐古拉山脉的西南侧，流经11个省市。纳百川千流，自西向东，横贯中国腹地,最后注入东海。

2. With a total length of 6300 kilometers, it is the longest river in China and the third longest river in the world, third only to the Nile and the Amazon River.

全长 6300 千米,是中国第一大河,是仅次于尼罗河和亚马孙河的世界第三大河流。

3. It breeds the ancient civilization of the Chinese nation, and integrates with mountains to form the magnificent Three Gorges of the Yangtze River.

它孕育了中华民族的古老文明,更与山融合而成了壮丽雄奇的长江三峡。

4. With a total length of 193 kilometers, the Three Gorges of the Yangtze River are composed of Qutang Gorge, Wu Gorge and Xiling Gorge.

长江三峡全长 193 千米,由瞿塘峡、巫峡、西陵峡组成。

5. Because of the precipitous location and numerous mountains on both sides, the Yangtze River has become a thin strip here. Looking up, you can only see a line of clouds and sky, but looking down, you can see rough waves.

由于这里地势险峻,两岸崇山无数,长江在这里变成了一条细带,向上看只能看到云天一线,向下看却看到波涛汹涌。

6. Now I know why some people compare Wu Gorge to a "circuitous landscape gallery".

我现在明白为什么巫峡被比作一条"迂回曲折的山水画廊"。

Exercises

1. Match the following Chinese with the correct English versions

(1) 发源于……   a. precipitous hills
(2) 波涛汹涌   b. turbulent waves
(3) 山势陡峭   c. originate from…
(4) 山水画廊   d. the Twelve Peaks of Wushan
(5) 崇山峻岭   e. the Goddess Peak
(6) 巫山十二峰   f. landscape gallery
(7) 神女峰   g. the white bone tower
(8) 白骨塔   h. the Three Gorges Dam
(9) 水流平稳   i. steady flow
(10) 三峡大坝   j. high and lofty hills

2. Translate the following Chinese into English

(1) 长江是我们的母亲河,是中国第一长河,世界第三长河。

(2) 长江三峡全长 193 千米,它以"瞿塘雄、巫峡秀、西陵险"而驰名。

(3) 长江三峡是世界大峡谷之一,是长江上最为奇秀壮丽的山水画廊,全长 200 千米左右。

(4) 瞿塘峡全长 8 千米,是三个峡中最短的,却是最雄伟壮观的。

(5) 白帝城是观"夔门天下雄"的最佳地点。

(6) 巫峡全长 45 千米，以幽深秀丽著称。

(7) 西陵峡以滩多水急而著称。

3. Fill in the blanks with appropriate words and expressions

The Three Gorges of the Yangtze River are a system of breathtaking gorges on China's longest river, which is also the ____(1)____ longest river in the world (after the Amazon and the Nile), stretching ____(2)____ 6300 kilometers.

The Qutang Gorge is best known for its steep precipices that form an enormous gateway over the river. The Wu Gorge is home to the famous twelve ____(3)____ of the Wushan. And the Xiling Gorge is known for its hidden reefs, perilous cliffs and tumbling rapids.

Qutang Gorge, the shortest and most ____(4)____ of the Three Gorges, winds five miles from Baidicheng in Fengjie County to Daxi Town in Wushan County. The two banks of the Qutang Gorge contain numerous scenic spots. As the peaks along the two banks are 3281 feet to 4921 feet high and the Yangtze River is only 109 yards to 219 yards wide, the deep gorge, fast-moving water, and chains of mountains form an imposing picture.

Wu Gorge is ____(5)____ for its deep valley and elegant beauty of forest-covered peaks. The twelve peaks of the Wushan lie at both banks of the gorge, among which the Goddess Peak in mist is the most ____(6)____. The rugged peaks, curious rocks and steep cliffs spread all over the gorge. It seems like a gallery ____(7)____ of many beautiful things. Because of the long and deep canyons in the Wu Gorge, the daily period of sunlight is short which impedes the dispersal of air borne moisture within the gorge and so creates clouds and fog in a variety of fantastic shapes. How wonderful it is!

Xiling Gorge is the longest gorge among the Three Gorges of the Yangtze River. Named ____(8)____ the mountain that at the endpoint of the Three Gorges —Mount Xiling, the gorge is historically famous for its natural scenes. Before the ____(9)____ of the Three Gorges Dam and Gezhouba Dam, it was known for being the most dangerous of the Three Gorges to travel through with numerous reefs and odd-shaped stones existing in rapid shoals. Scenery along the Xiling Gorge is spectacular. Some renowned streams, springs, stones and karst caves can be ____(10)____ along this section.

4. Role play

Situation: Suppose you are the local guide and are now guiding the guests to visit the Three Gorges of the Yangtze River. Make introductions and answer relevant questions.

IV Extended Reading

The Three Gorges of the Yangtze River Note

The Three Gorges of the Yangtze River

Module 11 Tour of Water Landscape

Task 2　A Trip to Jiuzhaigou

I Read and Match

a. the Pearl Shoal
b. the Mirror Lake
c. the Five-color Pond
d. the Wuhuahai Lake

(1)　　　　(2)

(3)　　　　(4)

II Situational Dialogues

A Trip to Jiuzhaigou

(As a local guide, Xiao Li is guiding the guests to Jiuzhaigou.)

L: Xiao Li, the local guide　　S: Ms. Sadie, the tourist

L: Ladies and gentlemen, today we will visit Jiuzhaigou. Located in Sichuan

Province, Jiuzhaigou stretches 80 kilometers in one direction and takes up an area of more than 60000 hectares. In the reserve there are perennially snow-topped mountain peaks, lush forests and stretches of serene lakes. It was listed in the World Heritage List in 1992.

S: Before we came, we heard an interesting Chinese saying, "You will never want to see any other water landscape after coming back from Jiuzhaigou."

L: Yes. This saying has well demonstrated the enchanting beauty of water landscape in Jiuzhaigou. It is no exaggeration that Jiuzhaigou is a world of water. It boasts many clear lakes, some of which are hidden in the valleys and some inlaid in the forests. Jiuzhaigou is composed of three main valleys arranged in a Y shape. Now we are entering Rize Valley. The Rize Valley is 18 kilometers long and is the southwestern branch of Jiuzhaigou. It contains the largest variety of sites. Going downhill from its highest point, we will pass the following sites: the Swan Lake, the Grass Lake, the Arrow Bamboo Lake, the Panda Lake, the Wuhuahai Lake, the Pearl Shoal, and the Mirror Lake. Due to the limited time, today we will focus on three scenic spots, the Panda Lake, the Pearl Shoal and the Wuhuahai Lake.

S: Panda Lake? Does it have anything to do with pandas? Can we see pandas there?

L: It is said that pandas in Jiuzhaigou like to wander here, drink water and look for food. Panda is regarded as an auspicious creature and is deeply loved by Tibetans in Jiuzhaigou. So this lake is called The Panda Lake.

S: What about the Pearl Shoal?

L: At the junction of the Rize Valley and the Nanri Valley, there is a flat shoal, where 100-meter-long torrent flows through the multi-level valley. Countless drops of water are splashed on the uneven milky yellow calcified shoal. In the sun, little drops of water are just like pearls in giant scallops. From a distance, you can get a view of white pearls flowing in the river. The Pearl Shoal is named after it.

S: The view is indeed breathtaking.

L: Now we have come to the Wuhuahai Lake, with the reputation of "the wonder of Jiuzhaigou" and "the essence of Jiuzhaigou". Here the water shows yellow, dark green, dark blue, navy blue and other colors.

S: Wow, I have never seen a lake like this. This must be the magic painting of nature.

L: Because there are more than 200 kinds of algae and minerals in the water, and because of the refraction and reflection of the sun's light, the color of the water is full of changes. You see, some dead old trees are floating in the water, and small trees and grass grow on the trunks, making the lake more beautiful and vigorous. Jiuzhai people believe that the Wuhuahai Lake is a magic pool, where its water is sprinkled;

there will be many flowers and forests, beautiful and lush. Now I will give you half an hour to appreciate the beauty of nature and take photos if you like.

S: Thank you. This is undoubtedly a haven of peace, leaving behind nothing but earthly troubles and worries.

Useful Expressions

1. It boasts many clear lakes, some of which are hidden in the valleys and some inlaid in the forests. Jiuzhaigou is composed of three main valleys arranged in a Y shape.

它有许多清澈的湖泊，或藏于深山，或嵌在森林。九寨沟由三条主沟组成，呈 Y 字形分布。

2. At the junction of the Rize Valley and the Nanri Valley, there is a flat shoal, where 100-meter-long torrent flows through the multi-level valley.

日则沟和南日沟的交界处有一片坡度平缓的浅滩，长约 100 米的水流在此流经多级河谷。

3. Countless drops of water are splashed on the uneven milky yellow calcified shoal. In the sun, little drops of water are just like pearls in giant scallops. From a distance, you can get a view of white pearls flowing in the river.

激流在凹凸不平的乳黄色钙化滩面上溅起无数水珠，阳光下，点点水珠就像巨型扇贝里的粒粒珍珠，远看河中好像流动着洁白的珍珠。

4. Because there are more than 200 kinds of algae and minerals in the water, and because of the refraction and reflection of the sun's light, the color of the water is full of changes.

因为水中有 200 多种藻类和矿物质，由于阳光的折射和反射，水的颜色充满了变化。

Exercises

1. Match the following Chinese with the correct English versions

(1) 珍珠滩   a. the Mirror Lake
(2) 五花海   b. the Five-color Pond
(3) 镜海   c. the Pearl Shoal
(4) 日则沟   d. snow-capped mountains
(5) 树正沟   e. the Wuhuahai Lake
(6) 原始森林   f. the Shuzheng Valley
(7) 五彩池   g. nature reserve
(8) 瀑布   h. the Rize Valley

(9) 雪峰　　　　　　　　　　　i. virgin forest
(10) 自然保护区　　　　　　　 j. waterfall

2. Translate the following Chinese into English

（1）九寨沟国家级自然保护区位于四川省，是中国第一个以保护自然风景为主要目的的自然保护区。

（2）九寨沟海拔在 2000 米以上，遍布原始森林，沟内分布 108 个湖泊。因有九个藏族村寨而得名。

（3）原始森林覆盖了九寨沟一半以上的面积。

（4）九寨沟四季景色迷人，被誉为"美丽的童话世界"。

（5）水是九寨沟景观的主角。色彩斑斓的湖泊和气势宏伟的瀑布令人目不暇接。

（6）日则沟风景线全长 18 千米，是九寨沟风景线中的精华部分。

（7）树正沟长 14 千米，共有各种海子 40 余个，约占九寨沟景区全部海子的 40%，被誉为九寨沟的缩影。

（8）五彩池是九寨沟最小的海子，但是色彩最为丰富，不同的角度和位置有不同的色彩。

3. Fill in the blanks with appropriate words and expressions

Jiuzhaigou boasts a number of unique features. The mountains, lakes, ＿＿(1)＿＿ forest, beautiful flowers all make Jiuzhaigou a ＿＿(2)＿＿. Mountains ranging 1980 to about 3100 meters in height are covered by a variety of trees and plants. Scenes change ＿＿(3)＿＿ to the season and the area is particularly ＿＿(4)＿＿ in autumn when the wind makes kilometers of tree belt along the lake undulate like sea waves. Waterfalls, lakes, springs, rivers and shoals add to the charming beauty and the green trees, red leaves, snowy peaks and blue skies are ＿＿(5)＿＿ from lakes and rivers. Trees grow in the water and flowers blossom in the middle of lakes.

It is a ＿＿(6)＿＿ that Jiuzhaigou can keep such a perfect and magical natural dream scene in modern society. This is closely ＿＿(7)＿＿ to the Benbo religion that Tibetan compatriots believe in. Tibetan people believe in gods. They believe that Jiuzhaigou is endowed with gods of grass, mountains and rivers.

4. Role play

Situation: Suppose you are the local guide and are now guiding the guests to visit Jiuzhaigou. Make introductions and answer relevant questions.

Ⅳ Extended Reading

Waterfalls in Jiuzhaigou

Module 11 Tour of Water Landscape

Task 3 A Trip to Qinghai Lake

I Read and Match

a. Qinghai Lake
b. Scaleless Carp
c. Bird Island
d. Chaka Salt Lake

(1)   (2)
(3)   (4)

II Situational Dialogues

A Trip to Qinghai Lake

(As a local guide, Xiao Li is guiding the guest to Qinghai Lake. He introduces the scenery on the way and answers relevant questions.)

L: Xiao Li, the local guide   S: Mr. Sadie, the tourist

L: Ladies and gentlemen, now we are on the way to Qinghai Lake. Qinghai Lake is located in the Qinghai Lake Basin in the northwest of Qinghai Province. High altitude is a major feature of Qinghai Lake. The lake is 3260 meters above sea level. Because of the high terrain, the climate here is very cool, even in midsummer. You have come at the best time of the year. The average daily temperature in July and August is only about 15 degrees.

S: We can feel it along the way. It is really an ideal summer resort.

L: Another characteristic of Qinghai Lake is its large size. It is the largest inland lake and the largest saltwater lake in China. It is estimated that Qinghai Lake is 106 kilometers long from east to west, 65 kilometers wide from north to south, and 360 kilometers long around, covering an area of 4340 square kilometers. To put it vividly, it can accommodate four Hong Kong.

S: How did Qinghai Lake form?

L: Qinghai Lake is the result of the uplift of Qinghai-Tibet Plateau after long-term collision and compression between Indian Ocean plate and Eurasian plate 40 million years ago.

S: What is to be seen in Qinghai Lake?

L: We are now in Erlangjian Scenic Area. Located on the southern shore of Qinghai Lake, Erlangjian Scenic Area has the best infrastructure. It's home to a shopping center, restaurants and hotels. There, you can get a great view of Qinghai Lake and take a yacht tour.

S: That is a good idea. I heard that Qinghai Lake is a paradise for birds, right?

L: Exactly. Qinghai Lake is notable for biodiversity. Qinghai Lake is a paradise for fish, a paradise for a variety of migratory birds, and a home for the world-class endangered Chinese gazelle. They coexist with Qinghai Lake and are the real masters of Qinghai Lake.

S: Look. There are so many fish in the lake.

L: Yes, that is the unique species of fish in Qinghai Lake, scaleless carp. As they live in salt lake, there is less food to eat and they grow very slowly. It is said that the fish will grow only one kilogram every ten years. It is also because of the existence of scaleless carps that hundreds of thousands of migratory birds can reproduce and live in Qinghai Lake. Qinghai Lake Bird Island, the first of the eight bird reserves in China, was established in 1975. Now we have approached Bird Island.

S: Wow, unbelievable. So many birds. That is amazing.

L: Bird Island is a paradise for birds near Qinghai Lake. More than 100000 migratory birds come to live here from April to June every year at the turn of spring and summer. It is also called Egg Island because it is full of bird eggs during the spawning period.

S: That is amazing.

L: Now we will go to Chaka Salt Lake. Chaka Salt Lake is a saltworks for more than 3000 years. Its water contains a lot of salt. It will naturally crystallize into a white lake surface, reflecting the sky, clouds and mountains on the opposite bank in the lake. It is very beautiful. Tourists can also walk barefoot to the lake to watch and take photos of their own reflection.

S: That is why the lake is also called the mirror of the sky.

L: That is right. Besides, there are many salt sculptures in the scenic area. You can also take a small train to the depth of the salt lake for sightseeing.

Useful Expressions

1. It is the largest inland lake and the largest saltwater lake in China.
它是中国最大的内陆湖和最大的咸水湖。

2. Qinghai Lake is the result of the uplift of Qinghai-Tibet Plateau after long-term collision and compression between Indian Ocean plate and Eurasian plate 40 million years ago.
青海湖是距今4千万年前，印度洋板块和欧亚板块经过长期碰撞和挤压，青藏高原隆起的结果。

3. Qinghai Lake is notable for biodiversity. Qinghai Lake is a paradise for fish, a paradise for a variety of migratory birds, and a home for the world-class endangered Chinese gazelle. They coexist with Qinghai Lake and are the real masters of Qinghai Lake.
青海湖是生物多样性的宝库。青海湖是鱼的乐园、多种候鸟的天堂、世界级濒危动物中华对角羚的家园，它们与青海湖共存，是青海湖真正的主人。

4. More than 100000 migratory birds come to live here from April to June every year at the turn of spring and summer. It is also called "Egg Island" because it is full of bird eggs during the spawning period.
每年4月至6月，春夏之交，有超过10万只候鸟来到这里栖息。它也被称为"蛋岛"，在产卵期岛上遍布鸟蛋。

5. Chaka Salt Lake is a saltworks for more than 3000 years.
茶卡盐湖是一座3000多年的盐场。

6. It will naturally crystallize into a white lake surface, reflecting the sky, clouds and mountains on the opposite bank in the lake.
湖水会自然结晶成为一片白色的湖面，将天空、云朵和对岸的山都倒映在湖里。

Exercises

1. Match the following Chinese with the correct English versions

（1）内陆湖　　　　　　　　a. plateau lake
（2）盐湖　　　　　　　　　b. habitat
（3）候鸟　　　　　　　　　c. inland lake

(4) 高原湖泊　　　　　　　　d. collision
(5) 栖息地　　　　　　　　　e. salt lake
(6) 鸟岛　　　　　　　　　　f. Qinghai-Tibet Plateau
(7) 二郎剑景区　　　　　　　g. biodiversity
(8) 碰撞　　　　　　　　　　h. migratory birds
(9) 生物多样性　　　　　　　i. Erlangjian Scenic Area
(10) 青藏高原　　　　　　　 j. Bird Island

2. **Translate the following Chinese into English**

(1) 海拔高是青海湖的一大特点，湖面海拔 3260 米。

(2) 由于这里地势高，气候十分凉爽，即使是在盛夏，日平均气温也只有 15℃ 左右。

(3) 作为中国最大的咸水湖与最大的内陆湖，青海湖是生物多样性的宝库。

(4) 青海湖流域是青藏高原候鸟迁徙途中的重要停歇地。

(5) 青海湖流域也是青藏高原特有物种青海湖裸鲤的唯一栖息地。

(6) 著名的鸟岛位于青海湖西部，面积只有 0.5 平方千米，春夏季节却栖息着 10 万只候鸟。

(7) 青海湖岸边有辽阔的天然牧场，这一带所产的马在春秋战国时期就很出名，雄壮善驰，被称为"秦马"。

(8) 茶卡盐湖以"天空之镜"而得名，是《国家旅游地理》杂志评选的"人一生要去的 55 个地方"之一。

3. **Fill in the blanks with appropriate words and expressions**

Qinghai Lake National Nature Reserve is located in the northeast of the Qinghai-Tibet ＿＿＿(1)＿＿＿ at the southern foot of the Qilian Mountains in Qinghai Province's most accessible northeast corner. It is 100-200 kilometers west of Xining City, the ＿＿＿(2)＿＿＿ of Qinghai Province, with convenient transportation.

Qinghai Lake has a breathtaking range of ＿＿＿(3)＿＿＿ — wetlands, grasslands, snow-capped mountains and deserts! Surrounded by snow-topped mountains, the lake is bounded with vast grasslands, wetlands, and some desert.

The lake is central to the popular Tour of Qinghai Lake professional bicycle racing event that is ＿＿＿(4)＿＿＿ every year in July at the same time as the Tour de France. So, it is already a favorite biking area in China.

The high ＿＿＿(5)＿＿＿, starting at about 3200 meters lakeside, makes biking around it strenuous. However, the rewards of seeing the beautiful scenery that sweeps outwards and soars upwards and seeing the local cultural mix make the strain worth it for many people.

As one of the seven largest wetlands in the world, Qinghai Lake wetland was listed as an internationally important ＿＿＿(6)＿＿＿ in 1992. It's a natural ＿＿＿(7)＿＿＿ of wetland ecosystems and wild animals. Qinghai Lake is a natural ＿＿＿(8)＿＿＿ of native birds and a paradise for migratory birds. Each year in late October, Qinghai Lake sees its peak of migratory bird activity, when more than 100000 migratory birds

Module 11 Tour of Water Landscape

gather at Qinghai Lake. There, you can have a closer ____(9)____ at nature, observe the birds, and learn a lot about animals and plants.

4. Role play

Situation: Suppose you are the local guide and are now guiding the guests to visit Qinghai Lake. Make introductions and answer relevant questions.

IV Extended Reading

Travel Tips in Qinghai Lake

Travel Tips in Qinghai Lake

Module 12
Tour of Historic Buildings

Learning Objectives

1. Master the vocabulary and sentence patterns of the tour of historic buildings.
2. Describe the scenery of historic buildings to the tourists.
3. Explore the cultural elements of famous historic buildings and constructions.
4. Summarize the main features of famous historic buildings.

Task 1 A Trip to the Forbidden City

Read and Match

a. the Hall of Supreme Harmony
b. the Hall of Central Harmony
c. the Hall of Preserving Harmony
d. the Palace of Heavenly Purity
e. the Hall of Union and Peace
f. the Palace of Earthly Tranquility

(1)

(2)

Module 12　Tour of Historic Buildings

(3)　　　　　　　　(4)

(5)　　　　　　　　(6)

‖ Situational Dialogue

A Trip to the Forbidden City

(As a local guide, Xiao Li is guiding the guests to the Forbidden City. He introduces the Forbidden City on the way and answers relevant questions.)

L: Xiao Li, the local guide　　G: Mrs. Gilma, the tourist

L: Ladies and gentlemen, now we are on the way to the Forbidden City. First, let me give you a brief introduction of the Forbidden city. It has a long history of over 800 years. Located in the middle of Beijing, it now houses the Palace Museum. For almost five centuries, it was the home of the emperor and his household. It was also the political center of Chinese government. It is really a must-see for any tour group coming to Beijing.

G: Why is it called the Forbidden City? To whom is it forbidden?

L: A good question. In the feudal society, emperors had supreme power, so his residence was certainly a forbidden place and the palace was once heavily guarded, and the common people were not allowed to enter.

G: So is it open to the public now?

扫码
听听力

L: Yes. After the last emperor of China left the palace, it later became a museum open to the public in 1925. Since then, the Forbidden City is no longer "forbidden", and now ordinary people are able to take a trip to see the secrets and luxury of the imperial life.

G: Thank you. Could you tell me something more about it? How large is it exactly?

L: It has 9900 bays of rooms under a total roof area of 150000 square meters. It is the largest and most well-preserved imperial residence in China. It is divided into two parts—the Outer Court for national affairs in the south and the Inner Court as living quarters in the north. It is not only an immense architectural masterpiece, but also a treasury housing a unique collection of 1.8 million pieces of art, including ancient calligraphy and painting, imperial artifacts, ancient books and archives. As a must-see in Beijing and the world's most visited museum, it is worth spending half to one day to visit the Forbidden City and appreciate the precious cultural heritage of China.

G: Wow, that is amazing. Unbelievable. What are the main spots that we will visit today?

L: We will first visit the Meridian Gate. It is the main entrance to the Forbidden City. It is also known as Wufenglou (Five-Phoenix Tower). Emperors in the Ming Dynasty held banquets here on the 15th day of the first month of the Chinese lunar year. Then we will visit the Hall of Supreme Harmony. There were a total of 24 emperors during the Ming and Qing Dynasties who were enthroned here. It is the biggest and most important piece of architecture in the Forbidden City. After that, we will go to the Hall of Central Harmony. It is the place where the emperors took a break before the ceremony and do a pre-exercise. At last, we will go the Hall of Preserving Harmony. It was used for Chinese New Year banquets and royal weddings.

G: Thank you. I cannot wait to see those wonderful buildings. Why are there so many yellow things? Is yellow the lucky color in China?

L: In fact, yellow is the symbol of the royal family in feudal China, so is the pattern of dragon and phoenix.

G: I see. We will have a good chance to feast our eyes today.

L: There are some points I would like to emphasize. First, as the Forbidden City is very large and there are thousands of visitors every day, please remember to stay close to our group. Do not wander away. It is really easy to get lost there, you know. So the guests with children please pay special attention to your children and remind them not to run around. Second, during the visit, you should take good care of your belongings. Third, please remember my phone number and call me if anything happens. I am always at your service.

G: Thank you for your reminding.

L: Now we are approaching the parking lot. Everyone, please get ready, take all your belongings. We will meet right here at about 12:00 and go back to the hotel. Please remember the number of the coach. Everyone, are you ready? Follow me please.

Useful Expressions

1. In the feudal society, emperors had supreme power, so his residence was certainly a forbidden place and the palace was once heavily guarded, and the common people were not allowed to enter.

在封建社会,皇帝有至高无上的权力,所以他的官邸肯定是禁地,宫殿曾经戒备森严,老百姓是不允许进入的。

2. It is the largest and most well-preserved imperial residence in China.

它是中国最大、保存最完好的皇宫。

3. It is divided into two parts—the Outer Court for national affairs in the south and the Inner Court as living quarters in the north.

它分为两个部分——位于南面处理朝政的外庭和位于北面的生活区内庭。

4. It is not only an immense architectural masterpiece, but also a treasury housing a unique collection of 1.8 million pieces of art, including ancient calligraphy and painting, imperial artifacts, ancient books and archives.

它不仅是一个巨大的建筑杰作,还是一个宝库,收藏了180万件独特的艺术品,包括古代书画、皇家文物、古籍和档案。

5. As a must-see in Beijing and the world's most visited museum, it is worth spending half to one day to visit the Forbidden City and appreciate the precious cultural heritage of China.

故宫是北京必看的景点,也是世界上参观人数最多的博物馆,花上半天或一天的时间游览故宫和欣赏中国珍贵的文化遗产是值得的。

6. Then we will visit the Hall of Supreme Harmony. There were a total of 24 emperors during the Ming and Qing Dynasties who were enthroned here.

然后我们将参观太和殿。明清时期共有24位皇帝在此登基。

Exercises

1. Match the following Chinese with the correct English versions

(1) 太和殿 　　　　a. the Outer Court and the Inner Court
(2) 中和殿 　　　　b. imperial palace
(3) 保和殿 　　　　c. the ruling center
(4) 皇家宫殿 　　　d. imperial wedding

（5）皇家婚礼　　　　　　　　e. central axis symmetry
（6）外庭和内庭　　　　　　　f. the Hall of Supreme Harmony
（7）对角线　　　　　　　　　g. the Hall of Central Harmony
（8）中轴对称　　　　　　　　h. the Hall of Preserving Harmony
（9）艺术宝库　　　　　　　　i. artistic treasury
（10）统治中心　　　　　　　 j. diagonal line

2. Translate the following Chinese into English

（1）故宫位于北京市中心，也称"紫禁城"。

（2）故宫曾居住过24个皇帝，是明清两代的皇宫，现辟为故宫博物院。

（3）故宫的宫殿建筑是中国现存最大、最完整的古建筑群，总面积达72万多平方米。

（4）一条中轴贯通着整个故宫，这条中轴又在北京城的中轴线上。

（5）故宫的主要建筑是太和殿、中和殿和保和殿。保和殿是科举考试举行殿试的地方。

（6）太和殿坐落在紫禁城对角线的中心，是现存中国古代建筑中最高大的建筑，是封建皇权的象征。

（7）故宫的正门叫"午门"，俗称"五凤楼"。午门是皇帝下诏书、下令出征的地方。

（8）故宫博物院藏有大量珍贵文物，据统计有180万件之多，占全国文物总数的1/6。

3. Fill in the blanks with appropriate words and expressions

　　The Forbidden City, is also ＿＿＿(1)＿＿＿ as the Palace Museum which is in the city ＿＿＿(2)＿＿＿ of Beijing, and was once the Chinese ＿＿＿(3)＿＿＿ palace of the Ming and Qing Dynasties. It was listed ＿＿＿(4)＿＿＿ the World Heritage List in 1987 and is the largest, best-preserved ancient timber-built palace complex in the world.

　　Constructed between 1406 and 1420, the Forbidden City was home to 24 ＿＿＿(5)＿＿＿ and their families and acted as the ceremonial and political ＿＿＿(6)＿＿＿ of ancient Chinese government throughout 500 years. Rectangular in shape, the Forbidden City is enormous, covering an ＿＿＿(7)＿＿＿ of 72 hectares. For comparison, the Forbidden City is four times the size of the Taj Mahal of India (18 hectares), which is mainly composed of gardens. Here the Forbidden City, with a multitude of palaces, has a building area even ＿＿＿(8)＿＿＿ than that of the Palace of Versailles in France (11 hectares).

4. Role play

　　Situation：Suppose you are the local guide and are now guiding the guests to visit the Forbidden City. Make introductions and answer relevant questions.

Ⅳ Extended Reading

Three Major Halls in the Forbidden City

Module 12　Tour of Historic Buildings

Task 2　A Trip to the Confucian Temple, Qufu

I Read and Match

a. Lingxing Gate
b. Apricot Altar
c. Kuiwen Pavilion
d. Thirteen Imperial Stele Pavilion

(1)

(2)

(3)

(4)

II Situational Dialogue

A Trip to the Confucian Temple, Qufu

(As a local guide, Xiao Li is guiding the guests to the Confucian Temple, Qufu.)

L: **Xiao Li, the local guide**　　G: **Ms. Galen, the tourist**

L: Ladies and gentlemen, we are now approaching the Confucian Temple. Have you ever heard of Confucius?

G: I know he was a famous and important figure in Chinese history.

L: Confucius was a great thinker, educator and founder of Confucianism. His ideology was developed to the influential Confucianism, which has had the most enduring and profound effect over Chinese culture. Besides, he founded the first private school in the history of Chinese education. He opened the door of school to ordinary people and broke the monopoly of education by the nobles. "In my classroom there is no class difference." That is why Confucius was called the teacher of teachers, the teacher for all ages.

G: He is a great person indeed. I remember there are many Temples of Confucius in China. What is special about the Confucian Temple in Qufu?

L: As Qufu is the hometown of Confucius, the Confucian Temple here is the most famous and the largest temple of its kind in memory of the sage. Together with the Summer Palace in Beijing and the Mountain Resort of Chengde, it is one of the three largest ancient architectural complexes in China.

G: When was it built?

L: The Confucian Temple started as three houses in the year of 478 BC, the second year after the death of Confucius. As Confucianism became the standard of Chinese culture, its scale was expanded accordingly. Sacrifices were often offered, either by emperors themselves, or by emperor-appointed high officials. The scale of offering sacrifices was as grand as that given to the heavens. This gives us an idea of the importance of the sage in history.

G: That is really without equals. How large is the temple? And the layout?

L: The existing temple was rebuilt and renovated during the Ming and Qing Dynasties. Patterned after a royal palace, it is divided into nine courtyards. The main buildings run along a north to south axis, with the attached buildings symmetrically in line. The whole group includes three halls, one pavilion, one altar, and three ancestral temples. Altogether there are 466 rooms and 54 gateways covering an area of 218000 square meters. The yellow tiles and red walls all covered with delicate decoration make the place extremely grand.

G: It is really magnificent.

L: Yes, indeed. However, the Confucian Temple in Qufu wins its fame not only for its grandness, but also for the rich cultural relics. The 2100 pieces of steles remaining from various dynasties make a fine exhibition of calligraphy and stone sculpture.

G: Great. We like Chinese calligraphy and sculptures.

L: Let us go inside. The buildings are divided into three parts. The central part is for offering sacrifices to Confucius, other scholars and sages. The eastern part is for sacrifices to his ancestors, while the west is for his parents.

(Entering Dacheng Hall)

L: We are now in the main hall, Dacheng Hall. This hall is 24.8 meters high on a base of 21 meters, and is the highest building in the temple in China. Dacheng means master with great achievement, which truly describes Confucius himself. This way, please.

(Going forward)

Please look at this stone tablet. There are two Chinese characters inscribed on it, which literally means apricot altar. Does anyone know the meaning?

G: We have no idea. How can apricot be connected with Confucius?

L: The Apricot Altar was built to commemorate Confucius' lecture. When the Confucian Temple was rebuilt and supervised by Kong Daofu, the 45th generation of Confucius' grandson, the main hall was moved back, the ground was removed as the altar, and apricots were planted around it, giving rise to the name "Apricot Altar". Apricot Altar is the symbol of Confucius' education. Let us move forward.

G: What is that pavilion for?

L: That is the Kuiwen Pavilion, a library. Kuixing was the legendary star responsible for literacy in ancient China. The upper story houses classic books and writings given by emperors and kings while the lower story houses items used by the emperors when offering sacrifices to Confucius.

G: Wow, look, so many steles.

L: More than 1000 pieces of steles have been preserved in the Confucius Temple since the Han Dynasty. The contents include the records of the feudal emperors' pursuit of posthumous titles, conferring titles, offering sacrifices to Confucius and building the Confucius Temple.

G: Only by coming here do we understand the life of Confucius and his role in Chinese culture.

L: I couldn't agree more.

Useful Expressions

1. His ideology was developed to the influential Confucianism, which has had the most enduring and profound effect over Chinese culture.

他的思想发展为影响深远的儒家思想,对中国文化产生了最为持久和深刻的影响。

2. "In my classroom there is no class difference." That is why Confucius was called the teacher of teachers, the teacher for all ages.

"有教无类",这就是为什么孔子被称为"老师的老师""万世师表"。

3. Together with the Summer Palace in Beijing and the Mountain Resort of Chengde, it is one of the three largest ancient architectural complexes in China.

它与北京颐和园和承德避暑山庄一起,是中国三大古建筑群之一。

4. Patterned after a royal palace, it is divided into nine courtyards. The main

buildings run along a north to south axis, with the attached buildings symmetrically in line. The whole group includes three halls, one pavilion, one altar, and three ancestral temples.

孔庙仿宫殿样式修建,前后九进院落。主要建筑沿南北轴线展开,附属建筑对称排列。整个建筑群包括三个大厅、一个亭子、一个祭坛、三个祠堂。

5. The 2100 pieces of steles remaining from various dynasties make a fine exhibition of calligraphy and stone sculpture.

历代遗存的 2100 块碑刻,是书法和石雕的精品展览。

6. The central part is for offering sacrifices to Confucius, other scholars and sages. The eastern part is for sacrifices to his ancestors, while the west is for his parents.

中心部分是祭祀孔子、先儒和先贤的场所,东边是祭祀孔子祖先的地方,西边是祭祀孔子父母的地方。

7. Kuixing was the legendary star responsible for literacy in ancient China. The upper story houses classic books and writings given by emperors and kings while the lower story houses items used by the emperors when offering sacrifices to Confucius.

魁星是中国古代的文曲星。上层专藏历代帝王御赐的经书、墨迹,下层专藏皇帝祭祀孔子时使用的物品。

8. When the Confucius Temple was rebuilt and supervised by Kong Daofu, the 45th generation of Confucius' grandson, the main hall was moved back, the ground was removed as the altar, and apricots were planted around it, giving rise to the name "Apricot Altar".

杏坛是为纪念孔子讲学而建,孔子第四十五代孙孔道辅监修孔庙时,将正殿后移,除地为坛,环植以杏,名曰"杏坛"。

9. More than 1000 pieces of steles have been preserved in the Confucius Temple since the Han Dynasty. The contents include the records of the feudal emperors' pursuit of posthumous titles, conferring titles, offering sacrifices to Confucius and building the Confucius Temple.

孔庙内保存汉代以来历代碑刻 1000 多块,内容有封建皇帝追谥、加封、祭祀孔子和修建孔庙的记录。

Exercises

1. Match the following Chinese with the correct English versions

(1) 孔庙　　　　　　　　　　a. Dacheng Hall
(2) 儒家思想　　　　　　　　b. Temple of Confucius
(3) 杏坛　　　　　　　　　　c. Thirteen Imperial Stele Pavilion
(4) 万世师表　　　　　　　　d. Kuiwen Pavilion

Module 12　Tour of Historic Buildings

（5）棂星门　　　　　　　　　　e. Confucianism
（6）大成殿　　　　　　　　　　f. Lingxing Gate
（7）碑林　　　　　　　　　　　g. Apricot Altar
（8）祭孔活动　　　　　　　　　h. the teacher for all ages
（9）奎文阁　　　　　　　　　　i. the Forest of Steles
（10）十三御碑亭　　　　　　　 j. activities of offering sacrifice to Confucius

2. Translate the following Chinese into English

（1）曲阜孔庙是祭祀中国古代著名思想家和教育家孔子的祠庙。
（2）曲阜孔庙始建于公元前478年。
（3）现存的建筑群绝大部分是明清两代完成的，前后九进院落。
（4）曲阜孔庙被建筑学家梁思成称为世界建筑史上的"孤例"。
（5）大成殿是孔庙的主体建筑，历朝历代皇帝的重大祭孔活动就在大殿里举行。
（6）棂星门是孔庙的大门。古代传说棂星是天上的文星，以此命名有国家人才辈出之意，因此古代帝王祭天时首先祭棂星，祭祀孔子的规格也如同祭天。
（7）奎文阁位于孔庙的中部，是一座藏书的楼阁。
（8）孔庙的杏坛相传是孔子讲学之所，位于大成殿前的院落正中。
（9）曲阜孔庙不仅是中国古代举行祭孔活动的场所，同时也是传承孔子思想、进行文化教育的教学场所。

3. Fill in the blanks with appropriate words and expressions

The temple, cemetery and family ＿＿＿（1）＿＿＿ of Confucius, the great philosopher, politician and ＿＿＿（2）＿＿＿ of the 6th-5th centuries BC, are located in Qufu, in Shandong Province. Built to commemorate him in 478 BC, the temple has been ＿＿＿（3）＿＿＿ and reconstructed over the centuries; today it comprises more than 100 buildings. The cemetery ＿＿＿（4）＿＿＿ Confucius' tomb and the remains of more than 100000 of his descendants. The small house of the Kong family developed into a gigantic aristocratic residence, of which 152 buildings remain. The Qufu complex of monuments has retained its outstanding artistic and historic character due to the devotion of successive Chinese ＿＿＿（5）＿＿＿ over more than 2000 years.

4. Role play

Situation：Suppose you are the local guide and are now guiding the guests to visit the Confucian Temple, Qufu. Make introductions and answer relevant questions.

Ⅳ Extended Reading

Confucius

Task 3　A Trip to the Museum of Terracotta Warriors and Horses

Read and Match

a. infantry　　b. crossbowman　　c. cavalry　　d. chariots

(1)　　(2)　　(3)　　(4)

Module 12　Tour of Historic Buildings

📖 ‖ Situational Dialogue

扫码
听听力

A Trip to the Museum of Terracotta Warriors and Horses

(As a local guide, Xiao Li is guiding the guests to the Museum of Terracotta Warriors and Horses. He introduces the museum and answers relevant questions.)

L: Xiao Li, the local guide　　G: Mrs. Green, the tourist

L: Ladies and gentlemen, today we will visit Emperor Qin Shi Huang's Mausoleum Site Museum, commonly known as the Museum of Terracotta Warriors and Horses. The Terracotta Army is no doubt a must-see for every visitor to Xi'an. It has been regarded as the most significant archeological excavations of the 20th century and listed in the World Heritage List by UNESCO.

G: Yes, we have long heard of it. Tell us more about Emperor Qin Shi Huang.

L: No problem. Qin Shi Huang established the first centralized state of China and so became the first emperor of the entire country. The determining factor of Qin State's transition from a small rather insignificant nation to the only power in the whole country was its strong army. Replicating the strong troops of the Qin Dynasty, the terracotta army was made with the glorious mission of protecting this great emperor in the underworld.

G: I see. It is said that it was accidently discovered by a group of farmers. Really?

L: Yes. In March, 1974, several broken life-sized clay figures were found near Xi'an by nine farmers as they were digging a well. After the excavation, this grand underground military troop came to light again.

G: That is indeed amazing. How many pits are there?

L: There are four pits in total, and from three of them terracotta figures have been unearthed. Now, in front of us is Pit 1. It is the largest one with a length of 230 meters and a width of 62 meters, equaling the size of two football fields. The military formation in it is made of chariots and infantry. There are over 6000 individual figures and 50 chariots in total.

G: It seems these warriors are quite high, higher than the common people.

L: The terracotta warriors are generally 1.8-1.9 meters high, while the tallest is about 2 meters. The average height of all the warriors is 1.85 meters, which is taller than modern Chinese people.

G: Does this mean that people in the old times were much taller?

L: Data from historical records and ancient human skeletons do show that ancient people were taller than modern people. But some people don't think so. The terracotta soldiers were made much taller for two reasons. During that period, on the one hand, the major form of battle was close combat, which required tall and strong warriors. On the other hand, the taller terracotta warriors are a more impressive representation of the majesty of this once dominant army.

G: The reasoning is well founded.

L: Now we are at the Pit 2. The Pit 2 covers half the size of the Pit 1. This pit has the most complete army units with chariots, infantry, cavalry and crossbowmen. And the Pit 3 is the headquarters of the formations in the above two pits, with 68 figures, 4 horses, 1 chariot, and 34 weapons unearthed at present.

G: That is indeed a formidable army.

L: It is extremely difficult to find two similar figures in the three pits. Every soldier has his own facial features, which means there are 8000 different faces in total. The 8000 distinctive faces were carved by craftsmen individually, which definitely took massive amount of manpower.

G: Yes, the artistry is really superb. I can hardly believe my eyes.

L: This way, please. Look at the Bronze Chariots and Horses. They are regarded as King of Bronze Ware. They were unearthed 18 meters west of the emperor's mausoleum in 1980. Before the excavation, they had already fallen into more than 1000 pieces. It took 8 years' renovation work to reproduce the original appearance of the chariots and horses. They are the largest and best-preserved bronze chariots in China with a half size of the real imperial chariots of Qin Shi Huang. The first set weighs 1061 kilograms with a length of 225 centimeters and a height of 152 centimeters. The second one is of 317 centimeters in length and 106 centimeters in height, with a weight of 1241 kilograms. Gold and silver were used to decorate the chariots and the accessories on the horses.

G: Now I understand why the discovery was praised as "the Eighth Wonder of the World".

Useful Expressions

1. It has been regarded as the most significant archeological excavations of the 20th century and listed in the World Heritage List by UNESCO.

它被认为是20世纪最重要的考古发掘，被联合国教科文组织列入《世界遗产名录》。

2. Replicating the strong troops of the Qin Dynasty, the terracotta army was made with the glorious mission of protecting this great emperor in the underworld.

兵马俑复制了秦朝强大的兵力,肩负着在阴间保护这位伟大皇帝的光荣使命。

3. This pit has the most complete army units with chariots, infantry, cavalry and crossbowmen.

这个坑里有最完整的军事编队,由战车、步兵、骑兵和弩手组成。

4. The 8000 distinctive faces were carved by craftsmen individually, which definitely took massive amount of manpower.

这8000张独特的面孔是由工匠们单独雕刻的,这无疑耗费了大量的人力。

5. They are the largest and best-preserved bronze chariots in China with a half size of the real imperial chariots of Qin Shi Huang.

它们是中国最大、保存最完好的青铜战车,只有秦始皇真正战车的一半大小。

6. Gold and silver were used to decorate the chariots and the accessories on the horses.

金银被用来装饰战车和马上的饰物。

Exercises

1. Match the following Chinese with the correct English versions

(1) 秦始皇陵　　　　　　a. Pit 1
(2) 兵马俑　　　　　　　b. Emperor Qin Shi Huang's Mausoleum
(3) 1号坑　　　　　　　c. Terracotta Warriors and Horses
(4) 青铜马车　　　　　　d. chariots
(5) 青铜之冠　　　　　　e. infantry
(6) 战车　　　　　　　　f. Bronze Chariots and Horses
(7) 步兵　　　　　　　　g. cavalry
(8) 骑兵　　　　　　　　h. King of Bronze Ware
(9) 弩手　　　　　　　　i. military headquarters
(10) 军事指挥所　　　　　j. crossbowman

2. Translate the following Chinese into English

(1) 秦始皇兵马俑博物馆位于陕西省西安市临潼区,它是在兵马俑坑原址上建立的遗址类博物馆,也是中国最大的古代军事博物馆。

(2) 兵马俑即用陶土制成兵马(战车、战马、士兵)形状的殉葬品。

(3) 秦始皇兵马俑博物馆共有1、2、3号三座兵马俑坑。

(4) 三座俑坑占地面积达2万多平方米,内有和真人、真马大小相似的陶俑、陶马近8000件。

(5) 俑坑内有战车、骑兵和步兵,排列整齐有序。

(6) 1号兵马俑坑内约埋藏陶俑、陶马6000件,同时还有大量的青铜兵器。

(7) 2号兵马俑坑内埋藏陶俑、陶马1300余件。2号俑坑较1号俑坑的内容更丰富,兵种更齐全。

(8) 3号俑坑的规模较小,坑内埋藏陶俑、陶马72件。

(9) 1987年,秦始皇陵及兵马俑坑被联合国教科文组织批准列入《世界遗产名录》,并被誉为"世界第八大奇迹"。

(10) 先后已有200多位国家领导人参观访问秦始皇陵及兵马俑坑,它成为中国古代辉煌文明的一张金字名片。

3. Fill in the blanks with appropriate words and expressions

Located in Lintong District of Xi'an, about 40 kilometers from downtown, the

Museum of Terracotta Warriors and Horses is no doubt a must-visit ___(1)___ for all tourists in Xi'an. This underground army remained undisturbed for over 2200 years until its ___(2)___ in 1974 by local ___(3)___ by chance. No sooner than the news was spread, it has shocked the whole world.

The Terracotta Army has been proved to be a part of the ___(4)___ of Emperor Qin Shi Huang, the first emperor in Chinese history. On one hand, it stands out of imperial tombs through all dynasties in terms of size, number of funerary pits, and variety of funerary objects. On the other hand, it shows the glorious lifetime of Emperor Qin Shi Huang. During Qin Shi Huang's ___(5)___ from 246 BC to 210 BC, he had made great ___(6)___ like unifying the separate vassal states, commanding the ___(7)___ of the Great Wall to defend against nomads, standardizing the measurement units and currencies. Standing in front of the Terracotta Warriors, the vivid scene of the first emperor of China and his army conquering other states will come into your mind easily. You can imagine how Qin Shi Huang ___(8)___ the military forces to complete the amazing feat of unifying the country.

The Qin Shi Huang Mausoleum covers a total area of 56.25 square kilometers, nearly 77 ___(9)___ larger than the Forbidden City. In 1987, Qin Shi Huang Mausoleum and the Terracotta Army were approved by UNESCO as a world cultural heritage and were hailed as the "Eighth ___(10)___ in the world". Archeologists also regard it as one of the ___(11)___ finds in the 20th century.

The Terracotta Army is not only a sketch of ancient Chinese military formation, but also a true epitome of the army in the Qin Dynasty. Up till now, about 8000 pottery warriors and horses have been found in total from the three ___(12)___ of the Terracotta Army. They made up a huge military array consisting of different arrays such as chariots, cavalry and ___(13)___. The terracotta warriors and horses, along with the unearthed bronze weapons, have provided concrete examples for many historical military puzzles such as the method of arranging military array, the establishment for the Qin army unit, and the weapons used by the Qin army.

4. Role play

Situation: Suppose you are the local guide and are now guiding the guests to visit the Museum of Terracotta Warriors and Horses. Make introductions and answer relevant questions.

The Terracotta Army
Note

IV Extended Reading

The Terracotta Army

Module 12　Tour of Historic Buildings

Task 4　A Trip to the Potala Palace

| Read and Match

a. White Palace
b. Red Palace
c. the Great East Hall
d. the East Chamber of Sunshine

(1)

(2)

(3)

(4)

|| Situational Dialogue

A Trip to the Potala Palace

(As a local guide, Xiao Li is guiding the guests in the Potala Palace. He introduces the palace and answers relevant questions.)

L: Xiao Li, the local guide　　F: Miss Ford, the tourist

L: Today we will visit the landmark of Tibet, the Potala Palace. It is considered to be a model of Tibetan architecture. It was originally built for one princess. Do you know which princess I am referring to?

F: I know. Princess Wencheng.

L: Yes, exactly. In 641, to greet his bride Princess Wencheng of the Tang Dynasty and let his descendants remember the event, Songtsen Gampo, ruler of the Tubo Kingdom in Tibet at that time, built a palace with a thousand rooms up on the Red Hill and named it Potala Palace. Princess Wencheng took with her medicines, books on science and technology, grain and vegetable seeds, and exquisite handicrafts of the Tang Dynasty. However, the original palace was destroyed due to a lightning strike and succeeding warfare. In the 17th century under the reign of the Fifth Dalai Lama, Potala was rebuilt. The Thirteenth Dalai Lama expanded it to today's scale. Now, Potala Palace has become a symbol of the cultural and economic communication of Tibetan people and Han People.

F: How large is the palace?

L: The palace occupies a building space of 130000 square meters. The Palace is composed of two parts, the Red Palace as the center and the White Palace as two wings. The palace was the religious and political center of ancient Tibet and the winter palace of Dalai Lamas.

F: What is the main difference between the White Palace and the Red Palace?

L: The former is for secular use while the latter is for religious use. The White Palace was once the office building of Tibet local government as well as the living quarters of Dalai Lama. Its wall was painted to white to convey peace. Look, there are three ladder stairs reaching inside of it. However, the central one was reserved for only Dalai Lamas and central government magistrates dispatched to Tibet. This way, please.

(Entering the White Palace)

Now we are on the fourth floor. This is the Great East Hall of the White Palace. Occupying a space of 717 square meters, it was the site for momentous religious and political events. This is the largest hall in the White Palace, where Dalai Lamas ascended the throne and ruled Tibet.

F: We may say this is the office area, right?

L: Yes. The fifth and sixth floors are used as the living quarters and offices of regents while the seventh floor, the top one, is the living quarters of Dalai Lama consisting of two parts named the East Chamber of Sunshine and the West Chamber of Sunshine due to the plentiful sunshine.

F: The layout is quite reasonable.

L: We have now come to the Red Palace. The Red Palace was constructed after the death of the Fifth Dalai Lama. The Red Palace is the highest part in the center that is completely devoted to religious study and Buddhist prayer.

F: Why is it called Red Palace?

L: It was painted to red to represent stateliness and power. That is where the name comes from. It consists of a complicated layout of different halls, chapels and libraries on many levels with an array of smaller galleries and winding passages: the Great West Hall, the Dharma Cave, the Saint's Chapel, the Tomb of the Thirteenth Dalai Lama, etc. The 725-square-meter Great West Hall is the largest hall, with beautiful murals painted on its inner walls. The Dharma Cave and the Saint's Chapel are the only two remained constructions of the 7th century with the statues of Songtsen Gampo, Princess Wencheng and Princess Bhrikuti inside.

F: These murals look interesting. What are these murals about?

L: These murals record the Great Fifth Dalai Lama's life. Look at this one. It is the scene of his visit to Emperor Shunzhi in Beijing in 1652. It is extraordinarily vivid, isn't it?

F: Yes, they are indeed the masterpiece of workmanship.

Useful Expressions

1. In 641, to greet his bride Princess Wencheng of the Tang Dynasty and let his descendants remember the event, Songtsen Gampo, ruler of the Tubo Kingdom in Tibet at that time, built a palace with a thousand rooms up on the Red Hill and named it Potala Palace.

641年，为了迎接他的新娘唐朝文成公主，让他的后代记住这件事，西藏吐蕃王朝统治者松赞干布在红山上建了一座千室宫殿，取名布达拉宫。

2. However, the original palace was destroyed due to a lightning strike and succeeding warfare.

然而，由于雷击和随后的战争，原来的宫殿被摧毁了。

3. The Palace is composed of two parts, the Red Palace as the center and the White Palace as two wings.

宫殿由两部分组成，红宫为中心，白宫为两翼。

4. The White Palace was once the office building of Tibet local government as well as the living quarters of Dalai Lama.

白宫曾经是西藏地方政府的办公楼，也是达赖喇嘛的生活区。

5. The former is for secular use while the latter is for religious use.

前者是世俗用途，后者是宗教用途。

6. The fifth and sixth floors are used as the living quarters and offices of regents while the seventh floor, the top one, is the living quarters of Dalai Lama consisting of two parts named the East Chamber of Sunshine and the West Chamber of Sunshine due to the plentiful sunshine.

五楼和六楼是达赖喇嘛的生活区和办公区，七楼是达赖喇嘛的寝宫日光殿，因阳光充足而得名，由东日光殿和西日光殿两部分组成。

7. It consists of a complicated layout of different halls, chapels and libraries on many levels with an array of smaller galleries and winding passages: the Great West Hall, the Dharma Cave, the Saint's Chapel, the Tomb of the Thirteenth Dalai Lama, etc.

它布局复杂，不同的大厅、小教堂和图书馆与一系列较小的画廊和蜿蜒的通道连接有西大殿、法王洞、圣观音殿、十三世达赖喇嘛墓等。

8. The Dharma Cave and the Saint's Chapel are the only two remained constructions of the 7th century with the statues of Songtsen Gampo, Princess Wencheng and Princess Bhrikuti inside.

法王洞和圣观音殿是7世纪仅存的两座建筑，里面有松赞干布、文成公主和尺尊公主的雕像。

III Exercises

1. Match the following Chinese with the correct English versions

（1）红宫　　　　　　　　　a. the White Palace
（2）白宫　　　　　　　　　b. the Dharma Cave
（3）东大殿　　　　　　　　c. stupa
（4）生活区　　　　　　　　d. religious use
（5）法王洞　　　　　　　　e. the Saint's Chapel
（6）圣观音殿　　　　　　　f. the Red Palace
（7）世俗用途　　　　　　　g. the Great East Hall
（8）宗教用途　　　　　　　h. secular use
（9）达赖喇嘛　　　　　　　i. living quarters
（10）灵塔　　　　　　　　　j. Dalai Lama

2. Translate the following Chinese into English

（1）7世纪初，松赞干布迁都拉萨后，为迎娶唐朝的文成公主，特别在红山之上修建了一座九层的千室宫殿楼宇，取名布达拉宫。

（2）整座宫殿具有藏式风格，高200余米，外观13层，实际只有9层。

（3）布达拉宫的主体建筑为白宫和红宫两部分。

（4）由松赞干布建立的吐蕃王朝灭亡之后，古老的宫堡也大部分被毁于战火。1645年，布达拉宫重建。

（5）这座古建筑群是汉藏文化交流的见证和代表。

（6）300余年来，布达拉宫大量收藏和保存了极为丰富的历史文物。其中有2500余平方米的壁画、近千座佛塔、上万座塑像、上万幅唐卡。

（7）白宫，是达赖喇嘛的冬宫，也曾是原西藏地方政府的办事机构所在地，高7层。

（8）红宫位于布达拉宫的中央位置，外墙为红色。红宫最主要的建筑是历代达赖喇嘛的灵塔殿。

Module 12 Tour of Historic Buildings

3. Fill in the blanks with appropriate words and expressions

The Potala Palace is considered as a ___(1)___ of Tibetan architecture. Located on the Red Hill in Lhasa, Tibet, this ancient architectural complex is 3700 meters above sea level and ___(2)___ an area of over 400000 square meters, measuring 360 meters from east to west and 270 meters from south to ___(3)___. The palace has 13 stories, and is 117 meters ___(4)___.

In 641, Songtsan Gambo, ___(5)___ of the Tubo Kingdom, had the Potala Palace built for Princess Wencheng of the Tang Dynasty, whom he was soon to marry. This structure was later burned to the ground during a war and was ___(6)___ in the 17th century by the Fifth Dalai Lama. Repeated repairs and expansions until 1645 finally brought the palace to its present scale. Over the past three centuries, the palace gradually became a place where the Dalai Lama lived and worked and a place for keeping the remains of successive Dalai Lama.

The stone-and-wood-structured Potala Palace ___(7)___ of the White Palace and the Red Palace. The White Palace, comprising halls, temples and courtyards, serves as the living quarters of the Dalai Lama. The Red Palace includes various chambers for ___(8)___ Buddha and chambers housing the eight stupa that contain the remains of fifth through thirteenth Dalai Lama. All the ___(9)___ are covered with gold foil. The most magnificent stupa belongs to the fifth Dalai Lama. It is 14.85 meters tall and inlaid with pearl and jade. The palace also collected a large number of sculptures, murals, scripture and other valuable cultural ___(10)___.

In 1994, the Potala Palace joined the list of world cultural heritage sites.

4. Role play

Situation: Suppose you are the local guide and are now guiding the guests to visit the Potala Palace. Make introductions and answer relevant questions.

IV Extended Reading

The Potala Palace

The Potala Palace

Module 13
Tour of Ancient Gardens

Learning Objectives

1. Master the vocabulary and sentence patterns of the tour of ancient gardens.
2. Describe the scenery of ancient gardens to the tourists.
3. Explore the cultural elements of ancient gardens.
4. Summarize the main features of ancient gardens.

Task 1　A Trip to the Summer Palace

Read and Match

a. Long Corridor
b. Longevity Hill
c. Marble Boat
d. 17-Arch Bridge

(1)

(2)

Module 13   Tour of Ancient Gardens

(3)

(4)

Situational Dialogue

扫码
听听力

A Trip to the Summer Palace

(Scene 1: As a local guide, Julie is guiding the guests to the Summer Palace. She introduces the palace and answers relevant questions.)

J: Julie, the local guide   P: Preston, tourist 1

P: Before I came to Beijing, I've heard that the Summer Palace is one of the most beautiful imperial gardens. Is that true?

J: I think you can confirm the impression by yourself after visiting it.

P: I really imagined several times that I had been here, now, my dream will come true.

J: Before we go into the Summer Palace, you'd better prepare for the crowdedness and the harmonious beauty.

P: Oh. I've got it. There will be so many people, right?

J: Yes. The Summer Palace, one of the hottest scenic spots in Beijing, is on the northwest outskirts of Beijing. It is about 20 kilometers away from the downtown. It covers a total area of over 290 hectares. It mainly consists of Longevity Hill and Kunming Lake. Their percentage is one quarter and three quarters respectively.

P: It must have taken a long time and great efforts to build such a big garden, I suppose.

J: That's true. Since the beginning of the 12th century, the garden had been constructed and reconstructed by different rulers and emperors. But until in the Qing Dynasty, the garden got the name of "Garden of Clear Ripples". And in 1750, Emperor Qianlong, the famous intelligent and capable emperor, ordered to rebuild it in order to celebrate his mother's 60th birthday. After that period, the hill and lake got the present name of Longevity Hill and Kunming Lake.

P: I see. The Longevity Hill was to show his wish of a long life for his mother.

Was Kunming Lake also specially meant in the Chinese culture?

J: The lake was called Kunming Lake because Emperor Qianlong wanted to follow the example of Emperor Wu Di in the Han Dynasty. Wu Di was an industrious and accomplished emperor in history; he trained his navy in Kunming Lake in Hans' capital Chang'an, the present Xi'an City, in Shaanxi Province.

P: When did the Summer Palace get its present name?

J: In 1888. Empress Dowager Cixi, the practical ruler of the Qing Dynasty at that time, pinched the navy fund to rebuild the garden which was plundered and destroyed by Anglo-French Allied Forces in 1860, and changed its name into the Summer Palace.

P: It's really affecting. The garden is so large. Do we have enough time to visit it through?

J: Nowadays, experts and scholars generally divide the Summer Palace into three parts according to their functions: the political area, the living area and the scenic area. We can choose some special spots of different areas to visit.

P: A good idea to grasp the masterpiece in a short time.

(Scene 2: Guiding the guests around the garden, Julie especially talks about what happened to the beautiful garden in the recent history.)

S: Stella, tourist 2   J: Julie, the local guide

S: From your description, I feel that the Summer Palace is the reflection of certain period of the Chinese history.

J: You are right. The evolution of the garden is the reflection of the development of the Chinese history. Since the 12th century, in the Liao and Jin Dynasties, the hill was called Golden Hill, the small lake located at the foot of the Golden Hill was called Golden Water Pond. In the Yuan Dynasty, the hill was changed to Jar Hill, and the lake was changed to Jar Hill Pond. In the later Ming Dynasty, the lake was called West Lake. And the wonderful scenery and structures continuously accumulated by ages provide a good foundation for the Qing Dynasty to enlarge and beautify it into Garden of Clear Ripples.

S: I heard that the beautiful and marvelous Garden of Clear Ripples was full of various kinds of structures and landscape design details as well as lots of treasures.

J: Just because of its beauty and treasures, the Anglo-French Allied Force invaded into the garden, plundered and set fire in 1860, thus the former wonder was leveled into ground.

S: It's not only a pity for the Chinese people, but also a pity for the world civilization.

J: What's more, after the reconstruction in 1888, the garden was changed into the name "Summer Palace", but it was again severely damaged by the Allied Forces of Eight Powers in 1900. In 1902, Empress Dowager Cixi ordered to reconstruct the Summer Palace for the second time. The Summer Palace today is more or less the same as the pattern rebuilt in 1903. With the ending of the Qing Dynasty, the Summer Palace was once treated as the private belongings of the Last Emperor Puyi. Later in 1928, the garden was officially opened to the public. And in 1948, the People's Government claimed the ownership.

S: From some old pictures, the Summer Palace was not as beautiful as today's scenery.

J: After the foundation of the People's Republic of China, the Chinese government gave many special protection and restoration to it for several times. In 1961, the Summer Palace was listed as one of the important historical monuments under special preservation by the Chinese government, and in 1998, it was listed in the World Heritage List by UNESCO.

S: I know it's one of the most popular parks in Beijing.

J: Yes. It's the best-preserved imperial garden in the world and one of the largest of its kind still in existence in China today.

Useful Expressions

1. The Summer Palace is one of the most beautiful imperial gardens.
颐和园是最美丽的皇家园林之一。

2. It mainly consists of Longevity Hill and Kunming Lake.
它主要由万寿山和昆明湖组成。

3. It must have taken a long time and great efforts to build such a big garden.
建造这么大的园林一定花了很长时间，付出了很大的努力。

4. Was Kunming Lake also specially meant in Chinese culture?
昆明湖在中国文化中也有特殊的含义吗？

5. When did the Summer Palace get its present name?
颐和园什么时候有了现在的名字？

6. The evolution of the garden is the reflection of the development of the Chinese history.
园林的演变反映了中国历史的发展。

7. After the reconstruction in 1888, the garden was changed into the name "Summer Palace".
1888年重建后，园林改名为颐和园。

8. It's the best-preserved imperial garden in the world and one of the largest of its kind still in existence in China today.
它是世界上保存最完好的皇家园林，也是中国现存规模最大的皇家园林之一。

Exercises

1. Match the following Chinese with the correct English versions

（1）听鹂馆　　　　　　　　　　a. Garden of Virtuous Harmony

(2) 永寿斋　　　　　　　　b. Chamber of Collecting Books
(3) 宜芸馆　　　　　　　　c. House of Eternal Longevity
(4) 文昌阁　　　　　　　　d. Fan-Shaped Hall
(5) 德和园　　　　　　　　e. the Hall for Listening to Orioles
(6) 苏州街　　　　　　　　f. Garden of Harmonious Interest
(7) 谐趣园　　　　　　　　g. Suzhou Street
(8) 铜牛　　　　　　　　　h. The six bridges on the West Dyke
(9) 西堤六桥　　　　　　　i. Bronze Ox
(10) 扇面殿　　　　　　　　j. Pavilion of Flourishing Culture
(11) 耶律楚材祠　　　　　　k. Spring Heralding Pavilion
(12) 知春亭　　　　　　　　l. Yelvchucai Temple

2. Translate the following Chinese into English

(1) 颐和园是北京最热门的景点之一,位于北京的西北郊。
(2) 它离市中心大约20千米。它的总面积超过290公顷。
(3) 直到清朝,这座花园才被称为"清漪园"。
(4) 1888年,当时的清朝实权统治者慈禧太后挪用海军经费,重建了1860年被英法联军掠夺和摧毁的花园,并将其更名为"颐和园"。
(5) 1888年重建后,清漪园更名为颐和园,但在1900年再次被八国联军严重破坏。

3. Fill in the blanks with appropriate words and expressions

　　The Summer Palace, up to now, is the best-　(1)　 and the largest 　(2)　 garden in China. It used to be an imperial 　(3)　 in the Qing Dynasty for the purpose of enjoying the picturesque 　(4)　 in Beijing. The Kunming Lake is the major scenic spot in the Summer Palace. Many views were 　(5)　 near the lake. To the west of the lake is the West 　(6)　, which were in 　(7)　 of the Su Causeway in the West Lake in Hangzhou. In the middle of the Summer Palace, you will come across many buildings along an 　(8)　 leading downhill, among which Foxiangge was the largest project in the Summer Palace, which commands a full view of the scenery in scores of miles. Moreover, the Long Gallery is the most 　(9)　 scene. It was added to the Guinness World Record for it is the 　(10)　 of its kind in the world.

4. Role play

　　Suppose you are the local guide. Try to introduce the scenic spots of the Summer Palace to your tourists.

Ⅳ Extended Reading

The Imperial Garden—The Summer Palace

Module 13 Tour of Ancient Gardens

Task 2 A Trip to the Humble Administrator's Garden

Read and Match

a. Hall of Distant Fragrance
b. 18 Camellias Hall
c. 36 Pairs of Mandarin Duck's Hall
d. Fragrant Islet

(1)

(2)

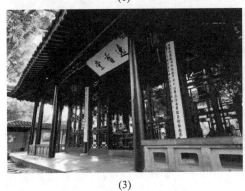

(3)

(4)

Situational Dialogue

A Trip to the Humble Administrator's Garden

(The tour guide and tourists are on the way to the Humble Administrator's Garden.)

G: the tour guide   T: the tourist

G: Our next destination is the Humble Administrator's Garden, which is also called Zhuozheng Garden.

T: Great! I heard that it is one of the four most famous gardens in China. I can't wait to get there.

G: Let's go!

T: By the way, can you tell us something about the four famous gardens in China?

G: Of course. The four famous gardens in China are the Summer Palace in Beijing, the Summer Resort of Chengde in Hebei Province, the Humble Administrator's Garden and the Lingering Garden in Suzhou.

T: Are there any differences?

G: The Summer Palace and the Summer Resort of Chengde are imperial gardens, while the Humble Administrator's Garden and the Lingering Garden are private gardens.

T: Imperial gardens must be much larger than private gardens. Are there any other differences between the imperial gardens and private gardens in China?

G: Yes. Since imperial gardens are much larger, there are always real lakes and hills in imperial gardens.

T: That must be very magnificent!

G: Sure, while there are ponds and rockeries in private gardens instead.

T: Interesting!

G: Imperial gardens were built for emperors, so the buildings there are magnificent. The idea of private gardens is to seek the quiet retreat from the hustle and bustle, so the buildings in private gardens are usually of simplicity.

T: The owners of private gardens must have lived a free, quiet and pleasant life.

G: It may be true. So let's go and have an unforgettable experience.

(They are arriving at the Humble Administrator's Garden.)

G: Now we are in front of the gate of the famous Humble Administrator's Garden.

T: Actually, I am interested in the owner of the Humble Administrator's Garden. Who built such a beautiful garden?

G: The garden's site was initially the residence and garden of Lu Guimeng, a Tang Dynasty scholar over 1100 years ago. Later in the Yuan Dynasty about 800 years ago, it became a monastery garden for Dahong Temple.

T: But I heard that the first owner was Wang Xianchen.

G: Yes. In the Ming Dynasty (1510), he retired to his native home of Suzhou after a long persecution by the East Imperial Secret Service, and began to work on the garden.

T: It's not an easy task for a person to build such a garden. How did he make it?

G: This garden, meant to express his fine taste, was designed in collaboration with his friend Wen Zhengming, the renowned artist, Suzhou native.

T: I know him. He was an artist as famous as Tang Bohu!

G: Right! The garden was built to its current size, with numerous trees and pavilions.

T: How long did it take to construct the garden?

G: It took 16 years until 1526 to complete the project.

T: Wow, but why did he name it "Humble Administrator's Garden"?

G: The name is from an essay called "To cultivate my garden and sell my vegetable crop is the policy of humble man". This verse symbolized Wang's desire to retire from politics and adopt an easy life.

T: Oh, I see.

G: Unfortunately, Wang died soon and Wang's son lost the garden to pay gambling debts, and it has changed hands many times since.

T: What a pity!

Useful Expressions

1. I heard that it is one of the four most famous gardens in China.
我听说它是中国四大名园之一。
2. Can you tell us something about the four famous gardens in China?
你能给我们讲讲中国四大名园吗?
3. Are there any other differences between the imperial gardens and private gardens in China?
中国皇家园林和私家园林还有什么不同之处吗?
4. How long did it take to construct the garden?
建造这个花园花了多长时间?

 Exercises

1. Match the following Chinese with the correct English versions

(1) 复园　　　　　a. Gui Tian Yuan Ju
(2) 兰雪堂　　　　b. Zhuiyun Peak
(3) 归田园居　　　c. Orchid Snow Hall
(4) 杜鹃花节　　　d. Tianquan Pavilion
(5) 缀云峰　　　　e. Fu Yuan
(6) 梧桐树　　　　f. Watching-clear-water Building
(7) 澄观楼　　　　g. Phoenix tree
(8) 天泉亭　　　　h. Pagoda Reflection Pavilion

(9) 雅石斋　　　　　　　　i. Azalea Festival

　　(10) 塔影亭　　　　　　　　j. Elegant Stone House

2. Translate the following Chinese into English

(1) 上有天堂，下有苏杭。

(2) 从外看，天泉亭是两层，但是进去看，你会发现它只有一层。

(3) 透过四周的玻璃往外看，人们可以清楚地看到周围的景色，仿佛在欣赏一幅长画卷。

(4) 这个园林刚建成时就和现在一般大小，种满了树，有许多亭子。

(5) 荷花出淤泥而不染。

3. Fill in the blanks with appropriate words and expressions

Chinese garden includes both the vast gardens of the ＿＿(1)＿＿ and smaller gardens built by scholars, ＿＿(2)＿＿, and former government officials. The gardens are filled with architecture: halls, pavilions, ＿＿(3)＿＿, galleries, bridges and towers, ＿＿(4)＿＿ a large part of the space. Chinese gardens are usually connected by ＿＿(5)＿＿ paths and zigzag galleries, so there is a "beautiful ＿＿(6)＿＿, anti-symmetry" in them. While the Western model is an ordered garden laid out in carefully ＿＿(7)＿＿ geometric and often symmetrical lines. Lawns and hedges in a Western formal garden need to be kept neatly clipped.

4. Role play

Situation: Suppose you are the guide of Humble Administrator's Garden, try to introduce the "borrowed view from afar" to the foreign tourists.

Ⅳ Extended Reading

Humble Administrator's Garden

Task 3　A Trip to Qinghui Garden

Ⅰ Read and Match

　　a. Cloud Reading Study　　　　　　b. Clear Riffle Pavilion
　　c. Boat Hall　　　　　　　　　　　d. Crystal Stream Thatched Cottage

Module 13 Tour of Ancient Gardens

(1) (2) (3) (4)

‖ Situational Dialogue

A Trip to Qinghui Garden

(The tour guide and tourists are on the way to Qinghui Garden.)

G: the tour guide   T: the tourist

G: Good morning, everyone. Today we are going to visit Qinghui Garden. Situated in Daliang Street, Shunde District, Foshan City, Guangdong Province. Built during the reign of Emperor Jiaqing, Qinghui (Pure Light) Garden is regarded as one of the four major gardens in Guangdong Province, the other three being the Shady Cottage of Panyu, Liang Garden in Foshan City, Keyuan Garden of Dongguan City.

T: It sounds great! It must have a long history and rich cultural heritage.

G: Yes. Qinghui was built on the garden of the Huang Residence. In 1607, a scholar called Huang Shijun came first in the imperial examination and was hence appointed the Director of the Board of Rites as well as the Grand Secretary in the imperial court. To glorify his family name, Huang as a most powerful official in 1621 had built the Ancestral Hall of the Huang Family, the Tianzhang Pavilion, and Ling Azhi Pavilion. During Emperor Qianlong's reign in the Qing Dynasty, the

Huang family declined and the courtyard became much deserted till Long Yingshi, another laureate candidate in the imperial examination bought it as the family residence. Long's son also performed well in the imperial examination in 1788 and was granted a high-ranking position. After his retirement, he had the family residence rebuilt. Comparing parental grace to the pure light of the sun, the three characters "Qing Hui Yuan" was written on the front door of the residence by Li Zhaoluo, the most renowned calligrapher in Jiangsu. After constant efforts by five generations of the Long Family, the landscape garden as a distinctive example of the Lingnan (the Pearl River Delta area) School took shape.

T: What are the characteristics of Qinghui Garden?

G: Qinghui Garden is featured firstly by its utilitarian considerations for the subtropical climate in southern China. To ensure ventilation, it adopts an innovative layout: buildings are so arranged that it is sparse in the front while dense at the back, low in the front while high at the back. Sparseness, however, is by no means void, density never congestion. Garden buildings are bright and brisk enjoying open space.

T: What are the differences between Qinghui Garden and other gardens?

G: Qinghui Garden exhibits typical features of the Pearl River Delta. First, waterscape takes a heavy weight in its layout. This is in conformity with the local landform of Shunde where rivers and streams form a network dotted with abounding blessed fishponds. Second, buildings are adorned with subtropical flowers and fruits such as bananas, pineapples and carambola carved on lime, wood or glass. Third, many of the buildings were ingeniously designed to exhibit the local flavor. In addition to the aesthetic value embodied in its layout, shape, color, texture and contour outline, the garden is known for its taste of fine arts, literature and calligraphy. Sculptures inlaid on walls or eaves, handwriting by master calligraphers made into plaques on the wall, poems or legendary figures engraved on latticed windows, all add to the cultural and aesthetic value of the structures, thus creating a space well-worth exploring.

T: What scenic spots are worth seeing in Qinghui Garden?

G: The most outstanding and best-known attractions in the Garden are the Muying Gulley, Phoenix Peak, Cloud Reading Study, Fragrance Hall, Crystal Stream Thatched Cottage, Clear Riffle Pavilion, Boat Hall and Bamboo Garden.

T: Wow. Let's go and take a look.

Useful Expressions

1. Comparing parental grace to the pure light of the sun, the three characters "Qing Hui Yuan" was written on the front door of the residence by Li Zhaoluo, the most renowned calligrapher in Jiangsu.

江苏最负盛名的书法家李兆洛将父母之恩比作太阳之光,将"清晖园"三个大字写在府邸的前门上。

2. Qinghui Garden is featured firstly by its utilitarian considerations for the subtropical climate in southern China.

对中国南方亚热带气候的实用性考虑是清晖园的首要特点。

3. Qinghui Garden exhibits typical features of the Pearl River Delta.

清晖园展现了珠江三角洲的典型特征。

4. In addition to the aesthetic value embodied in its layout, shape, color, texture and contour outline, the garden is known for its taste of fine arts, literature and calligraphy.

园林的美学价值除了体现在布局、形状、颜色、纹理和轮廓方面,还以其美术、文学和书法的品位而闻名。

5. What scenic spots are worth seeing in Qinghui Garden?

清晖园有哪些景点值得一看?

Exercises

1. Match the following Chinese with the correct English versions

（1）竹苑　　　　　　　a. Muying Gully
（2）沐英涧　　　　　　b. Phoenix Rockery
（3）凤来峰　　　　　　c. Fragrance Hall
（4）余荫山房　　　　　d. Bamboo Garden
（5）可园　　　　　　　e. the Shady Cottage
（6）留芬阁　　　　　　f. Liang Garden
（7）梁园　　　　　　　g. Keyuan Garden

2. Translate the following Chinese into English

（1）清晖园与番禺余荫山房、佛山梁园、东莞可园并称为"广东四大名园"。

（2）园的正门上方有江苏著名书法家李兆洛书写的"清晖园"三字,以喻父母之恩如日光和煦照耀。

（3）清晖园的造园特色首先在于园林的实用性,为适应南方炎热气候,形成前疏后密、前低后高的独特布局。

（4）清晖园有着鲜明的岭南建筑特色。

（5）园林的美学价值除了体现在布局、形状、颜色、纹理和轮廓方面,还以其美术、文学和书法的品位而闻名。

3. Fill in the blanks with appropriate words and expressions

Qinghui Garden Museum is a national key ＿＿＿(1)＿＿＿ relic preservation unit and a national 4A level scenic spot. It's also one of the Top Ten Classic Chinese Gardens, and one of the Top Four ＿＿＿(2)＿＿＿ Gardens. Profound in cultural background, Qinghui Garden initially used to be a ＿＿＿(3)＿＿＿ of Huang Shijun, who was a Zhuangyuan in Wanli Period of the Ming Dynasty. Zhuangyuan refers to the person who took the first place in the highest ____(4)____ examination. When it came to Qianlong Period of the Qing Dynasty, the mansion was ____(5)____ by a Jinshi, Long Yingshi. Jinshi refers to the person who gained a good score in the highest imperial examinations. Through generations of endeavors of Long's family, this garden formed its pattern and style. At the end of the 1990s, Shunde government put great manpower, material and financial resources to renovate and expand the garden to ____(6)____ its beauty as a famous ancient garden. At present, Qinghui Garden ____(7)____ an area of 22500 square meters.

4. Role play

Situation: As the guide of Qinghui Garden, you are guiding the foreign guests around the garden and introduce the view.

Ⅳ Extended Reading

Must-see Attractions in Qinghui Garden

Must-see Attractions in Qinghui Garden

Module 14
Tour of Ancient Cities and Ancient Towns

Learning Objectives

1. Master the vocabulary and sentence patterns of the tour of ancient cities and ancient towns.
2. Describe the scenery of ancient cities and ancient towns to the tourists.
3. Explore the cultural elements of ancient cities and ancient towns.
4. Summarize the main features of ancient cities and ancient towns.

Task 1   A Trip to Wuzhen

Read and Match

a. Wuzhen Ancient Stage
b. Fengyuan Double Bridge
c. Blue Cloth with Design in White
d. Former Residence of Mao Dun

(1)

(2)

(3)　　　　　　　　　　　　　　　(4)

Situational Dialogue

A Trip of Wuzhen

(The local guide Xiao Wang is taking his tour group around the town of Wuzhen.)

W: Xiao Wang, the local guide　　T: the tourist

W: Hello, everyone, welcome to Wuzhen. Chinese people say that unless you visit the Great Wall then you haven't been to China; for any visit south of the Yangtze River, one place not to be missed is the town of Wuzhen.

T: I am wondering why you compare Wuzhen with the Great Wall.

W: Sometimes I think that you may not visit the Great Wall, but you cannot miss the small town of Wuzhen. Over the past 1000 years, there were no obvious changes in the water systems and life styles in Wuzhen, which is a museum that shows the ancient civilization.

T: Can you tell me where Wuzhen lies?

W: It is located in the center of the six ancient towns south of the Yangtze River, 17 kilometers north of the city of Tongxiang.

T: What are the features of Wuzhen?

W: If you ask me about the features of Wuzhen, I suggest travelling there to see with your own eyes. Wuzhen displays its two-thousand-year history in its ancient stone bridge floating on mild water, its stone pathways between the mottled walls and its delicate wood carvings. Also, it gives a unique experience through its profound cultural background, setting it apart from other towns.

T: Tell us something more about the culture behind.

W: It is said that people have lived in Wuzhen for 7000 years and over time it has produced a galaxy of talents. Mao Dun, an outstanding modern Chinese writer, was born here and his masterpiece, *The Lin's Shop*, describes vividly the life of Wuzhen. In 2005, Wuzhen was acclaimed as one of the ten top famous towns in China, ranking first among the six ancient towns south of the Yangtze River.

T: What about the layout of Wuzhen?

W: Wuzhen's uniqueness lies in its layout, being 2 kilometers long and divided into six districts, which are as follows: Traditional Workshops District, Traditional Local-Styled Dwelling Houses District, Traditional Culture District, Traditional Food and Beverage District, Traditional Shops and Stores District, and Water Township Customs and Living District. Wandering along the circular route created by these six districts, you will enjoy the atmosphere of the traditional cultures and the original ancient features of the town that have been preserved intact.

T: It sounds great.

Useful Expressions

1. Chinese people say that unless you visit the Great Wall then you haven't been to China; for any visit south of the Yangtze River, one place not to be missed is the town of Wuzhen.

中国人常说,没有到过长城,就不算到过中国;而参观江南,一个不能错过的地方就是乌镇。

2. I am wondering why you compare Wuzhen with the Great Wall.

我想知道你为什么把乌镇和长城相提并论。

3. What are the features of Wuzhen?

乌镇有什么特色?

4. In 2005, Wuzhen was acclaimed as one of the ten top famous towns in China, ranking first among the six ancient towns south of the Yangtze River.

2005 年,乌镇被誉为中国十大名镇之一,位居江南六大古镇之首。

5. Wuzhen displays its two-thousand-year history in its ancient stone bridge floating on mild water, its stone pathways between the mottled walls and its delicate wood carvings.

浮在安静水面上的古石桥、斑驳墙壁之间的石道和精致的木雕,都是乌镇两千多年历史的体现。

6. What about the layout of Wuzhen?

乌镇的布局是怎样的?

7. Wandering along the circular route created by these six districts, you will enjoy the atmosphere of the traditional cultures and the original ancient features of the town that have been preserved intact.

沿着这六个区打造的环线漫步,你会感受到古城的传统文化氛围和被完整保留下来的原始古城风貌。

Exercises

1. Match the following Chinese with the correct English versions

（1）木雕陈列馆　　　　　　a. Hengyitang Chinese Medicine Shop

（2）江南百床馆　　　　　　b. Historic Wuzhen Post Office

（3）花鼓戏　　　　　　　　c. Yida Silk Store

（4）恒益堂药店　　　　　　d. Wood Carving Museum

（5）乌镇老邮局　　　　　　e. Jiangnan Hundred-bed Museum

（6）益大丝号作坊　　　　　f. Chinese Foot-binding Culture Museum

（7）中国三寸金莲馆　　　　g. Huagu Opera

2. Translate the following Chinese into English

（1）桐乡市以北17千米处就是江南六大古镇之一——乌镇。这里有古老的石桥、安静的河水、斑驳墙壁之间的石头小径，以及精美的石雕。

（2）乌镇有6万人口，尽管其中只有12000是常驻居民。

（3）这座古城有2千米长，分为六个区域：传统的手工作坊区、传统的当地特色住宅区、传统的文化区、传统的食物和饮料区、传统的商店区，以及水乡风俗和生活区。

（4）这里所有的建筑都面朝河流，水道就是街道，岸边就是市场。这座古镇拥有7000年历史，而且位于杭州、苏州和上海的三角地带。

（5）中国当代著名的作家茅盾就出生在乌镇，他著名的作品《林家铺子》写的就是乌镇的生活。

（6）1991年，乌镇被列为省级历史和文化古镇，在江南六大古镇中排名第一。

3. Fill in the blanks with appropriate words and expressions

East Street has been a prosperous ＿＿＿(1)＿＿＿ center of Wuzhen since ancient times. More than 700 local households are established along this street, most engaging in traditional ＿＿＿(2)＿＿＿ that visitors can admire and purchase.

Many interesting ＿＿＿(3)＿＿＿ centers are also here, including the Wood Carving Museum and Hundred-bed Museum. Take in the Huagu Opera ＿＿＿(4)＿＿＿ on a hundred-year-old stage, or delight in the daring acrobatics and martial arts that are performed on boats just offshore.

Several local workshops and stores that have been operating for over a century also ＿＿＿(5)＿＿＿ glimpses into a past life. Check out the Hengyitang Chinese Medicine Shop and the Historic Wuzhen Post Office.

For a look at the rich silk industry, visit the Yida Silk Store, ＿＿＿(6)＿＿＿ from 1875, to see beautiful brocades being hand-woven by skilled ＿＿＿(7)＿＿＿.

4. Role play

Suppose you are the local guide of Wuzhen, your American friend Harry comes to visit Wuzhen the first time. And now you arrive at the Former Residence of Mao Dun.

Module 14　Tour of Ancient Cities and Ancient Towns

Ⅳ Extended Reading

The Town's Name Origin

Task 2　A Trip to Zhouzhuang

I Read and Match

a. Shen Wansan's Underwater Tomb　　b. Shen House
c. Quanfu Tower　　　　　　　　　　d. Twin Bridges

(1)

(2)

(3)

(4)

Situational Dialogue

A Trip to Zhouzhuang

(The tour guide and tourists arrive at a towering archway and begin to have their tour of the First Water Town in China.)

G: the tour guide   T: the tourist

G: Now we arrive at Zhouzhuang, "the First Water Town in China".

T: Why do people call it the first one?

G: A good question. You'll see it is surrounded and divided by lakes and rivers, 14 stone bridges crossing the rivers, showing distinctive views of the water town. It's really worth its reputation.

T: Oh, I see. What about other water towns? Are they as beautiful as the first one?

G: Well, other water towns include Zhouzhuang's neighbours Tongli, Luzhi, Guangfu and Mudu, also Wuzhen and Xitang in Jiaxing, Zhejiang Province and so on. As to their beauty, I would say each has its own merits.

T: I've never been to other water towns, but I think visiting Zhouzhuang here is just enough for me to enjoy riverside towns and scenery in China.

G: Absolutely right. It's the most typical one and we call it "Venice of the Orient". Look ahead, please.

T: Is this an archway?

G: Yes, it bears four Chinese characters "Zhen Feng Ze Guo". They are handwriting of Shen Peng, a famous calligrapher.

T: Are there any special meanings about these characters?

G: Yeah, "Ze Guo" means a place which is surrounded by water. It indicates Zhouzhuang is a water town.

T: You've told us Zhouzhuang was called Zhenfengli in ancient times on the way. Is it the name of the old town?

G: Exactly.

T: What about these characters in green? I've noticed they are equal in number on both pillars.

G: Well, we call it antithetical couplet, or poetic couplet. It's usually seen on both sides of doors.

T: Really interesting.

G: Zhouzhuang is also renowned for its typical southern China riverside scenery, elegantly-crafted bridges, murmuring streams and classical dwellings.

T: Sounds wonderful and I'd like to see it with my own eyes.

Module 14 Tour of Ancient Cities and Ancient Towns

G: Let's enjoy its beautiful scenery. Follow me, please.

(The tour guide and tourists arrive at Shuang Qiao, also called the Twin Bridges)

G: Now we have come to the Twin Bridges. They are old bridges built in Wanli's reign of the Ming Dynasty and have a history of about 500 years. They are the symbol of Zhouzhuang.

T: What wonderful bridges! They remind me of Chen's painting exhibited in a gallery of New York in 1984. I remember the title of the painting is *Memory of Hometown*.

G: You really have a good memory. And now let me introduce the Twin Bridges. I think you have noticed there are two bridges, Shide Bridge and Yong'an Bridge.

T: Why do people call them Twin Bridges? Do they look like each other?

G: Well, Shide Bridge is east-west and has a round arch, while Yong'an Bridge is north-south and has a square arch. They span over two criss-cross rivers and connect at the middle, so people call them the Twin Bridges.

T: And I know they have got another name of Key Bridge.

G: Yes, linked together, they look like an ancient key, right?

T: Oh. I see. It's really unique in style in China, even over the world.

G: That's why people call them the symbol of Zhouzhuang.

T: The bridges really deserve their reputation. Look, a boat is gliding through Shide Bridge. And what is the lady singing about?

G: You mean the barge-woman? Well, she's singing a local boat song.

T: It's really wonderful just standing here. I'd like to take photos here. Would you do me a favor?

G: OK. Attention, please! Perfect!

T: Thank you. Some students are painting here, but their paintings are not about the Twin Bridges.

G: Let me see. It's Taiping Bridge. That would be another story and I will tell you on the way.

Useful Expressions

1. Why do people call it the First Water Town in China?
为什么人们叫它中国第一水乡?

2. What about other water towns? Are they as beautiful as the first one?
其他水乡呢?它们和第一水乡一样漂亮吗?

3. Are there any special meanings about these characters?
这些字有什么特别的意思吗?

4. Why do people call them Twin Bridges?
为什么人们叫它们双桥?

5. And I know they have got another name of Key Bridge.

我知道它们还有另一个名字——钥匙桥。

Exercises

1. Match the following Chinese with the correct English versions

(1) 新牌楼　　　　　　　　　a. Zhengu Hall New Archway
(2) 江南人家　　　　　　　　b. Zhang House
(3) 周庄博物馆　　　　　　　c. Taiping Bridge
(4) 古牌楼　　　　　　　　　d. Ancient Archway
(5) 贞固堂　　　　　　　　　e. Zhouzhuang Museum
(6) 古戏台　　　　　　　　　f. Old Opera Stage
(7) 太平桥　　　　　　　　　g. Southern Yangtze River Family
(8) 富安桥　　　　　　　　　h. Fu'an Bridge
(9) 张厅　　　　　　　　　　i. Ye Chuchen's Former Residence
(10) 叶楚伧故居　　　　　　 j. New Archway

2. Translate the following Chinese into English

(1) 周庄是一个有着900多年历史的江南水乡古镇。
(2) 周庄是典型的江南水乡，有人把它比作"东方威尼斯"。
(3) 石牌楼上面镌刻有"贞丰泽国"四个字，为著名书法家沈鹏所写。
(4) 世德桥是东西走向的圆形拱桥，永安桥是南北走向的正方形拱桥。它们横跨两条交叉的河流，并在中间连接，所以人们称它们为"双桥"。
(5) 这条古街俗称"一步街"，因为它很窄，一步就可以跨过。

3. Fill in the blanks with appropriate words and expressions

In Suzhou's suburbs, there are some well-preserved old towns. Among them, more than 900-year-old Zhouzhuang is the most famous one, _____(1)_____ as the First Water Town in China.

This old town owes its fame to the oil _____(2)_____ entitled *Memory of Hometown* and its bridge scenery _____(3)_____ on the First Day Cover for the United Nations' 1985 International Stamp Festival.

Actually, Zhouzhuang was well known in China as _____(4)_____ as the Song Dynasty, about 1000 years ago, when southern China was as prosperous as northern China. There has been a popular _____(5)_____ that up above there is paradise, down below there are Suzhou and Hangzhou, and between them there is a town known as Zhouzhuang. During that time, _____(6)_____ China has been much stable, so more and _____(7)_____ northerners moved here to avoid the epidemic wars. They also brought the advanced culture to southern China where people were mild by nature. _____(8)_____ on, architecture art of its own style in the areas south of the Yangtze River has been developed, with water town as the most typical.

Module 14 Tour of Ancient Cities and Ancient Towns

4. Role play

Situation: Suppose you are the local guide of Zhouzhuang, your American guest Harry comes to visit Zhouzhuang the first time. And now you arrive at the Twin Bridges.

Ⅳ Extended Reading

Natural Features of Zhouzhuang

Task 3   A Trip to the Old Town of Lijiang

Ⅰ Read and Match

a. Mosuo people   b. Classic Naxi Music
c. The Ancient Tea Horse Road d. Dongba Symbols

(1)

(2)

(3)

(4)

Situational Dialogue

A Trip to Lijiang

(Sarah, a tourist, is talking with Xiao Wang, the local guide about Classic Naxi Music Concert in Lijiang.)

W: Xiao Wang, the local guide　　S: Sarah, tourist 1　　D: Danny, tourist 2

S: Excuse me. May I ask where we could get the tickets for the Classic Naxi Music Concert?

W: Do you mean the concert hosted by Mr. Xuan Ke?

S: Yes.

W: Go all the way down the street, turn left when you see the post office, and turn right when you see a yogurt place. Then you will see the box office and the theater 100 meters away. Maybe a lot of people are standing in a line to buy the tickets now.

S: Wow, you know this place well. Thank you very much!

W: Hmm, I have been here for ten years already.

S: What do you think of the people in this place?

W: People in this place are not busy at all. Lijiang used to be a trade center on the Ancient Tea Horse Road, but now it is a representative of the slow-down lifestyle. Everyone here is not in a hurry. We get up when we wake up, we wander in the town leisurely, and we enjoy the tea without thinking about anything.

S: Your description is absolutely right. Some people here are kind of party animals and go to bed until they are too tired to drink and sing songs.

W: Oh, yes. You can find great singers, dancers and bars here.

(On the second day)

W: How was the concert yesterday?

S: Very good. The spirit that Mr. Xuan Ke did his best to preserve Naxi classic music inspired us.

D: I admired all the players. They are preserving as well as passing down the art. The clear voice of the soprano is still in my ears.

S: Could you please tell us more about Dongba Symbols?

W: Dongba Symbols are a system of pictographic glyphs used by the Naxi people. They were developed in the 7th century, and are also called "the living fossil" together with Naxi Classic Music.

D: When did the Ancient Tea Horse Road come into being?

W: About one thousand years ago, tea in Yunnan, one of the first tea-producing regions, was transported to India, Tibet and central China by people and horses. The network of horse caravan paths among the mountains in Southwest China was named the Ancient Tea Horse Road.

D: I found that the architecture style in Lijiang is different from buildings in other places of China. Am I right?

W: Yes. The Lijiang Old Town is famous for its orderly system of waterways and bridges.

S: I found it easy to get lost in the Old Town.

W: The Old Town is a maze of winding cobblestone streets, built by Mu Family, who ruled the town during the Ming and Qing Dynasties. The layout of the town was established to conform to the flow of three streams in adherence to Feng Shui design. But there is no need to worry, because every turn leads one to some new interesting spots.

Useful Expressions

1. May I ask where we could get the tickets for the Classic Naxi Music Concert?
我想问问我们在哪里能买到纳西古乐音乐会的票呢？
2. Could you please tell us more about Dongba Symbols?
你能给我们讲讲东巴文吗？
3. When did the Ancient Tea Horse Road come into being?
茶马古道是什么时候形成的？
4. The Lijiang Old Town is famous for its orderly system of waterways and bridges.
丽江古城以它规划齐整的水路和桥闻名。

 ||| **Exercises**

1. Match the following Chinese with the correct English versions

（1）城墙　　　　　　　a. residential house
（2）木府　　　　　　　b. city wall
（3）三眼井　　　　　　c. totem column
（4）石拱桥　　　　　　d. Sifang Street
（5）四方街　　　　　　e. Three-Eye Well
（6）民居　　　　　　　f. Mu's Mansion
（7）图腾柱　　　　　　g. stone arch bridge

2. Translate the following Chinese into English

（1）丽江曾经是茶马古道上重要的贸易中心，现在它是一种慢节奏生活的代表。
（2）我们睡到自然醒，在镇子里闲逛，静静地喝茶，什么也不想。

(3) 东巴文是纳西族人使用的一套象形符号。东巴文早在7世纪时被发明,现在和纳西古乐一起被称为"活化石"。

(4) 古城像一座鹅卵石铺就的蜿蜒小路的迷宫。这座城是明清两代统治此地的木家建造的。

(5) 丽江是中国保存最完好的古城之一,1997年被列入《世界遗产名录》。

3. Fill in the blanks with appropriate words and expressions

Now, we are at the center of the town—Sifang Street. This is an open market of about 400 ____(1)____ meters. It takes the shape of a square official seal. From here, five streets lead to every ____(2)____ of the town. The town ____(3)____ to be the market center on the Ancient Tea Horse Road. The houses in Lijiang are a superb synthesis of the ancient ____(4)____ of dwellings found in the Central Plains and those of the Bai and Tibetan peoples. The houses have tiled roofs and external corridors or verandas. The most common forms are called "sanfang yi zhaobi and sihe wu tianjing". The former design ____(5)____ of a main house, two side buildings. And a screen wall ____(6)____ the main house. The latter consists of a main house and houses on each of the other three sides. Naxi people have also developed their own unique style ____(7)____ on local conditions and traditions. They are innovative in different ____(8)____, such as design, earthquake resistance, sun protection, and décor.

4. Role play

Situation: Suppose you are the local guide of Lijiang, your American guest Harry comes to visit Lijiang the first time. And now you arrive at the Sifang Street.

Ⅳ Extended Reading

Picturesque Lijiang

Picturesque Lijiang

Task 4　A Trip to the Ancient City of Pingyao

Ⅰ Read and Match

a. Zhenguo Temple　　　　　b. Rishengchang Exchange Shop
c. Qiao's Compound　　　　 d. Shuanglin Temple

Module 14 Tour of Ancient Cities and Ancient Towns

(1)　　　　　　　　　　(2)

(3)　　　　　　　　　　(4)

📖 ‖ Situational Dialogue

A Trip to the Ancient City of Pingyao

(Wang Jing is taking Judy around the Pingyao Ancient City. They are walking along Nandajie Street of the Pingyao Ancient City.)

W: Wang Jing, the guide   J: Judy, the tourist

W: Judy, here we are, the Pingyao Ancient City.

J: Well, I want to know more about the Chinese culture. I don't want to take photos only. I believe Pingyao Ancient City has a long history and a brilliant culture.

W: Very good. Now, we are walking along Nandajie Street. It is also called Ming and Qing Street. It is one of the best places where you can explore the ancient Chinese culture.

J: Marvelous! I love these traditional Chinese buildings. I don't like the concrete forest in the city. Look! What are the rows of shops along the street?

W: The place where we are standing is a bazaar. Here are over 700 stores and shops. Most of these time-honored stores continue to thrive to this day.

J: What are available in the shops? It seems to me they are all curiosity shops.

W: There is a dazzling array of art wares: antiques, furniture, ancient coins, Chinese paintings, jade ware, lacquer ware and traditional folk clothing, etc. You can buy some souvenirs if you like.

J: I'd like to, but I want to go sightseeing first. The traditional buildings here are really attractive. If I had enough money, I would have bought one of the compounds, not souvenirs only.

W: By the way, do you know which one is the earliest bank in China? You can find the answers when you enter the Rishengchang Exchange Shop.

J: The question you asked is just the answer. I guess it is Rishengchang Exchange Shop, am I right?

W: You are right. By the way, you told me just now you haven't enough money to buy a compound in Pingyao. Why not borrow some money from this bank?

J: I'd like to. I hope that you could help me if the bank asks me to provide the financial guarantee.

W: I'm afraid that I cannot. I'm only a poor guide. However, Pingyao used to be the financial center of China. You may borrow some money here.

J: Really?

W: There were twenty-two banks in Pingyao out of the total fifty-one in China during the Qing Dynasty. Among these many banks, Rishengchang at No. 105 in Nandajie was the most famous.

J: I see. The first bank must be the most famous one.

(Judy is standing in front of the Rishengchang Exchange Shop. Wang Jing continues to introduce the glory of the banking business in Pingyao. He also briefly introduces the security company which used to protect the property of the bankers.)

W: Here is the Rishengchang Exchange Shop. It used to be the most prestigious bank in Pingyao Ancient City, as well as in the North China.

J: Oh. What a surprise! This bank looks like a Chinese classic garden. I think the value of the building itself is more than that of the deposits in the bank.

W: You're right. Unfortunately, the bank became bankrupt 100 years ago. However, Rishengchang Exchange Shop is very important because it was the first bank in China.

J: But it looks like a Chinese garden. I have mistaken it for a big garden if you hadn't told me it was a bank.

W: The structure of the house is typical of a bank. Three rooms in the middle courtyard are the exchange center. The counters are arranged on either side of the front yard. Guest rooms are located in the wings beside the main hall.

J: It's really a big banking mansion. The complex is worthy of a lot of money, and the banker must be an upstart.

W: Yes, he was. Now, would you please get in to borrow some money?

Module 14 Tour of Ancient Cities and Ancient Towns

J: You're kidding me. I cannot offer to buy a compound in China. I only want to see more traditional Chinese buildings. What's the shop over there? It is an elegant and beautiful building.

W: Actually, it's not a shop, but a museum. The house used to be the Tongxinggong Armed Escort Company. In ancient times, the armed escort service played an important role in the development of Chinese business.

J: Why did people establish armed escort firms? Were there a lot of robberies?

W: Like the security companies in your country, many bankers need security service. The merchants in Pingyao employed armed escorts to safeguard their property. The armed escort business was prosperous in Shanxi Province in the mid-19th century.

J: I have no interest in such business. I'm told Pingyao is popular for the folk houses. I'd like to see more Chinese architectures in Pingyao.

W: OK. Then, I will take you around one of the famous compounds—Qiao's Compound. It is not far away from here, some twenty kilometers north of Pingyao. What about having a look?

J: Of course. Thank you.

Useful Expressions

1. It is one of the best places where you can explore the ancient Chinese culture.
它是你探索中国古代文化的最好地方之一。
2. The place where we are standing is a bazaar.
我们站的地方是市集。
3. Do you know which one is the earliest bank in China?
你知道中国最早的银行是哪家吗？
4. Rishengchang Exchange Shop is very important because it is the first bank in China.
日升昌票号非常重要，因为它是中国第一家银行。
5. I'll take you around one of the famous compounds—Qiao's Compound.
我将带你参观其中一个著名的大院——乔家大院。

Exercises

1. Match the following Chinese with the correct English versions

（1）明清商业街　　　　a. City Tower
（2）票号博物馆　　　　b. Museum of Lacquer Art
（3）市楼　　　　　　　c. Shopping Street from Ming and Qing Dynasties
（4）古镖局　　　　　　d. traditional quadrangles

(5) 漆器艺术馆　　　　　　e. Museum of Draft Banks
(6) 城隍庙　　　　　　　　f. County Office
(7) 县衙署　　　　　　　　g. Town God Temple
(8) 传统四合院民居　　　　h. An Ancient Escort Agency

2. Translate the following Chinese into English

(1) 平遥古城中心的主要路段两旁有很多不错的纪念品商店,还有一些古董店。

(2) 过去在平遥人看来,商业上的成功更值得他们骄傲,而学者的地位还不如农民和军人。

(3) 平遥经济的主体是农业,这里的牛肉非常出名。

(4) 慈禧太后当年路过平遥时品尝了这里的牛肉,对其大加赞赏。

(5) 很多旅店都具有明清风格,建筑精妙、装修华贵,环境舒适,游客在这里很容易感受到平遥古城的古色古香。

(6) 平遥古城在中国历史的发展中为人们展示了一幅非同寻常的经济、文化、社会及宗教发展的画卷。

(7) 明清时期,商人各自组建商帮在全国范围内做生意,其中以平遥为中心的山西商帮最为重要。

3. Fill in the blanks with appropriate words and expressions

The city wall stretches for about six kilometers. The town is ＿＿(1)＿＿ by a city moat, both three meters deep and ＿＿(2)＿＿. Outside the city is a drawbridge. Within the city, 4 big streets and 8 small streets radiate to ＿＿(3)＿＿ with 72 lanes.

Preserved in the ancient city are near 4000 traditional quadrangle residences of common people, over 400 of which are fairly intact, in ＿＿(4)＿＿ to the few even more cherished houses of Ming ＿＿(5)＿＿ and those rare proto-types of Yuan Dynasty. These shelters are typical of northern China and ＿＿(6)＿＿ Province, specifically with the following features: perfect combination of cave dwelling and quadrangle courtyard; rectangle layout with an enclosed but elaborate space; mostly shed or flat roofed; grand courtyard as a whole ＿＿(7)＿＿ elegant inside; carefully observing Chinese geomancy as ＿＿(8)＿＿ as other customs.

4. Role play

Situation: Suppose you are the local guide of Pingyao, your American guest Harry comes to visit Pingyao the first time. And now you arrive at the Rishengchang Exchange Shop.

Ⅳ Extended Reading

The Origin of Shanxi Business—Ancient City of Pingyao

Module 14　Tour of Ancient Cities and Ancient Towns

Task 5　A Trip to the Three Lanes and Seven Alleys

I　Read and Match

a. Ermei Study
b. Former Residence of Lin Juemin
c. Former Residence of Yan Fu
d. Former Residence of Shen Baozhen

(1)

(2)

(3)

(4)

II　Situational Dialogue

A Trip to the Three Lanes and Seven Alleys

(The local guide Xiao Wang shows the tour group around the Three Lanes and Seven Alleys.)

W: Xiao Wang, the local guide　　T: the tourist

W: Hello, everyone! Welcome to Fuzhou, the capital city of Fujian Province. I am your guide Wang from Sunshine Travel Agency. Our bus driver is Mr. Lin. We hope you will have a wonderful journey with us.

T: We're glad to be here in Fuzhou.

W: Today, we will visit Sanfang Qixiang, literally meaning "Three Lanes and Seven Alleys". It is one of the most rewarding places to visit in the heart of Fuzhou. Three Lanes and Seven Alleys is an architectural complex of the Ming and Qing Dynasties. It enjoys a reputation of "the Museum of the buildings of the Ming and Qing Dynasties", and it is also regarded as a living fossil of the walled district system of ancient China. The district covers an area of 40 hectares with 268 ancient houses.

T: What do three lanes and seven alleys refer to?

W: Well. The three lanes are Yijin Lane, Wenru Lane and Guanglu Lane. The seven alleys are Yangqiao Alley, Langguan Alley, Anmin Alley, Huang Alley, Ta Alley, Gong Alley and Jibi Alley. The lanes and alleys lie along both sides of Nanhou Street, the central axis of the block, forming a traditional checkered street pattern. Jibi Alley, Yangqiao Alley and Guanglu Lane have been converted into driveways in the city development, leaving some famous old sites hidden among modern buildings, such as "Guanglu Recital Platform" which was a favorite retreat of Chinese literati to enjoy and share their social lives over the centuries. So there actually remain two lanes and five alleys.

T: By the way, can you tell us what the historical value of the three lanes and seven alleys is?

W: Yes. The Three Lanes and Seven Alleys is of high value for historical research because it is a place with typical architectural features of its time and has been the residence of many outstanding people.

T: What are the architectural features of Three Lanes and Seven Alleys?

W: As for its architectural features, the Three Lanes and Seven Alleys retain the street pattern of the Tang and Song Dynasties from over thousand years ago. Houses are symmetrically distributed along the axis. The number of buildings well preserved from the Ming and Qing Dynasties and Republic of China Period amounts to 200, in which 9 are rated as the National Cultural Relics Protection Units, including Waterside Stage, former residences of Yanfu and Shen Baozheng. The Three Lanes and Seven Alleys highly represent the characteristics of Fujian traditional dwelling-houses. The architectural layout reflects the family's traditional ethic notion, and the building materials used were especially designed for the humid climate of Fuzhou. The exquisite designs of gardens reflect the owner's preference for a landscape with hills and waters. Each building is featured by their distinguished wood carvings on the windows and the doors. Those vivid and lively carvings, such as carvings of animals and flowers, reveal the excellent handcraft of local craftsmen.

T: And what is the cultural deposit of Three Lanes and Seven Alleys?

W: In addition to the buildings, the rich cultural deposit here is far more amazing. Since the Jin and Tang Dynasties, many nobles and scholar-officials settled down here. A number of people who had tremendous impacts on modern China like Lin Zexu, Shen Baozheng, Yan Fu, Bin Xin, Yu Dafu and so on, once lived here.

T: So, this place is really worth seeing.

W: Yes. The unique historical and cultural heritage of the city should be under careful protection during urban development. By the turn of the century, the old buildings in the Three Lanes and Seven Alleys were nearly sacrificed to the commercial real estate development in the old city reconstruction project. Fortunately, the government timely terminated the project. In recent years, the preservation and restoration of the Three Lanes and Seven Alleys received great technical and financial support from the government. The Three Lanes and Seven Alleys was included on the list of "Top ten historical and cultural streets in China", awarded by the Ministry of Culture and State Bureau for Preservation of Cultural Relics in June, 2009.

T: Wow, we can't wait to see it.

W: OK. Let's start today's journey from Yangqiao Alley.

Useful Expressions

1. It is one of the most rewarding places to visit in the heart of Fuzhou.
它是福州市中心值得一看的景点之一。
2. Three Lanes and Seven Alleys is an architectural complex of the Ming and Qing Dynasties.
三坊七巷集合了明清以来保留下的众多建筑。
3. The district covers an area of 40 hectares with 268 ancient houses.
整个街区占地 40 亩,共有古建筑 268 座。
4. In addition to the buildings, the rich cultural deposit here is far more amazing.
除建筑外,更令人惊叹的是它的文化底蕴。
5. Each building is featured by their distinguished wood carvings on the windows and the doors.
每一栋建筑的窗户和门上都有独特的雕刻。
6. The unique historical and cultural heritage of the city should be under careful protection during urban development.
在城市发展过程中,城市的独特历史文化遗产应得到良好的保护。

 **Exercises**

1. Match the following Chinese with the correct English versions
(1) 衣锦坊　　　　　　　　a. Huang Alley

(2) 文儒坊　　　　　　　b. Jibi Alley
(3) 光禄坊　　　　　　　c. Langguan Alley
(4) 杨桥巷　　　　　　　d. Ta Alley
(5) 郎官巷　　　　　　　e. Anmin Alley
(6) 安民巷　　　　　　　f. Guanglu Lane
(7) 黄巷　　　　　　　　g. Yijin Lane
(8) 塔巷　　　　　　　　h. Yangqiao Alley
(9) 宫巷　　　　　　　　i. Wenru Lane
(10) 吉庇巷　　　　　　 j. Gong Alley

2. Translate the following Chinese into English

(1) 街巷分布在街区中轴线南后街两侧，形成了传统的棋盘式街道格局。
(2) 三坊七巷高度代表了福建传统民居的特点。
(3) 建筑布局体现了家族的传统伦理观念，使用的建筑材料专门针对福州潮湿的气候而设计。
(4) 精致的园林设计反映了主人对山水景观的偏好。
(5) 三坊七巷入选"中国十大历史文化街区"。

3. Fill in the blanks with appropriate words and expressions

Yangqiao Alley is the northernmost alley in the attraction. A century ago, it was a small ＿＿(1)＿＿ connecting Dongjiekou and Shuangpao Bridge. During the 1960's the alley was converted into a road to ＿＿(2)＿＿ traffic flow in the area.

Shuangpao Bridge was once the convergence of two ＿＿(3)＿＿ waterways. One is the Yuanshuai Miao River; the other is the Baima River. A couple of Banyan trees on opposite banks of the river near the bridge are also a ＿＿(4)＿＿ attraction. The two Banyan trees, poetically named Embracing Trees, grow in opposite directions with their branches and leaves embracing each other, ＿＿(5)＿＿ people of the romantic story of a pair of young lovers committing suicide for love in the river. ＿＿(6)＿＿ to the city construction and river diversion, Shuangpao Bridge has been ＿＿(7)＿＿ into a pavilion on the sidewalk. With the Embracing Trees offering wide shade, Shuangpao Bridge becomes a popular stop for passersby to take a ＿＿(8)＿＿ and have some tea.

4. Role play

Situation: Suppose you are the local guide of Three Lanes and Seven Alleys, your American friend Harry comes to visit Three Lanes and Seven Alleys the first time. And now you arrive at Former Residence of Lin Juemin.

Ⅳ Extended Reading

Former Residence of Lin Juemin

Module 15
Tour of Chinese Culture

Learning Objectives

1. Master the vocabulary and sentence patterns of the tour of typical Chinese culture.
2. Describe the features of typical Chinese culture to the tourists.
3. Explore the representative elements of typical Chinese culture.
4. Summarize the main features of typical Chinese culture.

Task 1 Traditional Chinese Festivals

Read and Match

a. Water-splashing Festival
b. Double Third Festival
c. Dragon Boat Festival
d. Torch Festival

(1)

(2)

(3)   (4)

Situational Dialogues

➢ Dialogue 1

Dragon Boat Festival

(Xiao Li, a local guide, is on the way to a scenic spot along the Puxia River of Fuzhou with a group. The tourists are quite interested in dragon boat race and want to know more about the Dragon Boat Festival.)

L: Xiao Li, the local guide   T: the tourists

L: ladies and gentlemen, in front of us is the Puxia River in Fuzhou, or Dragon-boat River. Each year a great dragon boat race is held here during the Dragon Boat Festival.

T: We have heard about Dragon Boat Festival. Can you tell us something more about it?

L: Of course. Dragon Boat Festival, or Duanwu Festival, is regarded as one of the four great traditional festivals for Han people in China. The other three are Chinese New Year, Mid-Autumn Festival and Qingming Festival. Dragon Boat Festival is on the 5th day of the 5th month in Chinese lunar calendar.

T: It's said that there is a core idea behind each Chinese festival. What's the core idea of Dragon Boat Festival?

L: It's a special day to commemorate Qu Yuan, an ancient Chinese patriotic poet. It is also a day to get rid of diseases, avoid disaster and wish for good health.

T: How do you celebrate Dragon Boat Festival?

L: China, as the origin of the Dragon Boat Festival, celebrates it at the largest scale with many activities for over 2000 years. People usually have the dragon boat race, eat Zongzi, drink realgar wine, hang calamus and wormwood in front of the gate, wear perfume pouches and bath in herbal water, etc.

T: I have seen the dragon boat race before. It's very excited.

L: The boat is in a shape of traditional Chinese dragon. One team member sits at the front of the boat to beat a drum. The rowers can maintain morale and keep in time with one another with the rhythm of the drumbeat. Now it has turned to be a sport event not only held in China. Some other countries in Asia, like Japan, South Korea, Vietnam, Singapore and Malaysia, also celebrate it with some different features.

T: Why do people hang calamus and wormwood in front of the door?

L: The Dragon Boat Festival falls in hot summer, which breeds germs easily and pests are active. Both calamus and wormwood can clean the air and drive out mosquitoes and insects with special fragrance, so people can keep the diseases and epidemics at bay.

T: What's Zongzi?

L: Every major festival in China has its special food and for the Dragon Boat Festival, sticky rice dumplings, or zongzi are taken. They are made in a variety of grains, fillings in triangles or pillow-sized packages. In northern China people prefer sweet zongzi filled with red bean paste or red dates while in southern China they like salty zongzi stuffed with roast pork, eggs and shrimp.

T: Oh, I'm a little hungry now. Can we taste zongzi today?

L: Yes, the day after tomorrow is the Dragon Boat Festival. So I have prepared delicious zongzi for you today. I hope you'll like it.

T: You are so considerate.

➢ Dialogue 2

Water-splashing Festival

(Li Mei, a local guide, is on the way to a scenic spot with a group. The tourists will attend the Water-splashing Festival of Dai People. They seem to be quite interested in it and want to know more about the Water-splashing Festival.)

扫码
听听力

L: Li Mei, the local guide   T: the tourists

L: Good morning, this is our first visit in Yunnan. Everyone is on the bus now. I will give you a brief introduction of Yunnan Province. Yunnan Province is located on the most southwest of China. Yunnan means beautiful clouds in the southwest. It is a land of natural beauty and mystery with grand mountains, clean rivers and kind people.

T: Many friends told me there are plenty of ethnic minorities and ethnic festivals in Yunnan Province.

L: Yunnan is home to 26 ethnic minorities. They give a rich color to the land with their colorful costumes, their traditional songs and dances. The Water-splashing Festival of Dai nationality, the March Fair of Bai nationality, the Torch Festival of Yi nationality, will make you forget to leave. In some ethnic groups, apart from the common and important festivals, different branches have different festivals as well.

T: I'm looking forward to the Water-splashing Festival we are going to experience. Would you give me more details?

L: Water-splashing Festival usually lasts for three days. In the first two days, they hold dragon boat competitions to say farewell to the old year; on the third day, they carry out the "lucky" activities welcoming the New Year.

T: I have heard that the Water-splashing Festival is related to Buddha.

L: All people in a village will take a bath and put on new clothes and go to worship Buddha in the first morning of the Water-splashing Festival. People meet in the Buddhist temple, building a tower with sand. Then all people sit around the tower and listen to the chanting of Buddhist scripture. Then again a Buddhist statue will be carried out into the yard and splashed by all women in the village, which is so-called bathing for the Buddha.

T: How do people celebrate the festival?

L: The occasion is marked by a variety of activities, including singing and dancing, fireworks display, boat racing, exhibiting Kongming lanterns, bathing the Buddha, and parades and fairs. But the most popular event is water-splashing. After such religious rite, all young people will go out of the temple and splash water on each other for pleasure. All visitors involved in water splashing and congratulations are expressed onto each other. Spray flies everywhere, and everyone is shouting for fun. The water brings good luck and happy cheers to all the villages around.

T: Will other ethnic group celebrate the festival?

L: Water-splashing Festival is not only the first Buddhist festival at the beginning of a new year but also the most important festival of the Dai people, De-ang people and A-chang people.

T: Thank you for your introduction.

Useful Expressions

1. It's said that there is a core idea behind each Chinese festival.

据说每个中国节日的背后都有一个核心理念。

2. It's a special day to commemorate Qu Yuan, an ancient Chinese patriotic poet. It is also a day to get rid of diseases, avoid disaster and wish for good health.

端午节是纪念中国古代爱国诗人屈原的特殊日子,也是驱邪避灾、祈求健康的日子。

3. People usually have the dragon boat race, eat Zongzi, drink realgar wine, hang calamus and wormwood in front of the gate, wear perfume pouches and bath in herbal water, etc.

通常有赛龙舟、吃粽子、喝雄黄酒、在门前挂菖蒲和艾草、佩带香囊、泡草药浴等活动。

4. Both calamus and wormwood can clean the air and drive out mosquitoes and insects with special fragrance, so people can keep the diseases and epidemics at bay.

菖蒲和艾草带有特殊的香味，可以净化空气、驱除蚊虫，使人们远离疾病和流行病。

5. Yunnan is a land of natural beauty and mystery with grand mountains, clean rivers and kind people.

云南有雄伟的高山、干净的河流、善良的人民，是美丽而神秘的地方。

6. In some ethnic groups, apart from the common and important festivals, different branches have different festivals as well.

一些少数民族除了有共同的重要节日外，不同的分支也有不同的节日。

7. I'm looking forward to the Water-splashing Festival we are going to experience.

期待我们即将体验的泼水节。

8. A Buddhist statue will be carried out into the yard and splashed by all women in the village, which is so-called bathing for the Buddha.

人们将一尊佛像抬进院子里，村里的妇女们为佛像泼水，即所谓的浴佛。

9. The occasion is marked by a variety of activities, including singing and dancing, fireworks displays, boat racing, exhibiting Kongming lanterns, bathing the Buddha, parades and fairs.

活动丰富多彩，包括歌舞、烟花表演、赛艇、孔明灯展、浴佛、游行和集市等。

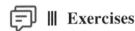 Exercises

1. Match the following Chinese with the correct English versions

(1) 除夕　　　　　　　a. Chinese New Year's Eve
(2) 腊八节　　　　　　b. Lantern Festival
(3) 七夕节　　　　　　c. Qingming Festival
(4) 重阳节　　　　　　d. Dragon Boat Festival
(5) 元宵节　　　　　　e. Double Seventh Festival
(6) 春节　　　　　　　f. Mid-Autumn Festival
(7) 清明节　　　　　　g. Double Ninth Festival
(8) 端午节　　　　　　h. Winter Solstice
(9) 中秋节　　　　　　i. Laba Festival
(10) 冬至　　　　　　　j. the Spring Festival

2. Translate the following Chinese into English

(1) 除夕之夜，人们辞旧迎新。
(2) 春节，也就是中国的新年，从农历正月初一开始至正月十五结束。
(3) 元宵节吃元宵、赏花灯、猜灯谜。
(4) 清明节，江南地区的人吃青团。青团是用糯米做成的深绿色的食物，口感柔软、香甜。
(5) 相传七月初七，喜鹊在天河中飞翔，为牛郎织女搭鹊桥。

3. Fill in the blanks with appropriate words and expressions

Double Ninth Festival, also known as Chong Jiu festival, is a Han Chinese

_____(1)_____ festival. The celebration activities include sightseeing, climbing mountains, watching chrysanthemum, wearing cornel, drinking chrysanthemum wine, etc. The meaning of Chong Yang is _____(2)_____ from the *Book of Changes*. Because the ancient "Book of Changes" defined "six" as negative numbers and the "nine" as _____(3)_____ numbers. Ancients thought that Chong Jiu is the auspicious day which is worth celebrating. Today's Double Ninth Festival has been given a new _____(4)_____. In 1989, the 9th day of the 9th lunar month of each year was set up as the elderly festival, becoming a chance to _____(5)_____ and care for the elderly.

4. Role play

Situation: Suppose you are the local guide and are now guiding the guests to explore Mid-Autumn Festival. Make introductions and answer relevant questions.

Ⅳ Extended Reading

Chinese Ethnic Minority Festivals

Task 2　Traditional Chinese Operas

Ⅰ Read and Match

a. Kunqu Opera　　　　b. Huangmei Opera
c. Beijing Opera　　　　d. Xiang Opera

(1)

(2)

(3)　　　　　　　　　　　　　　(4)

📖 ‖ Situational Dialogues

➢ Dialogue 1

Beijing Opera

(As a local guide, Xiao Ling is taking the tour group to the National Grand Theater to enjoy Beijing Opera. She introduces Beijing Opera on the way and answers relevant questions.)

L: Xiao Ling, the local guide　　T: the tourist

L: Ladies and gentlemen, we are now on the way to the National Grand Theater to enjoy Beijing Opera. Anyone knows the origin of Beijing Opera?

T: Beijing Opera is considered as the national opera of China. It has a history of more than 200 years.

L: Yes, it has a history of over 200 years. Beijing Opera gradually came into being after 1790 when the famous four Anhui opera troupes came to Beijing. Beijing Opera underwent fast development during the reign of Emperor Qianlong and the Empress Dowager Cixi, and eventually became more accessible to the common people.

T: What are the skills of performing?

L: To become a good Beijing Opera performer, one has to master four basic skills: singing, dialogue, acting and combating.

T: What are the main roles in Beijing Opera?

L: The types of roles in Beijing Opera fall into four major groups: Sheng, Dan, Jing and Chou.

T: I have no idea of them.

L: Sheng is the male role, Dan is the female role, Jing is the supporting male role with different looks and Chou is the funny or evil role.

T: Can we distinguish by their voice?

L: I'm afraid not. The performing artists of the Western grand opera are distinguished by their vocal range while Beijing Opera performing artists are rather differentiated according to the characters they play. Sheng means the male role, includes Laosheng, Xiaosheng and Wusheng. Laosheng usually refers to a middle-aged or an old-aged character who wears an artificial beard in the play.

T: So Xiaosheng is a young male character?

L: That's right. And Wusheng stands for a combating male role.

T: I know Dan is the female role.

L: Dan is divided into Qingyi, Huadan, Wudan and Laodan. Qingyi usually refers to the virtuous wives and good mothers. Huadan usually refers to girls. Wudan refers to a combating female while Laodan an aged female.

T: I hope I can recognize their roles during the performance.

L: I'm sure you will. It's not difficult to distinguish these roles by their costumes and facial paintings.

T: With your help and introduction, I'm sure we will enjoy the performance.

➢ Dialogue 2

Huangmei Opera

(As a local guide, Xiao Ling is taking the tour group back to the hotel from the National Grand Theater to enjoy Beijing Opera. The tourists are inquiring Xiao Ling about the local operas in China and Xiao Ling is answering the relevant questions.)

L: Xiao Ling, the local guide   T: the tourist

L: Ladies and gentlemen, have you enjoyed the performance just now?

T: Yes, I'm impressed by the facial make-ups.

L: A foreigner who watches a Beijing Opera performance for the first time is very likely to be stunned by the colorful facial make-ups.

T: Chinese operas are so different from the Western operas. How many operas are there in China?

L: Chinese opera has a long history and a wide variety of types. According to the 2015 Census by the Ministry of Culture, there are 348 local operas in China.

T: Can you introduce some famous operas?

L: Of course. Chinese operas are traditional dramas combining literature, music, dance, martial art and acrobatics, such as Sichuan Opera, Henan Opera, Shaoxing Opera, Guangdong Opera and Huangmei Opera.

T: I have heard about Sichuan Opera, but I have never heard Huangmei Opera. What is Huangmei Opera?

L: Huangmei Opera is one of the most famous traditional operas in China. It originated in Huangmei County, Hubei Province and has spread in Anhui, Jiangxi and Hubei provinces. Nowadays, the opera has spread both at home and abroad. Huangmei fans can be found not only on the Chinese mainland but also in Malaysia, Japan and even Europe.

T: Why is it so famous and popular?

L: Huangmei Opera is easy to understand and learn. Like other Chinese local operas, Huangmei Opera also adopts the local dialect. Its language is a mixture of northern and southern styles, therefore it's easy to imitate and pleasant to native ears.

T: Maybe we can enjoy it on the Internet after we arrive at the hotel.

L: I recommend The Heavenly Maid and the Mortal. It's a love story. I'm sure you will be attracted by its sweet melodies, graceful sounds and beautiful costumes.

T: Thanks for your recommendation.

Useful Expressions

1. To become a good Beijing Opera performer, one has to master four basic skills: singing, dialogue, acting and combating.

要成为一名优秀的京剧演员，必须掌握四项基本技能：唱、念、做、打。

2. Sheng is the male role, Dan is the female role, Jing is the supporting male role with different looks and Chou is the funny or evil role.

生是男性角色，旦是女性角色，净是品貌特异的男配角，丑是滑稽或邪恶的角色。

3. The performing artists of the Western grand opera are distinguished by their vocal range while Beijing Opera performing artists are rather differentiated according to the characters they play.

西方歌剧的表演艺术家以音域区分，而京剧表演艺术家则根据他们所扮演的角色区分。

4. Chinese opera has a long history and a wide variety of types. According to the 2015 Census by the Ministry of Culture, there are 348 local operas in China.

中国戏曲历史悠久，种类繁多。文化部2015年的普查显示，中国有地方戏曲348种。

5. Chinese operas are traditional dramas combining literature, music, dance, martial art and acrobatics, such as Sichuan Opera, Henan Opera, Shaoxing Opera, Guangdong Opera and Huangmei Opera.

中国戏曲是结合文学、音乐、舞蹈、武术和杂技的传统戏剧，如川剧、豫剧、越剧、粤剧、黄梅戏等。

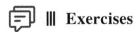 **Exercises**

1. Match the following Chinese with the correct English versions

(1) 唱腔   a. music

(2) 脸谱   b. performance
(3) 扯脸   c. literature
(4) 武术   d. aria
(5) 音乐   e. Wiping Mask
(6) 表演   f. Blowing Mask
(7) 戏剧   g. Pulling Mask
(8) 抹脸   h. martial art
(9) 吹脸   i. Facial Painting
(10) 文学   j. drama

2. Translate the following Chinese into English

(1) 第一次看京剧表演的外国人，经常会被表演者五彩斑斓的妆容惊艳到。

(2) 脸谱具有不同的含义。脸谱的颜色包括红色、粉色、紫色、黑色、灰色、蓝色、黄色、绿色和白色。

(3) 红色代表忠诚和正义；粉色代表直接和资历；紫色代表谨慎和稳重；黑色代表正直和诚实；白色代表机智和狡猾；黄色代表敏锐和凶猛；蓝色代表勇敢和傲慢；绿色代表顽固和残忍。

(4) 人物的性格是通过面部化妆的不同颜色的组合来表现的，所以当他上台时，观众很快就知道他是一个什么样的人。

3. Fill in the blanks with appropriate words and expressions

The Peony Pavilion is a love story that transcends time and space. Du Liniang, the heroine, falls asleep in her family garden and has a vivid ____(1)____: she is impressed by Liu Mengmei's refined and cultured image and falls in love with the handsome young ____(2)____. After she wakes up, she is possessed by this dream's imagery regardless of others' advice. She wastes away after her dream lover until she dies. A few days after Du Liniang's ____(3)____, her dream lover stops in the garden while he's traveling to take his civil service exam. He sees the heroine's portrait and falls in love with it. Du's ghost visits him and tells him she is actually buried in the ____(4)____ and if he will only disinter her she can ____(5)____ to life. Liu digs up her corpse and it's well preserved; she comes back to life.

4. Role play

Situation: Suppose you are the local guide and are now guiding the guests to enjoy Sichuan Opera. Make introductions and answer relevant questions.

Ⅳ Extended Reading

Magical Face Changes in Sichuan Opera

Magical Face Changes in Sichuan Opera

Module 15 Tour of Chinese Culture

Task 3   Chinese Ceramics

Read and Match

a. Jingdezhen Porcelain
b. White Porcelain
c. Tri-Colour Glazed Pottery
d. Cloisonné

(1)

(2)

(3)

(4)

Situational Dialogues

> Dialogue 1

An Introduction about Jingdezhen Porcelain

(As a local guide, Xiao Li is guiding the guests to Jingdezhen. He introduces

Jingdezhen porcelain on the way and answers relevant questions.)

L: **Xiao Li, the local guide**　　S: **Ms. Sara, the tourist**

L: Ladies and gentlemen, we are now on the way to Jingdezhen. Have you ever heard of this town?

S: Jingdezhen is famous for its wonderful porcelain.

L: Yes. Jingdezhen Porcelain is the most well-known type of Chinese porcelain. It is known for its fine quality, graceful shapes and elaborate patterns. It's the highlight of the classical ceramic art all around the world.

S: It's said Jingdezhen porcelain has a long history.

L: That's right. It has a history of more than 1600 years.

S: How to make Jingdezhen porcelain? What makes it different from other porcelains?

L: 72 procedures are needed to make clay into a fine piece of Jingdezhen Porcelain. Today I will introduce the 5 basic core steps for you. The first step is wheel throwing. This procedure is to make the prototype of the porcelain. The craftsman needs to place a lump of wet clay on a spinning base and mold it into the wanted shape. The second step is fine trimming. After the basic clay body is finished, various tools, such as knives and files, are needed to rub or polish the clay to ensure an even thickness and a symmetrical shape. And the third step is glazing. This procedure will make the final porcelain shiny and solid.

S: What kind of mineral will be painted during the step?

T: The glaze material is made up of ground talc, quartz and other minerals. They will be painted on the surface of the clay body before firing.

S: So the fourth step is firing.

T: In fact before firing, painting should be done first. Cobalt oxide is used as an indigo pigment to paint the patterns or write Chinese characters on the clay body.

S: So firing is the last step.

T: Yes. Usually, the clay body will be placed on the furnace floor and fired at a temperature of 1270-1300 ℃ for at least 24 hours.

S: Where is Jingdezhen Porcelain used nowadays?

T: Jingdezhen Porcelain has been massively used for making tableware, tea set, coffee set and drinking vessel. Of course, it can also be used widely as building materials like tiles, or house decorations like vases and sculptures, etc.

S: That is marvelous. Maybe I can buy a set of coffee set for my new home.

T: That's a good idea.

➢ Dialogue 2

An Introduction about White Porcelain of Dehua

(Xiao Li, the local guide, is visiting National Museum with his tour group. He is making a brief introduction now.)

L: Xiao Li, the local guide   S: Ms. Smith, the tourist

L: Ladies and gentlemen, now we are at National Museum. The Exhibition of Dehua Porcelain Art is held recently, so we have a good chance to appreciate the "Chinese White".

S: What's Chinese White?

L: Dehua Porcelain is a type of white porcelain. Famed as Ivory White and Down White, it enjoys a unique position in Chinese porcelain culture. The French keen on Chinese porcelain have a special name for the Ming Dehua white porcelain "Blanc De Chine" (Chinese White), meaning it is the top grade of Chinese porcelain.

S: So Dehua porcelain has been exported abroad many years ago.

L: Yes, Dehua ware was exported in large quantities to Southeast Asia and in the 18th century to Europe.

S: How long will the Exhibition of Dehua Porcelain Art be held?

T: The exhibition exhibits 181 works by 106 artists from August 20 to September 1. It is divided into two sections. The first section is themed on the Vast Mysterious World where porcelain carvings of religious figures including Guanyin, arhats and Nryana are displayed, reflecting the sacred religious culture full of mercy. The second section is themed on the Kaleidoscopic World of Mankind, showing the daily life of the emperors and ministers, fair ladies, and common people.

S: The exhibition will bring the visitors to have a close view of the simple and elegant beauty of Dehua white porcelain.

T: Yes. And the exhibition has expanded the impact of such cultural brands as Chinese White and the World Porcelain City, and showcased the marvelous porcelain-making techniques and the exquisite porcelain art.

S: It's the combination of tradition and innovation.

T: The Dehua white porcelain has a history of 1000 years. Today, it combines the traditional art and novel creation. Dehua porcelain culture plays a very important role in the implementation of the Belt and Road Initiative and international communication.

Useful Expressions

1. Famed as Ivory White and Down White, it enjoys a unique position in Chinese porcelain culture.

德化白瓷素有"象牙白""鹅绒白"等美称,在我国陶瓷文化体系中享有独特的地位。

2. The French keen on Chinese porcelain have a special name for the Ming Dehua white porcelain "Blanc De Chine" (Chinese White), meaning it is the top grade of Chinese porcelain

热爱中国瓷器的法国人甚至专门为明代德化白瓷造了一个词——Blanc de Chine

"中国白",意为"中国瓷器之上品"。

3. Dehua ware was exported in large quantities to Southeast Asia and in the 18th century to Europe.

德化瓷器大量出口到东南亚,并从 18 世纪开始出口到欧洲。

4. The first section is themed on the Vast Mysterious World where porcelain carvings of religious figures including Guanyin, arhats and Nryana are displayed, reflecting the sacred religious culture full of mercy.

展览的第一个主题是"云端高淼",主要展示和宗教相关的观音、罗汉、力士等瓷雕作品,表现宗教文化的圣洁和慈悲。

5. The second section is themed on the Kaleidoscopic World of Mankind, showing the daily life of the emperors and ministers, fair ladies, and common people.

第二个主题为"人间万象",展示帝王将相、窈窕淑女以及市井百姓的日常生活等题材的作品。

6. And the exhibition has expanded the impact of such cultural brands as Chinese White and the World Porcelain City, and showcased the marvelous porcelain-making techniques and the exquisite porcelain art.

本次展览扩大了德化瓷"中国白""世界陶瓷之都"等文化品牌的影响力,展现了德化陶瓷精湛的制作技艺和精美的陶瓷艺术。

Exercises

1. Match the following Chinese with the correct English versions

(1) 青花瓷　　　　　　　　　a. ceramic
(2) 玲珑瓷　　　　　　　　　b. black pottery
(3) 高岭石　　　　　　　　　c. blue and white porcelain
(4) 官窑　　　　　　　　　　d. clay
(5) 长石　　　　　　　　　　e. kaolinite
(6) 黏土　　　　　　　　　　f. feldspar
(7) 陶瓷　　　　　　　　　　g. silica
(8) 黑陶　　　　　　　　　　h. painted pottery
(9) 彩陶　　　　　　　　　　i. glowing porcelain
(10) 硅石　　　　　　　　　 j. Guan Kiln

2. Translate the following Chinese into English

(1) 第一步是做坯。是制作器物的雏形。
(2) 第二步是修坯。将经过印坯工艺后的粗坯旋削,使之厚度均匀、形状对称。
(3) 第三步是施釉。在器坯内外上一层玻璃质釉,使之光润。
(4) 第四步是画坯。用青花料在坯胎上绘画或写青花字。
(5) 第五步是烧窑。将装有成坯的匣钵按窑位置放在窑床上,以 1270—1300 ℃的温度烧至少 24 小时。

3. Fill in the blanks with appropriate words and expressions

The five basic core steps to make clay into a fine piece of Jingdezhen ___(1)___ are as the following. The first step is ___(2)___. This procedure is to make the prototype of the porcelain. The craftsman needs to place a lump of wet clay on a spinning base and mold it into the wanted shape. The second step is ___(3)___. After the basic clay body is finished, various tools, such as knives and files, are needed to rub or polish the clay to ensure an even thickness and a symmetrical shape. And the third step is ___(4)___. This procedure will make the final porcelain shiny and solid. The fourth step is painting. Cobalt oxide is used as an indigo pigment to paint the patterns or write Chinese characters on the clay body. The fifth step is ___(5)___. The clay body will be placed on the furnace floor and fired at a temperature of 1270-1300 ℃ for at least 24 hours.

4. Role play

Situation: Suppose you are the local guide and are now guiding the guests to visit Dehua Museum. Make introductions and answer relevant questions.

Ⅳ Extended Reading

Chinese Porcelain

Chinese Porcelain

Module 16
Red Tour

Learning Objectives

1. Master the vocabulary and sentence patterns of the red tour.
2. Describe the scenery of red tour site to the tourists.
3. Explore the cultural elements of the red tour site.
4. Summarize the main features of the red tour site.

Task 1   A Trip to Mount Jinggang

Read and Match

a. Five Fingers (Wuzhi) Peak
b. Dragon Pond Waterfalls
c. monument and memorial
d. military statues

(1)

(2)

(3)

(4)

Situational Dialogue

A Trip to Mount Jinggang

(As a local guide, Xiao Li is visiting Mount Jinggang with his tour group. He introduces Mount Jinggang and answers relevant questions.)

L: Xiao Li, the local guide   S: Ms. Smith, the tourist

L: Ladies and gentlemen, we are now at Mount Jinggang. Mount Jinggang lies on the common boundary of Jiangxi and Hunan, 352 kilometers southwest from Nanchang, the capital city of Jiangxi Province. The mountain is quite different from the other sights.

S: What's the difference?

L: Mount Jinggang has great significance in modern Chinese history. It was here that important events took place during the Chinese revolution. It's here that forces led by Zhu De joined those headed by Mao Zedong. The combined forces of the CCP (Chinese Communist Party) marched on to the victory of establishing the new China under the chairmanship of Mao Zedong.

S: What are the main attractions here?

T: Mount Jinggang scenic spot is divided into 11 major sections, such as Ciping, Longtan, Huangyangjie, Five Fingers (Wuzhi) Peak, Dragon Pond Waterfalls, Maoping, etc. The best route is Huangyangjie-Longtan-Revolutionary Martyrs Cemetery-Revolution Museum.

S: What is the highest peak?

T: Five Fingers Peak is the highest in the Jinggang range. The peak has the appearance of five extended fingers, so it got the name Five Fingers Peak. It is also the largest and considered to be the most beautiful sight on the mountain.

S: Can we climb to the peak?

T: There is no path to climb. The virgin forest on the mountain is almost without any trace of human beings, so it remains the home of rare animal species.

S: What a pity!

T: Tourists may climb up to the Sightseeing Platform on the opposite, which is the best view point for seeing its majestic appearance.

S: OK. And just now you said the best tour route is from Huangyangjie. And will we visit Huangyangjie today?

T: Yes, today our first stop is Huangyangjie. It is one of the five famous sentries here. The well-known Defence of Huangyangjie happened here and Mao Zedong's poem—*Xijiang Moon* was written to commemorate it. The monument to the Defence of Huangyangjie is made up of an upright stele and a transverse stele, on which the inscriptions of Mao Zedong and Zhu De are carved. The old residences of the Red Army leaders remain here.

S: Is Huangyangjie the center of the scenic spot?

T: The center of the Mount Jinggang area is Ciping Town. It's the red revolution base of China and the location of the highest leading department. Now many places of interest in connection with the revolution can be seen here, such as the Mount Jinggang Revolution Museum, the Tower of the Revolutionary Martyrs and military statues. OK, now please follow me to explore the revolution base.

Useful Expressions

1. Mount Jinggang scenic spot is divided into 11 major sections, such as Ciping, Longtan, Huangyangjie, Five Fingers (Wuzhi) Peak, Dragon Pond Waterfalls, Maoping, etc.

井冈山风景名胜区分为茨坪、龙潭、黄洋界、五指峰、龙潭瀑布群、茅坪等11个大景区。

2. There is no path to climb. The virgin forest on the mountain is almost without any trace of human beings, so it remains the home of rare animal species.

山上没有任何可攀登的路。山上的原始森林几乎没有任何人类的踪迹，它仍然是珍稀动物物种的家园。

3. The well-known Defence of Huangyangjie happened here and Mao Zedong's poem—*Xijiang Moon* was written to commemorate it.

著名的黄洋界保卫战就发生在这里，毛泽东写下《西江月·井冈山》纪念这次战役。

Exercises

1. Match the following Chinese with the correct English versions

(1) 瀑布　　　　　　　　　　　　a. force

(2) 纪念碑　　　　　　　　　　　b. rare animal species

(3) 中国革命　　　　　　　　　c. fall
(4) 石碑　　　　　　　　　　　d. poem
(5) 部队　　　　　　　　　　　e. rhododendron
(6) 烈士　　　　　　　　　　　f. monument
(7) 珍稀动物　　　　　　　　　g. Chinese revolution
(8) 诗词　　　　　　　　　　　h. stele
(9) 哨所　　　　　　　　　　　i. martyr
(10) 杜鹃花　　　　　　　　　 j. sentry

2. **Translate the following Chinese into English**

(1) 1927年10月,老一辈无产阶级革命家率领中国工农红军来到井冈山。

(2) 他们创建了中国第一个农村革命根据地。

(3) 他们开辟了"以农村包围城市、武装夺取政权"的具有中国特色的革命道路。

(4) 井冈山被誉为"中国革命的摇篮"和"中华人民共和国的奠基石"。

(5) 井冈山作为中国爱国主义教育示范基地之一,也已成为进行革命传统教育和爱国主义教育的理想课堂。

3. **Fill in the blanks with appropriate words and expressions**

Maoping is ＿＿＿(1)＿＿＿ in the north foot of Huangyangjie with many revolutionary sites. Here we have Bajiao Lou (a two-story building), those who are familiar with Chinese history may recall that Mao Zedong lived, ＿＿＿(2)＿＿＿ and finished two splendid ＿＿＿(3)＿＿＿ works here. The first hospital of the base was established in Panlong Shuyuan (a classical academy in ancient times) of Maoping. You can visit the treatment room, medicine room and see some of the equipment ＿＿＿(4)＿＿＿ at the time. Another site that provided support to the base is bedclothes ＿＿＿(5)＿＿＿ which mainly produced the army clothes, hats and bullets bags. Each of these sites made a contribution to the achievements of the Red Army.

4. **Role play**

Situation: Suppose you are the local guide and are now guiding the guests to visit Huangyangjie Scenic Area. Make introductions and answer relevant questions.

Ⅳ Extended Reading

Mount Jinggang

Mount Jinggang

Task 2　A Trip to the Memorial Hall of the First National Congress of the CPC

I | Read and Match

a. Memorial Hall
b. the Communist Party of China
c. Shikumen style
d. the Red Boat

(1)

(2)

(3)

(4)

II | Situational Dialogue

The Memorial Hall of the First National Congress of the CPC

(As a local guide, Xiao Li is guiding the guests to the Memorial Hall of the First National Congress of CPC. He introduces the site on the way and answers relevant questions.)

Module 16 Red Tour

L: Xiao Li, the local guide   S: Ms. Sara, the tourist

L: Good morning, everyone. What we are going to visit this morning is the Memorial Hall of the First National Congress of CPC, the birthplace of the Communist Party of China. The Congress was held in Shanghai on July 23, 1921.

S: It's said that Shanghai is the key to modern history of China. Can you tell us the reasons?

T: Of course. Shanghai is the key to modern China and a microcosm of the whole country. Shanghai is a city with a glorious revolutionary tradition and a city that has attracted worldwide attention. The older generation of proletarian revolutionaries, such as Mao Zedong, Zhou Enlai, Liu Shaoqi, Deng Xiaoping, Chen Yun, etc., has left immortal traces of revolutionary struggle in Shanghai.

S: How long will it take us to get the site?

T: The site is located at No. 76 and 78, Jinxingye Road. It will take us about half an hour to get there. The building is lined up with two two-story brick-wood structures along the street. It is a typical Shanghai Shikumen style building.

S: What is Shikumen style building?

T: This kind of building absorbs a large number of styles of Jiangnan dwellings, and uses stone as the door frame. Lacquered solid thick wood was used for the door leaf, and this building is named "Shikumen". Although the exterior of the building is just the Shikumen style of ordinary Shanghai residents, it embodies extraordinary heritage. The 18-square-meter living room downstairs of the building was the meeting place at that time.

S: Who attended the meeting at that time?

T: The representatives at the meeting were Mao Zedong, Dong Biwu, Deng Enming, Li Da, He Shuheng, Chen Tanqiu, Wang Jinmei, Li Hanjun, Liu Renjing, Zhang Guotao, Zhou Fohai, Chen Gongbo, and Bao Huiseng, representing 53 Party members across the country. Marin and Nikolsky, the international representatives of the Communist Party, also attended the conference.

S: What decisions have been made during the meeting?

T: The conference passed the Party platform and resolutions, elected the Central Bureau and announced the establishment of the Communist Party of China. The Congress closed on a boat on Nanhu Lake in Jiaxing City, Zhejiang Province. It marks the founding of the Party, and July 1 was later designated as the date to commemorate the anniversary.

S: No wonder this place is called the birthplace of the Communist Party of China.

Useful Expressions

1. What we are going to visit this morning is the Memorial Hall of the First National Congress of CPC, the birthplace of the Communist Party of China.

早上我们要去参观的是中国共产党的诞生地——中共一大会址。

2. Shanghai is the key to modern China and a microcosm of the whole country.

上海是近代中国的钥匙,也是全国的一个缩影。

3. Shanghai is a city with a glorious revolutionary tradition and a city that has attracted worldwide attention.

上海是一个具有光荣革命传统的城市,是一个举世瞩目的城市。

4. The older generation of proletarian revolutionaries has left immortal traces of revolutionary struggle in Shanghai.

老一辈无产阶级革命家都在上海留下了不朽的革命斗争足迹。

5. This kind of building absorbs a large number of styles of Jiangnan dwellings, and uses stone as the door frame. Lacquered solid thick wood is used for the door leaf, and this building is named "Shikumen".

这种建筑大量吸收了江南民居的式样,以石头做门框,以乌漆实心厚木做门扇,这种建筑因此得名"石库门"。

6. Although the exterior of the building is just the Shikumen style of ordinary Shanghai residents, it embodies extraordinary heritage.

这幢大楼外表虽然只是普通上海居民石库门式风格,但是却体现了非凡的底蕴。

7. The conference passed the Party platform and resolutions, elected the Central Bureau and announced the establishment of the Communist Party of China.

大会通过了党纲和决议,选举了中央局,宣告了中国共产党的成立。

8. It marks the founding of the Party, and July 1 was later designated as the date to commemorate the anniversary.

党的一大宣告中国共产党成立。7月1日被确定为中国共产党诞生纪念日。

Ⅲ Exercises

1. Match the following Chinese with the correct English versions

(1) 发起人　　　　　　　　　a. revolution
(2) 缩影　　　　　　　　　　b. dwelling
(3) 纪念日　　　　　　　　　c. program
(4) 革命　　　　　　　　　　d. representative
(5) 发源地　　　　　　　　　e. initiator
(6) 共产党　　　　　　　　　f. microcosm
(7) 代表　　　　　　　　　　g. anniversary
(8) 会议　　　　　　　　　　h. the Communist Party
(9) 住宅　　　　　　　　　　i. congress
(10) 纲领　　　　　　　　　　j. birthplace

2. Translate the following Chinese into English

(1) 这种石库门建筑大量吸收了江南民居的式样，以石头做门框。

(2) 这幢大楼外表是普通上海民居的石库门式风格。

(3) 本次大会宣告了中国共产党的成立。

(4) 7月1日是中国共产党的生日。

(5) 沿街的这两幢两层砖木结构的建筑就是中共一大会址。

3. Fill in the blanks with appropriate words and expressions

After the founding of the People's ___(1)___ of China, the Party and the government attached great importance to the restoration of this house. In 1952, the site was restored, and a memorial hall was established and ___(2)___ to the public. In 1961, the State Council designated the site as a national key cultural relics protection unit. Deng Xiaoping also inscribed the name of the site "the ___(3)___ Hall of the First National Congress of CPC". In 1996, the site was expanded. Jiang Zemin also wrote the phrase "without the ___(4)___ Party, there would be no new China" for the meeting site. So this place is called the ___(5)___ of our Party.

4. Role play

Situation: Suppose you are the local guide and are now guiding the guests to visit the Memorial Hall of the First National Congress of CPC. Make introductions and answer relevant questions.

IV Extended Reading

The National Congress of the CPC

The National Congress of the CPC

Task 3 A Trip to the Site of the Gutian Congress

I Read and Match

a. exhibition hall
b. the meeting hall
c. the Party flag
d. the reviewing stand

(1) (2) (3) (4)

📖 Ⅱ Situational Dialogue

A Trip to the site of the Gutian Congress

(As a local guide, Xiao Li is guiding the guests to site of the Gutian Congress. He introduces the site on the way and answers relevant questions.)

L: Xiao Li, the local guide   T: the tourist

L: Ladies and gentlemen, we are now at the site of Gutian Congress. The Gutian Congress is a milestone in the history of army building of the Communist Party. It is regarded as the "holy land of Chinese communism".

T: What are the words above the building?

L: The splendid eight Chinese characters means that the eternal glory of the Gutian Congress.

T: Is the meeting site its original state?

L: Today the congress hall has been restored to its original state. As you see, the seats, the banner, the rostrum, the slogan signs, the Party flag, the wall clock and the pictures of Karl Marx and Lenin are all in their places as the congress was held in 1929.

T: What's the room used for? It's like an office.

L: It's served as Chairman Mao's office. He drafted proposals, issued document and met delegates who attended the meeting. And there is a well and lotus pond on the left and Chairman Mao often took a walk after dinner.

T: The layout is reasonable.

L: Have you noticed there is a large lawn on the right? It's used to be the parade ground of the Red Army. According to historical record, Mao Zedong, Zhu De and Chen Yi, leaders of the Fourth Front Red Army, once held a grand parade here.

T: What a large lawn. It's a good place to hold a party.

L: Yes. They also staged an evening party here to welcome the New Year after the congress was closed. OK, now follow me please. I will show you around the Memorial of the Gutian Congress and the Headquarter of the Fourth Front Red Army.

Useful Expressions

1. The Guantian Congress is a milestone in the history of army building of the Communist Party. It is regarded as the "holy land of Chinese communism".

古田会议是中国共产党建军史上的一座里程碑，被称为"中国共产主义的圣地"。

2. The splendid eight Chinese characters means that the eternal glory of the Gutian Congress.

八个光彩夺目的大字意为"古田会议永放光芒"。

3. The seats, the banner, the rostrum, the slogan signs, the Party flag, the wall clock and the pictures of Karl Marx and Lenin are all in their places as the congress was held in 1929.

座位、会议标志、主席台、会议标语、党旗、壁钟，以及马克思与列宁的肖像等物品的摆放都是1929年举行会议时的原貌。

4. He drafted proposals, issued document and met delegates who attended the meeting.

他就是在这里起草、批阅并发布文件，接见与会代表。

5. According to historical record, Mao Zedong, Zhu De and Chen Yi, leaders of the Fourth Front Red Army, once held a grand parade here.

据史料记载，当年毛泽东、朱德、陈毅等红四军领导在这里举行了盛大的阅兵仪式。

Exercises

1. Match the following Chinese with the correct English versions

（1）草坪　　　　　　　a. ancestral temple
（2）纪念馆　　　　　　b. primary school
（3）陈列室　　　　　　c. document

(4) 肖像　　　　　　　　d. slogan sign
(5) 宗祠　　　　　　　　e. lawn
(6) 文物　　　　　　　　f. memorial
(7) 小学　　　　　　　　g. cultural relic
(8) 标语　　　　　　　　h. showroom
(9) 油画　　　　　　　　i. oil painting
(10) 文件　　　　　　　　j. portrait

2. Translate the following Chinese into English

(1) 首先，我向大家介绍一下古田会议会址的历史。
(2) 接下来，我向大家介绍一下古田会议的时代背景。
(3) 红四军多次突破敌人的封锁，成功地在赣南和闽西建立了革命根据地。
(4) 正堂包括庭院、前厅、后厅和厢房。
(5) 整座建筑共有大厅 3 个、小厅 6 个、天井 9 个，以及各类房间 53 间。

3. Fill in the blanks with appropriate words and expressions

Today the meeting hall has been ＿＿＿(1)＿＿＿ to the original scene with such things in place as the seats, logo, rostrum, slogans, the Party flag, wall clock and pictures of Karl Marx and Lenin. The left wingroom ＿＿＿(2)＿＿＿ as Mao Zedong's office. And the mark left on the ground still ＿＿＿(3)＿＿＿ people of the scene of the delegates warming themselves by the fire. Outside, on the right side is the reviewing stand. On the left are a lotus ＿＿＿(4)＿＿＿ and a well. Erected behind the house is a board with big red ＿＿＿(5)＿＿＿ reading "Eternal Glory of the Gutian Congress".

4. Role play

Suppose you are the local guide and are now guiding the guests to visit Memorial of the Gutian Congress. Make introductions and answer relevant questions.

IV Extended Reading

The Site of the Gutian Meeting

Module 17
City Tour

Learning Objectives

1. Master the vocabulary and sentence patterns of thecity tour.
2. Describe the city tour to the tourists.
3. Explore the cultural elements of the city tour.
4. Summarize the main features of the city tour.

Task 1 A Trip to the Oriental Pearl TV Tower

Read and Match

a. Jinmao Tower
b. World Financial Center
c. the Bund
d. the Oriental Pearl TV Tower

(1)

(2)

(3)

(4)

Situational Dialogue

A Trip to the Oriental Pearl TV Tower

(As a local guide, Xiao Li is visiting the Oriental Pearl TV Tower with his tour group. He introduces the building and answers relevant questions.)

L: Xiao Li, the local guide   S: Ms. Sadie, the tourist

L: Ladies and gentlemen, in front of us is the Oriental Pearl TV Tower, the most famous landmark of Shanghai. It lies at No. 1 Century Avenue on the tip of Lujiazui, just opposite the Bund. It's 468 meters, used to be the tallest building in China from 1995 to 2007.

S: What is the tallest building in China now?

T: It's Shanghai Tower, with a height of 632 meters.

S: Is it one of "The Three Giants" in Shanghai?

T: Yes. "The Three Giants" refer to Jinmao Tower, Shanghai Tower and Shanghai World Financial Center. These giants with neighboring skyscrapers make Pudong New Area the most desired place in China.

S: People say a trip to Shanghai is never complete without visiting the Oriental Pearl TV Tower. What makes it so special?

T: As you see, the tower is composed of the tower base with three batter posts and three standing pillars. With 11 spheres of different sizes, it creates the poetic conception of large and small pearls dropping into a jade plate. And the order of visiting the Oriental Pearl Tower is from top to bottom.

S: So will we go up to the upper now?

T: Yes, please follow me. We'll take the elevator to the upper sphere. As there are lots of visitors here, I will give you detailed introduction when we arrived at the upper sphere.

(After getting to the upper sphere)

S: How amazing! Too fast, I feel a little tinnitus.

T: The upper sphere is 250 meters from the ground and it just took us 40 seconds to get here just now. The tower is equipped with 6 elevators, which send about 7500 visitors on a daily average.

S: How big is the sphere?

T: The upper sphere is 45 meters in diameter with 9 floors. The highlight is the revolving restaurant at 267 meters and the transparent sightseeing gallery. The revolving restaurant completes one circle with one hour. The transparent sightseeing gallery offers tourists a chance to experience "walking in the air".

S: That's exciting. Let's explore it.

Module 17 City Tour

Useful Expressions

1. "The Three Giants" refer to Jinmao Tower, Shanghai Tower and Shanghai World Financial Center. These giants with neighboring skyscrapers make Pudong New Area the most desired place in China.

"魔都三巨头"是指金茂大厦、上海中心大厦和上海环球金融中心。它们与周边摩天大楼使浦东新区成为中国最令人向往的地方。

2. People say a trip to Shanghai is never complete without visiting the Oriental Pearl TV Tower.

人们都说,不上东方明珠电视塔就没来过上海。

3. The tower is composed of the tower base with three batter posts and three standing pillars.

塔身由塔座、三根斜撑、三根立柱组成。

4. With 11 spheres of different sizes, it creates the poetic conception of large and small pearls dropping into a jade plate.

由11颗大小不一的球体构成,构成了充满"大珠小珠落玉盘"诗情画意的壮美景观。

5. The highlight is the revolving restaurant at 267 meters and the transparent sightseeing gallery.

亮点是位于塔上267米处的旋转餐厅和透明的观光廊。

Exercises

1. Match the following Chinese with the correct English versions

(1) 外观   a. skyscraper
(2) 瓷器精品   b. financial center
(3) 回廊   c. residence
(4) 内部   d. porcelain artwork
(5) 摩天大楼   e. vaulted stone door
(6) 瓷砖   f. cloister
(7) 金融中心   g. exterior
(8) 民居   h. interior
(9) 刺绣   i. embroidery
(10) 石拱门   j. tile

2. Translate the following Chinese into English

(1) 当地人通常以在外滩锻炼身体开始一天的生活。在这里,你可以看到他们散步、慢跑、练太极或放风筝等。

(2) 游览外滩最经典的路线要么是从北端向南端漫步,要么从南端向北端漫步。

(3) 在新天地有高档餐厅,供应法国、巴西、美国、日本、德国和意大利等不同国家的美食。

(4) 参观上海迪士尼乐园时,建议在到达地铁站时购买回程票,以免晚上排长队。

(5) 您将体验到20世纪20年代的上海和21世纪现代都市人的生活方式。

3. Fill in the blanks with appropriate words and expressions

In the morning we visit the Shanghai Urban Planning Exhibition Hall, showing detailed information of the ___(1)___, present and future of Shanghai. After that, go deeper to learn more by ___(2)___ Shanghai Museum, presenting you the profound history and culture of China. In the afternoon, have a relaxing time rambling in the ___(3)___ Yu Garden. After that you will come to the Bund area. Located on the ___(4)___ of Huangpu River, travelers come to the Bund not only for the charming riverside ___(5)___, but the unique Western and gothic architectures also deserve a look. You have some free time to stroll around the Bund and take some photos.

4. Role play

Situation: Suppose you are the local guide and are now guiding the guests to visit Shanghai World Financial Center (SWFC). Make introductions and answer relevant questions.

Ⅳ Extended Reading

Shanghai Nightlife

Task 2　A Trip to Kulangsu

Ⅰ Read and Match

a. steamship　　b. electric golf carts　　c. wharf　　d. villa

(1)

(2)

Module 17　City Tour　265

(3)

(4)

📖 Situational Dialogue

扫码
听听力

A Trip to Kulangsu

(As a local guide, Xiao Li is guiding the guests to the Piano Museum on Kulangsu. He introduces the Piano Museum and answers relevant questions.)

L: **Xiao Li, the local guide**　　S: **Ms. Sara, the tourist**

L: Ladies and gentlemen, Kulangsu covers an area of less than 2 square kilometers with 20000 permanent residents. They enjoy a comfortable, relaxing life and the environment free from the noise and pollution of combustion engines as only electric-powered vehicles are permitted on Kulangsu. It is called the Architecture Museum with classical and romantic European style architectures. It is also known as "the Cradle of Musicians" and "Island of Music" because of its reputation for music appreciation. Now we are at the Piano Museum.

S: Oh, we'll have a delightful tour here with the melodious sound of the pianos.

T: The Piano Museum displays early piano donated by Mr. Hu Youyi, a Chinese-Australian piano collector born on Kulangsu.

S: How many pianos here?

T: There are over 100 world famous antique pianos from the UK, the US, France, German, Austria and Australia. Here you can also find the world's largest upright piano, the oldest vertical piano, an auto-performing piano, an 8-pedal piano and the oldest square piano.

S: That's marvelous. Look, the two pianos in the center of the hall are so attractive.

T: Yes, the two pianos are decorated with traditional Chinese patterns of flowers and birds. Musicians play the piano every half an hour in the museum.

S: The Island of Music is worth visiting again and again. Can you tell us the detailed information of the wharves? We plan to travel here again in our free time.

T: There are five main wharves to get to Kulangsu in day time. There are three options for tourists: Xiamen International Cruise Terminal (Dongdu Youlun Matou) to Sanqiutian Wharf, Xiamen International Cruise Terminal (Dongdu Youlun Matou) to Neicuo'ao Wharf and Songyu Wharf to Neicuo'ao Wharf. Different wharves have different prices and running time, you can check it on the Internet before you set off.

S: How about the evening?

T: In the evening there is only one choice for tourists: Lundu Ferry Terminal to Sanqiutian Wharf. Passengers should depart at the No. 2 hall of Lundu Ferry Terminal in the evening. The frequency of both wharves mentioned above will be changed to 30 minutes after 21:00 every evening due to fewer customers.

S: Thanks for your information.

T: It is my pleasure. It seems the musicians will play the piano. Let's enjoy the musical atmosphere of the Music Islet.

Useful Expressions

1. They enjoy a comfortable, relaxing life and the environment free from the noise and pollution of combustion engines as only electric-powered vehicles are permitted on Kulangsu.

鼓浪屿岛上禁止机动车辆通行,只有电动交通工具可以通行,所以岛上的居民能够享受舒适轻松的生活和没有内燃机噪声污染的环境。

2. It is also known as "the Cradle of Musicians" and "Island of Music" because of its reputation for music appreciation.

因其深厚的音乐底蕴,鼓浪屿被誉为"音乐家的摇篮""音乐之岛"。

3. Here you can also find the world's largest upright piano, the oldest vertical piano, an auto-performing piano, an 8-pedal piano and the oldest square piano.

在这里你可以看到世界上最大的直立式钢琴、最古老的立式钢琴、自动演奏钢琴、8个踏板的古钢琴和最古老的四角钢琴。

4. The two pianos are decorated with traditional Chinese patterns of flowers and birds. Musicians play the piano every half an hour in the museum.

这两架钢琴琴身装饰着传统的中国花鸟图案。每隔半小时有钢琴师在馆内现场演奏钢琴。

Exercises

1. Match the following Chinese with the correct English versions

(1) 弥勒佛　　　　　　　　　a. seafood

(2) 观音　　　　　　　　　　b. vegetarian cake

（3）十八罗汉   c. oyster omelet
（4）海蛎煎   d. fish ball
（5）台湾香肠   e. patriotic overseas Chinese
（6）海鲜   f. satay noodle
（7）沙茶面   g. Taiwanese sausage
（8）鱼丸   h. Maitreya
（9）素饼   i. Guanyin
（10）爱国华侨   j. Eighteen Arhats

2. **Translate the following Chinese into English**

（1）鼓浪屿不仅是个景点，还是个社区，我们鼓励当地居民参与保护工作。

（2）为了更好地呈现鼓浪屿的文化资源，岛上新开设了几座博物馆。

（3）政府将继续鼓励改善岛上居民的生活以及游客体验。

（4）环岛路全长31千米，又称"五色公路"，因为有蓝色的大海、金色的沙滩、绿色的草地、红色的跑道、灰色的公路。

（5）每日的游客数量上限将遵循世界遗产委员会的人流控制要求。

3. **Fill in the blanks with appropriate words and expressions**

  Xiamen mainly consists of Xiamen Island, Kulangsu Island, the north bank area of the Jiulong River and Tong'an District. The city has been ＿＿＿(1)＿＿＿ the Egret Island because of the hundreds of thousands of egrets inhabiting there. It is an ideal tourist ＿＿＿(2)＿＿＿ for you. It is a typical coastal city with abundant tourist attractions such as islands, mountains, temples and parks, etc., providing you with a full ＿＿＿(3)＿＿＿ schedule.

  The well-known Kulangsu Island, South Putuo Temple, Baicheng Beach and other areas like Jimei, Hulishan Fortress, Wanshiyan, are highly recommended for a tour. To promote its tourism industry, it has established not only the corresponding infrastructures, but also a great ＿＿＿(4)＿＿＿ of entertainment centers. This city, with distinct oriental culture and ＿＿＿(5)＿＿＿ Fujian features, welcomes you from all over the world.

4. **Role play**

Situation: Suppose you are the local guide and are now guiding the guests to visit Kulangsu. Make introductions and answer relevant questions.

IV Extended Reading

Shuzhuang Garden

Shuzhuang Garden

Task 3　A Trip to Chimelong Tourist Resort

I Read and Match

a. international circus
b. safari park
c. water park
d. crocodile park

(1)

(2)

(3)

(4)

II Situational Dialogue

A Trip to Chimelong Tourist Resort

(As a local guide, Xiao Li is guiding the guests to enjoy the performance in Chimelong International Circus. He introduces Chimelong International Circus before the performance and answers relevant questions.)

L: Xiao Li, the local guide   S: Ms. Sara, the tourist

L: Ladies and gentlemen, tonight we will enjoy the wonderful performance in Chimelong International Circus. It has been classified as the "Most Competitive Cultural Brand in Guangzhou", "China's Culture Card", and "the Best Night Entertainment in Guangzhou". The performance will begin half an hour later. Now let me make a brief introduction of the circus. It has the largest live-action circus stage in the world, which was listed into the Guinness Book of Records.

S: It's said that the circus has the most performers and animals on the show.

L: Yes. It has 300 award-winning performers from over 20 countries in Asia, America, Europe and Africa and more than 500 animals of 40 different species.

S: How many seats does the circus have? It looks so large.

L: It is equipped with a seating capacity of 8000. The performance stage makes use of all sorts of lamps and other lighting equipment up to more than 2000. The luxury lighting system makes a variety of effects from early in the morning, during the day and the dusk to night, greatly enhancing the richness of stage effect and the sense of space and time.

S: It's regarded as the most luxurious and professional international circus. It was not until I visited the place that I found it really worthy of the reputation.

T: The opening hours of the circus are from 5:00 pm to 9:00 pm. The circus show starts from 7:30 pm to 9:00 pm, so the visitors can get into the stage 1.5 hours earlier to wait for the start of the performance. Now it's 7:20 and the performance will begin soon. Please take your seats and enjoy the most professional circus.

S: That is marvelous. I feel so excited.

Useful Expressions

1. Chimelong International Circus has been classified as the "Most Competitive Cultural Brand in Guangzhou", "China's Culture Card", and "the Best Night Entertainment in Guangzhou".

广州长隆国际大马戏被评为"广州最具竞争力的文化品牌""中国文化名片""羊城夜游首选"。

2. Chimelong International Circus has the largest live-action circus stage in the world, which was listed into the Guinness Book of Records.

广州长隆国际大马戏拥有全球最大实景式马戏舞台,被列入吉尼斯世界纪录。

3. Chimelong International Circus has 300 award-winning performers from over 20 countries in Asia, America, Europe and Africa and more than 500 animals of 40 different species.

拥有来自20多个国家,横跨亚洲、美洲、欧洲、非洲共300余名的马戏精英以及多达40余种500多只珍奇动物同台献技。

4. The luxury lighting system makes a variety of effects from early in the

morning, during the day and the dusk to night, greatly enhancing the richness of stage effect and the sense of space and time.

奢华的灯光营造了从清晨、白天、黄昏到夜间的多种效果,极大地增强了舞台效果的丰富性和时空感。

Exercises

1. Match the following Chinese with the correct English versions

(1) 欢乐世界　　　　　　　　　a. tourist resort
(2) 水上乐园　　　　　　　　　b. scenic area
(3) 野生动物园　　　　　　　　c. destination
(4) 鳄鱼公园　　　　　　　　　d. water park
(5) 主题公园　　　　　　　　　e. safari park
(6) 度假区　　　　　　　　　　f. crocodile park
(7) 会展中心　　　　　　　　　g. paradise
(8) 目的地　　　　　　　　　　h. theme park
(9) 娱乐中心　　　　　　　　　i. convention center
(10) 旅游景区　　　　　　　　　j. entertainment center

2. Translate the following Chinese into English

(1) 作为华南地区最重要的国际贸易中心,广州自1957年以来每年举办两次广交会。

(2) 天河城、中华广场等大型购物中心为您提供来自世界各地的一流产品的便捷通道。

(3) 在批发市场购物时讨价还价是一种独特的体验,但在大型购物中心无法讨价还价。

(4) 喝早茶是当地人,特别是老年人的传统习惯。工夫茶和美味的点心是早茶的完美搭配。

(5) 广州一年四季绿树成荫,花团锦簇。

3. Fill in the blanks with appropriate words and expressions

When night comes, it is easy to find a place to relax in Guangzhou. The top things to do for Guangzhou ＿＿＿(1)＿＿＿ include cruising along Pearl River to enjoy the night scenes, watching Cantonese Opera to ＿＿＿(2)＿＿＿ Cantonese culture, meeting young and experiencing the lively Guangzhou nightlife in one of the many bars, and watching a circus performance in Chimelong Resort.

The night scene on two sides of the Pearl River is so enchanting that you must have a ＿＿＿(3)＿＿＿. The best way is by boat. Tourists can take a night ＿＿＿(4)＿＿＿ on the Pearl River from one of the five wharfs. Along the cruise, you will pass by many shining buildings decorated by ＿＿＿(5)＿＿＿, such as Canton Tower, Xinghai

Concert Hall, Haiyin Bridge, various Western style buildings in Shamian Island.

4. Role play

Situation: Suppose you are the local guide and are now guiding the guests to visit Chimelong Tourist Resort. Make introductions and answer relevant questions.

IV Extended Reading

Chimelong Tourist Resort

Chimelong Tourist Resort

参考文献
References

[1] 赖春梅. 涉外导游英语实训[M]. 厦门:厦门大学出版社,2016.
[2] 袁智敏,仇向明. 领队英语[M]. 5版. 北京:旅游教育出版社,2016.
[3] 朱宁,王伟民. 导游服务能力100问(英汉对照)[M]. 北京:旅游教育出版社,2016.
[4] 王青. 英语导游实训教程[M]. 北京:中国人民大学出版社,2017.
[5] 郑毅,刘惠波. 旅游英语视听说[M]. 北京:外语教学与研究出版社,2011.
[6] 吴云,沈莉. 出境旅游领队英语[M]. 北京:旅游教育出版社,2016.
[7] 曲琳娜. 实用旅游英语[M]. 北京:旅游教育出版社,2019.
[8] 褚琴. 江苏导游英语[M]. 北京:中国旅游出版社,2016
[9] 裴冠金,陈薇薇,米玉琴,等. 新实用北京导游英语听说教程[M]. 北京:北京交通大学出版社,2014.
[10] 陈洪富. 福建省主要旅游景区景点英语导游词[M]. 厦门:厦门大学出版社,2014.
[11] 郑张敏,陆金英. 21世纪大学旅游英语视听说综合教程[M]. 上海:复旦大学出版社,2014.
[12] 吴云. 导游英语口译[M]. 上海:上海交通大学出版社,2016.
[13] 胡强. 华东线导游训练教程[M]. 北京:旅游教育出版社,2017.
[14] 李长安. 旅游英语实用教程[M]. 西安:西安电子科技大学出版社,2015.
[15] 朱华. 旅游英语视听说[M]. 北京:北京大学出版社,2020.
[16] 易玉婷,汪锋. 英语导游实务——导游业务部分[M]. 北京:国防工业出版社,2012.
[17] 朱华. 英语导游听说教材[M]. 北京:北京大学出版社,2021.
[18] 叶宏,郭红芳,柳波. 旅游实用英语[M]. 武汉:华中科技大学出版社,2018.
[19] 苏静,范作为. 导游英语[M]. 北京:化学工业出版社,2013.

本书练习题参考答案

Exercises 参考答案

教学支持说明

为了改善教学效果,提高教材的使用效率,满足高校授课教师的教学需求,本套教材备有与纸质教材配套的教学课件(PPT 电子教案)和拓展资源(案例库、习题库、视频等)。

为保证本教学课件及相关教学资料仅为教材使用者所得,我们将向使用本套教材的高校授课教师赠送教学课件或相关教学资料,烦请授课教师通过电话、邮件或加入旅游专家俱乐部 QQ 群等方式与我们联系,获取"教学课件资源申请表"文档,准确填写后反馈给我们,我们的联系方式如下:

地址:湖北省武汉市东湖新技术开发区华工科技园华工园六路

邮编:430223

电话:027-81321911

传真:027-81321917

E-mail:lyzjjlb@163.com

旅游专家俱乐部 QQ 群号:758712998

旅游专家俱乐部 QQ 群二维码:

群名称:旅游专家俱乐部5群
群　号:758712998

电子资源申请表

填表时间：_____年___月___日

1. 以下内容请教师按实际情况填写，★为必填项。
2. 相关内容可以酌情调整提交。

★姓名		★性别	□男 □女	出生年月		★职务	
						★职称	□教授 □副教授 □讲师 □助教

★学校		★院/系	
★教研室		★专业	
★办公电话		家庭电话		★移动电话	
★E-mail				★QQ号/微信号	
★联系地址				★邮编	

★现在主授课程情况	学生人数	教材所属出版社	教材满意度
课程一			□满意 □一般 □不满意
课程二			□满意 □一般 □不满意
课程三			□满意 □一般 □不满意
其 他			□满意 □一般 □不满意

教 材 出 版 信 息						
方向一		□准备写	□写作中	□已成稿	□已出版待修订	□有讲义
方向二		□准备写	□写作中	□已成稿	□已出版待修订	□有讲义
方向三		□准备写	□写作中	□已成稿	□已出版待修订	□有讲义

请教师认真填写下列表格内容，提供申请教材配套课件的相关信息，我社将根据每位教师填表信息的完整性、授课情况与申请课件的相关性，以及教材使用的情况赠送教材的配套课件及相关教学资源。

ISBN（书号）	书名	作者	申请课件简要说明	学生人数（如选作教材）
			□教学 □参考	
			□教学 □参考	

★您对与课件配套的纸质教材的意见和建议有哪些，希望我们提供哪些配套教学资源：